Marry Me a Little

a graphic memoir

ROB KIRBY

graphic mundi

Library of Congress Cataloging-in-Publication Data

Names: Kirby, Robert, 1962– author.
Title: Marry me a little : a graphic memoir / Rob Kirby.
Description: University Park, Pennsylvania : Graphic Mundi, [2023]
Summary: "A graphic memoir exploring the author's personal and political feelings about his decision to marry his longtime partner when same-sex marriage became legal"—Provided by publisher.
Identifiers: LCCN 2022030821 | ISBN 9781637790397 (paperback)
Subjects: LCSH: Kirby, Robert, 1962—Comic books, strips, etc. | Same-sex marriage—United States—Comic books, strips, etc. | Gay couples—United States—Comic books, strips, etc. | LCGFT: Autobiographical comics. | Graphic novels.
Classification: LCC HQ1034.U5 K57 2023 | DDC 306.84/4092 [B]—dc23/eng/20220721
LC record available at https://lccn.loc.gov/2022030821

Printed in Lithuania by BALTO Print
Published by The Pennsylvania State University Press, University Park, PA 16802–1003

10 9 8 7 6 5 4 3 2 1

graphic mundi
drawing our worlds together

Graphic Mundi is an imprint of The Pennsylvania State University Press.

#snowflake originally appeared on Pen America, 2017, https://pen.org/snowflake/.

The Pennsylvania State University Press is a member of the Association of University Presses.

It is the policy of The Pennsylvania State University Press to use acid-free paper. Publications on uncoated stock satisfy the minimum requirements of American National Standard for Information Sciences—Permanence of Paper for Printed Library Material, ANSI Z39.48–1992.

For John
I'd still marry you a lot.

THE FIRST TIME I SAID IT (DEC. 2013)

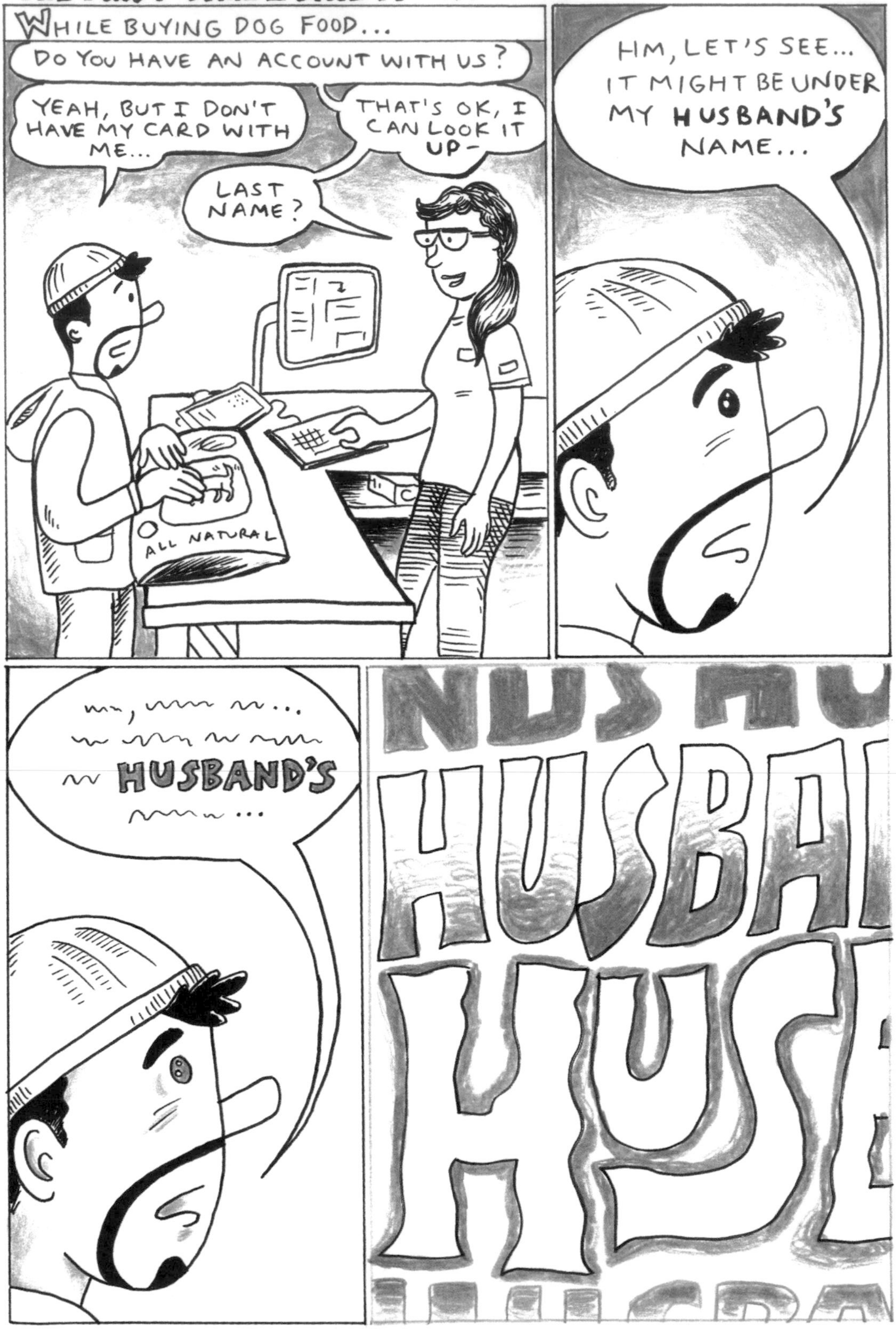
WHILE BUYING DOG FOOD...
DO YOU HAVE AN ACCOUNT WITH US?
YEAH, BUT I DON'T HAVE MY CARD WITH ME...
THAT'S OK, I CAN LOOK IT UP-
LAST NAME?
ALL NATURAL
HM, LET'S SEE... IT MIGHT BE UNDER MY HUSBAND'S NAME...
HUSBAND'S

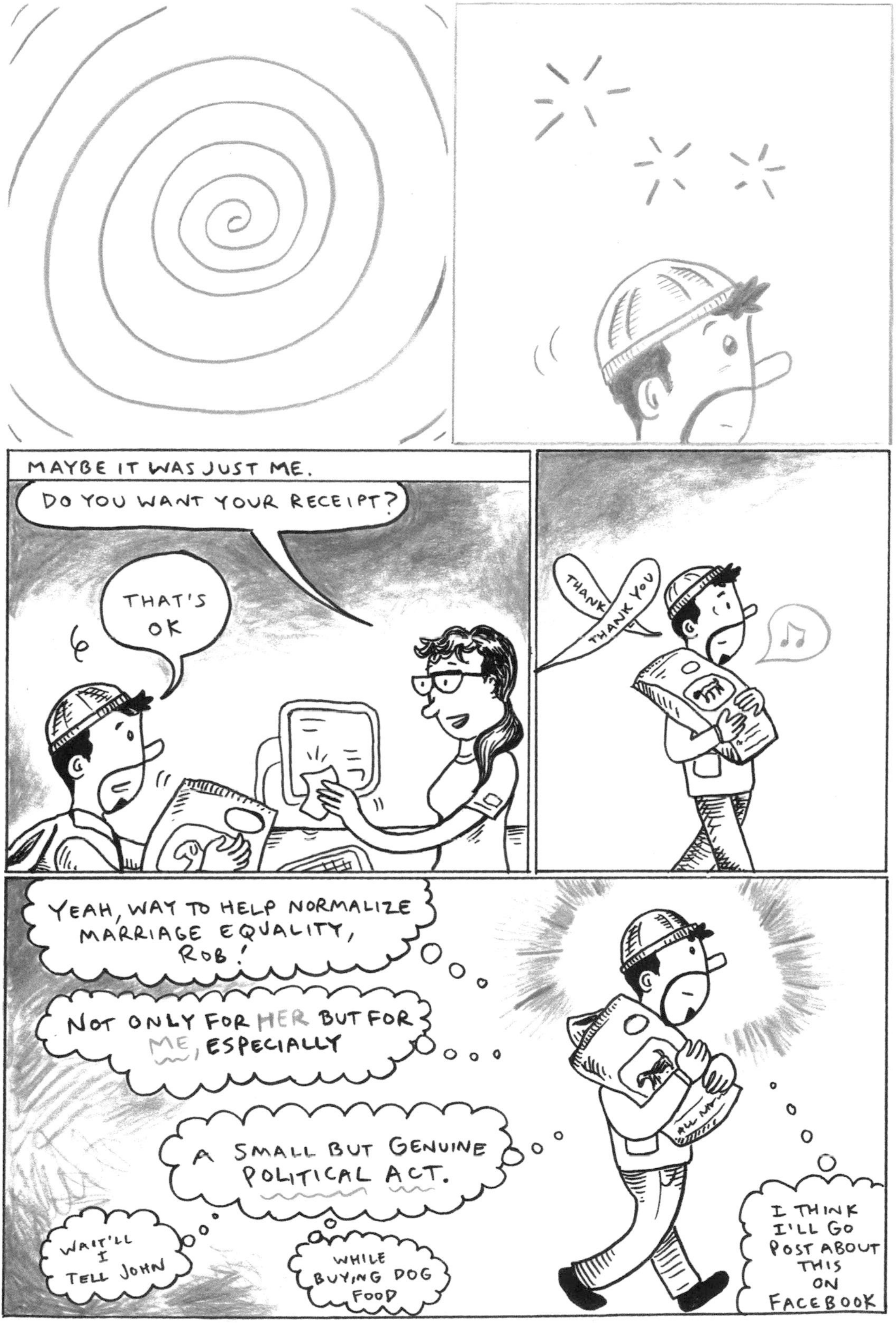
MAYBE IT WAS JUST ME.
DO YOU WANT YOUR RECEIPT?
THAT'S OK
THANK THANK YOU
YEAH, WAY TO HELP NORMALIZE MARRIAGE EQUALITY, ROB!
NOT ONLY FOR HER BUT FOR ME, ESPECIALLY
A SMALL BUT GENUINE POLITICAL ACT.
WAIT'LL I TELL JOHN
WHILE BUYING DOG FOOD
I THINK I'LL GO POST ABOUT THIS ON FACEBOOK

On October 3rd, 2013,
I got married.

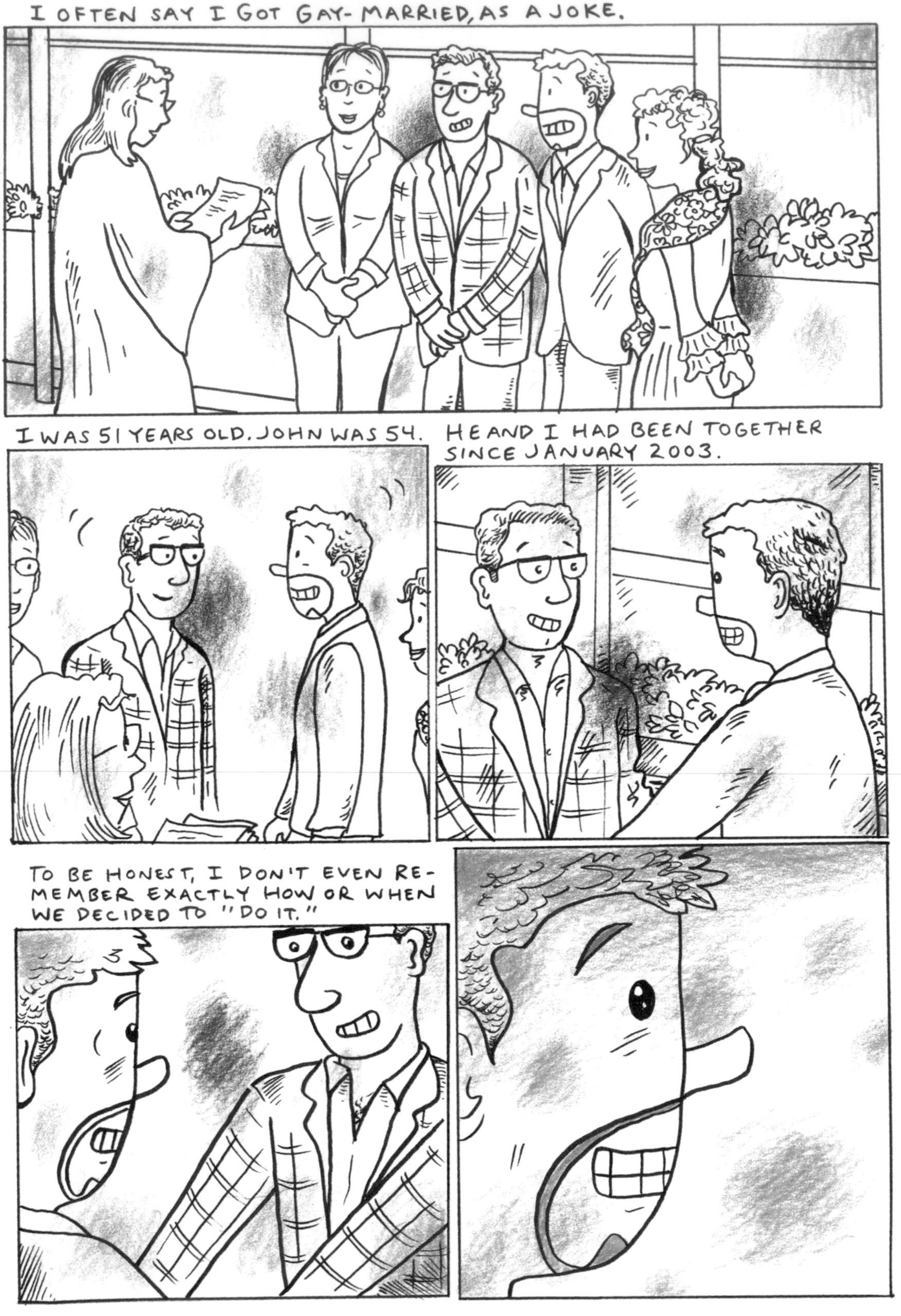
I OFTEN SAY I GOT GAY-MARRIED, AS A JOKE.
I WAS 51 YEARS OLD. JOHN WAS 54.
HE AND I HAD BEEN TOGETHER SINCE JANUARY 2003.
TO BE HONEST, I DON'T EVEN REMEMBER EXACTLY HOW OR WHEN WE DECIDED TO "DO IT."

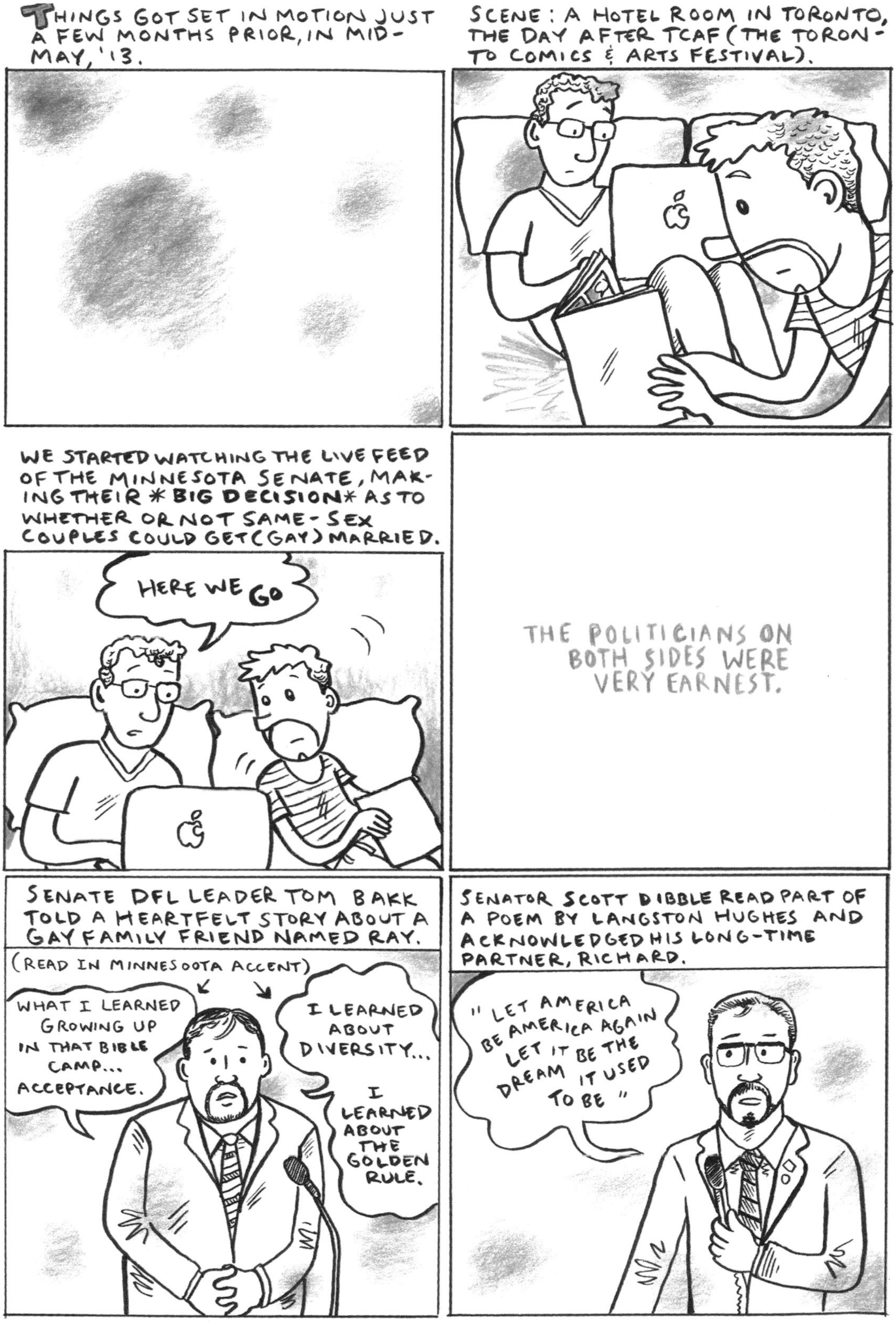
THINGS GOT SET IN MOTION JUST A FEW MONTHS PRIOR, IN MID-MAY, '13.
SCENE: A HOTEL ROOM IN TORONTO, THE DAY AFTER TCAF (THE TORONTO COMICS & ARTS FESTIVAL).
WE STARTED WATCHING THE LIVE FEED OF THE MINNESOTA SENATE, MAKING THEIR *BIG DECISION* AS TO WHETHER OR NOT SAME-SEX COUPLES COULD GET (GAY) MARRIED.
HERE WE GO
THE POLITICIANS ON BOTH SIDES WERE VERY EARNEST.
SENATE DFL LEADER TOM BAKK TOLD A HEARTFELT STORY ABOUT A GAY FAMILY FRIEND NAMED RAY.
(READ IN MINNESOOTA ACCENT)
WHAT I LEARNED GROWING UP IN THAT BIBLE CAMP... ACCEPTANCE.
I LEARNED ABOUT DIVERSITY...
I LEARNED ABOUT THE GOLDEN RULE.
SENATOR SCOTT DIBBLE READ PART OF A POEM BY LANGSTON HUGHES AND ACKNOWLEDGED HIS LONG-TIME PARTNER, RICHARD.
" LET AMERICA BE AMERICA AGAIN LET IT BE THE DREAM IT USED TO BE "

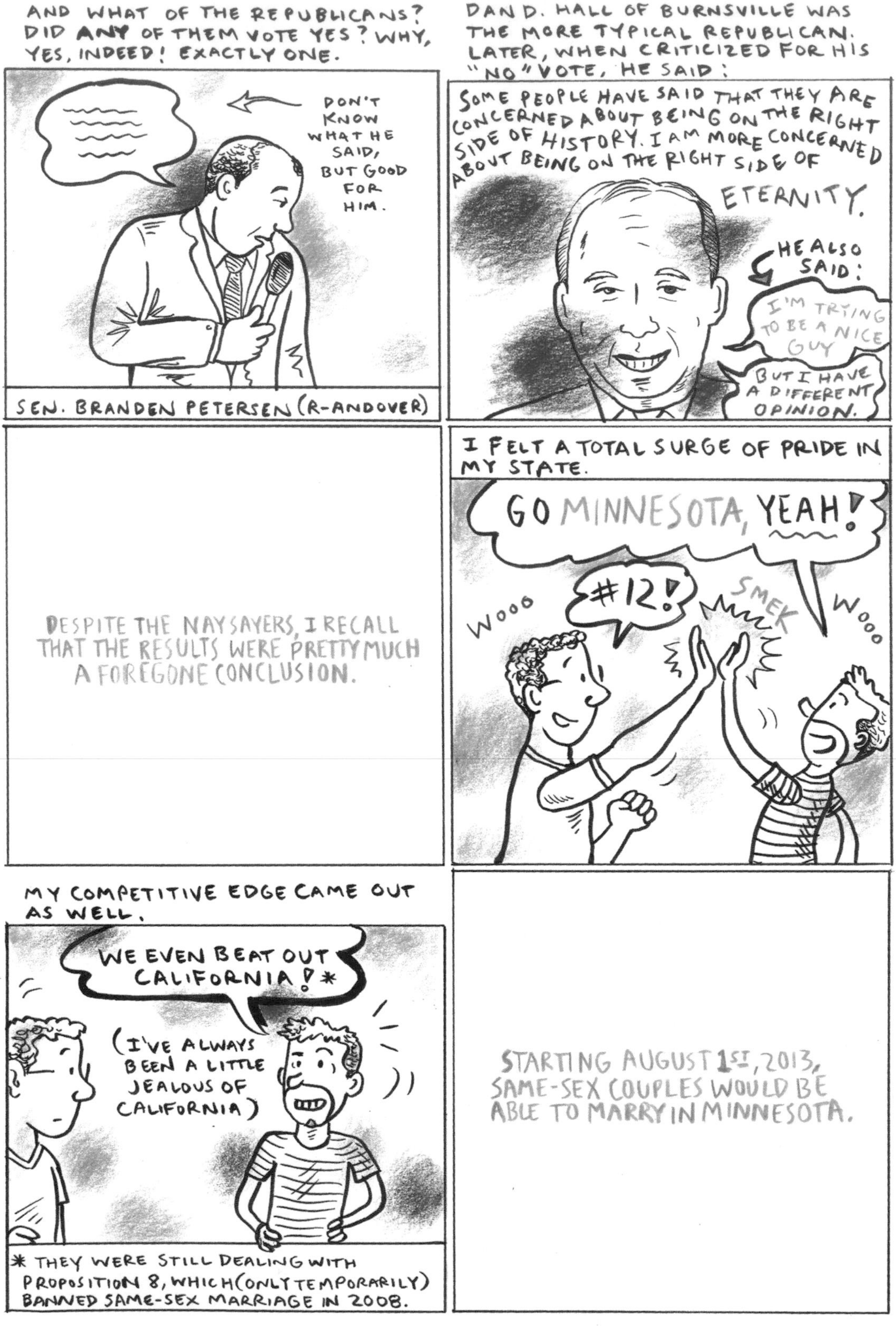
AND WHAT OF THE REPUBLICANS? DID ANY OF THEM VOTE YES? WHY, YES, INDEED! EXACTLY ONE.
DON'T KNOW WHAT HE SAID, BUT GOOD FOR HIM.
SEN. BRANDEN PETERSEN (R-ANDOVER)
DAN D. HALL OF BURNSVILLE WAS THE MORE TYPICAL REPUBLICAN. LATER, WHEN CRITICIZED FOR HIS "NO" VOTE, HE SAID:
SOME PEOPLE HAVE SAID THAT THEY ARE CONCERNED ABOUT BEING ON THE RIGHT SIDE OF HISTORY. I AM MORE CONCERNED ABOUT BEING ON THE RIGHT SIDE OF ETERNITY.
HE ALSO SAID:
I'M TRYING TO BE A NICE GUY
BUT I HAVE A DIFFERENT OPINION.
DESPITE THE NAYSAYERS, I RECALL THAT THE RESULTS WERE PRETTY MUCH A FOREGONE CONCLUSION.
I FELT A TOTAL SURGE OF PRIDE IN MY STATE.
GO MINNESOTA, YEAH!
#12!
SMEK
WOOO
WOOO
MY COMPETITIVE EDGE CAME OUT AS WELL.
WE EVEN BEAT OUT CALIFORNIA!*
(I'VE ALWAYS BEEN A LITTLE JEALOUS OF CALIFORNIA)
* THEY WERE STILL DEALING WITH PROPOSITION 8, WHICH (ONLY TEMPORARILY) BANNED SAME-SEX MARRIAGE IN 2008.
STARTING AUGUST 1ST, 2013, SAME-SEX COUPLES WOULD BE ABLE TO MARRY IN MINNESOTA.

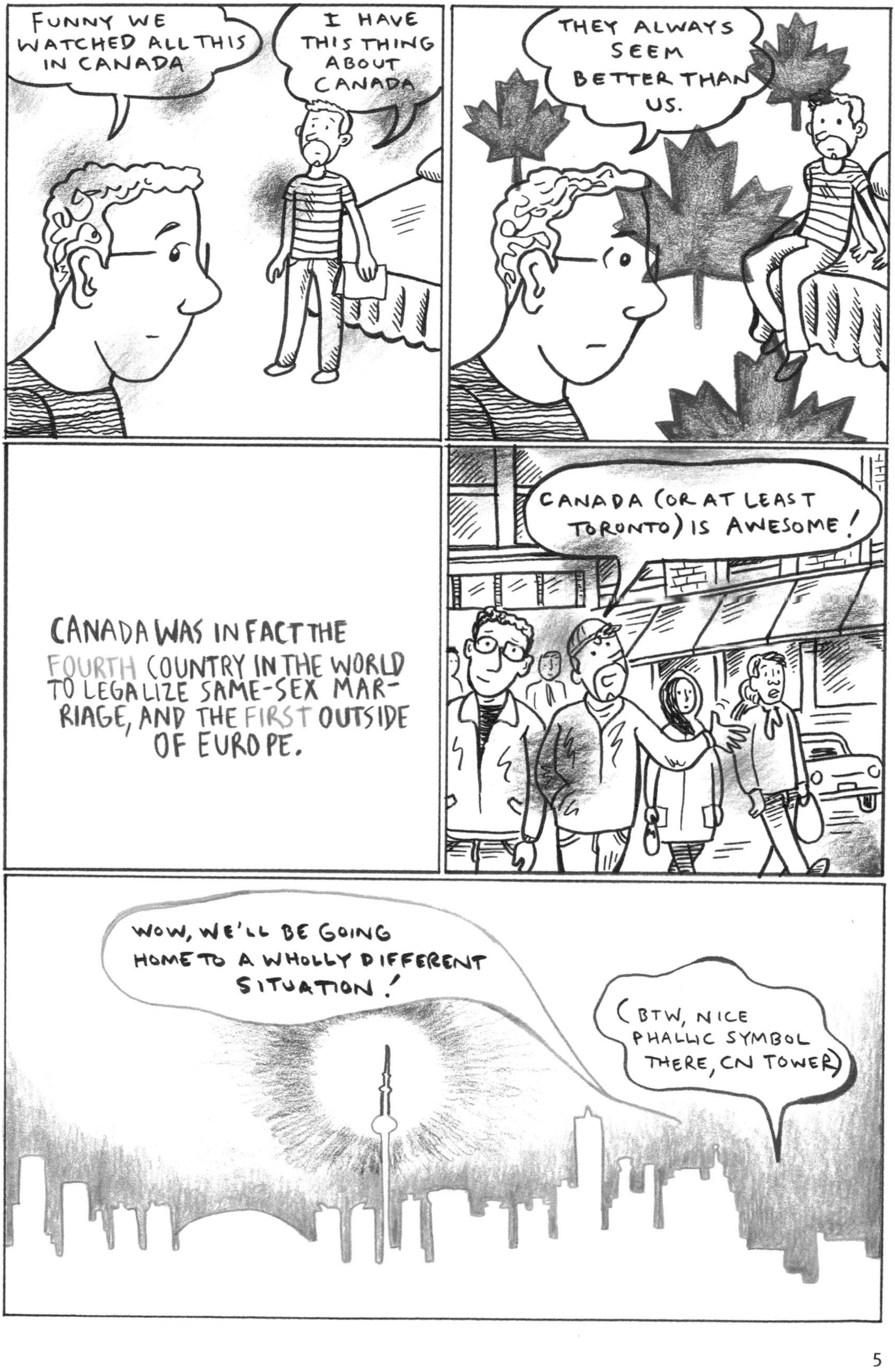
FUNNY WE WATCHED ALL THIS IN CANADA
I HAVE THIS THING ABOUT CANADA
THEY ALWAYS SEEM BETTER THAN US.
CANADA WAS IN FACT THE FOURTH COUNTRY IN THE WORLD TO LEGALIZE SAME-SEX MARRIAGE, AND THE FIRST OUTSIDE OF EUROPE.
CANADA (OR AT LEAST TORONTO) IS AWESOME!
WOW, WE'LL BE GOING HOME TO A WHOLLY DIFFERENT SITUATION!
(BTW, NICE PHALLIC SYMBOL THERE, CN TOWER)

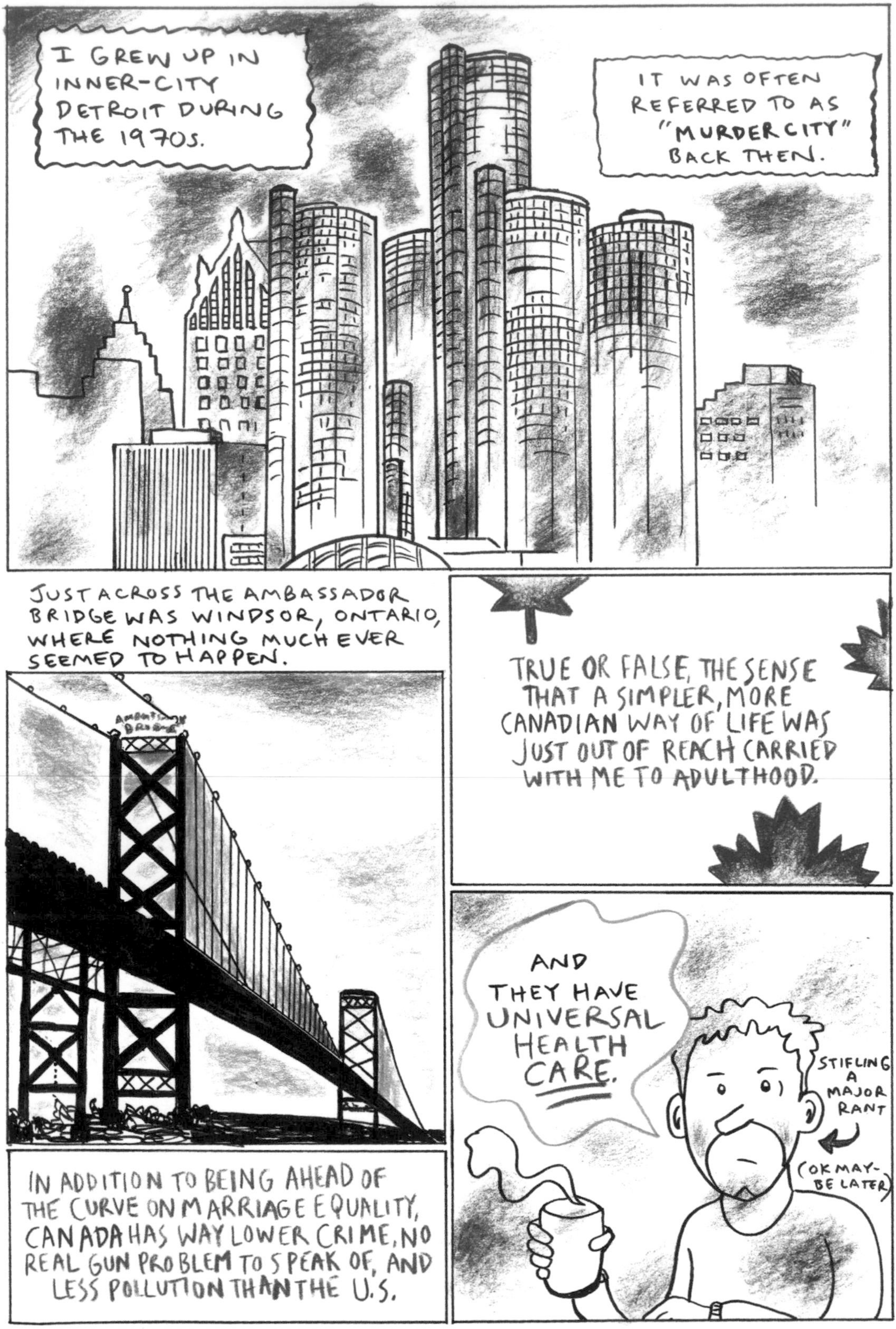
I GREW UP IN INNER-CITY DETROIT DURING THE 1970S.
IT WAS OFTEN REFERRED TO AS "MURDER CITY" BACK THEN.
JUST ACROSS THE AMBASSADOR BRIDGE WAS WINDSOR, ONTARIO, WHERE NOTHING MUCH EVER SEEMED TO HAPPEN.
TRUE OR FALSE, THE SENSE THAT A SIMPLER, MORE CANADIAN WAY OF LIFE WAS JUST OUT OF REACH CARRIED WITH ME TO ADULTHOOD.
IN ADDITION TO BEING AHEAD OF THE CURVE ON MARRIAGE EQUALITY, CANADA HAS WAY LOWER CRIME, NO REAL GUN PROBLEM TO SPEAK OF, AND LESS POLLUTION THAN THE U.S.
AND THEY HAVE UNIVERSAL HEALTH CARE.
STIFLING A MAJOR RANT
(OK MAYBE LATER)

NO MATTER WHAT ANYONE THINKS ABOUT ANY RIVALRY BETWEEN THE TWO COUNTRIES, I BET THE MAJORITY OF PEOPLE WOULD AGREE THAT IN THE HEALTHCARE DEPT, CANADA HAS IT ALL OVER THE U.S.A.

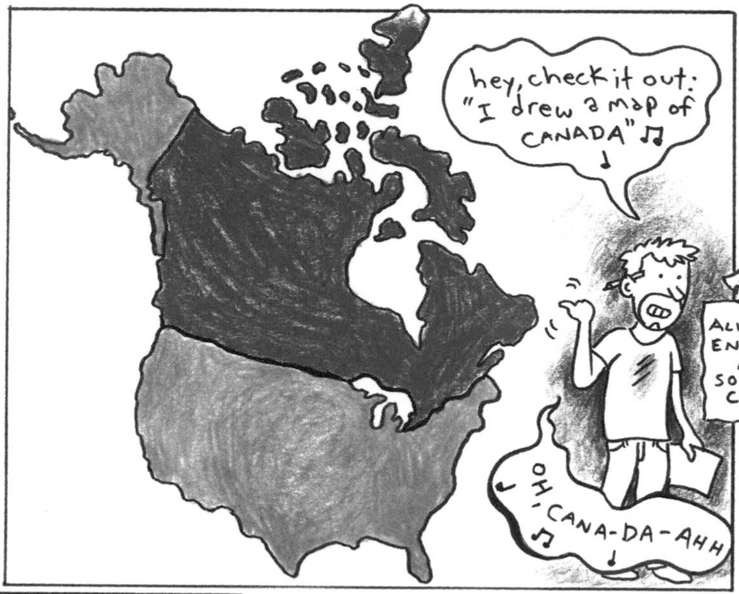

hey, check it out: "I drew a map of CANADA" ♫
ALWAYS ENJOYS A SONG CUE
OH, CANA-DA-AHH

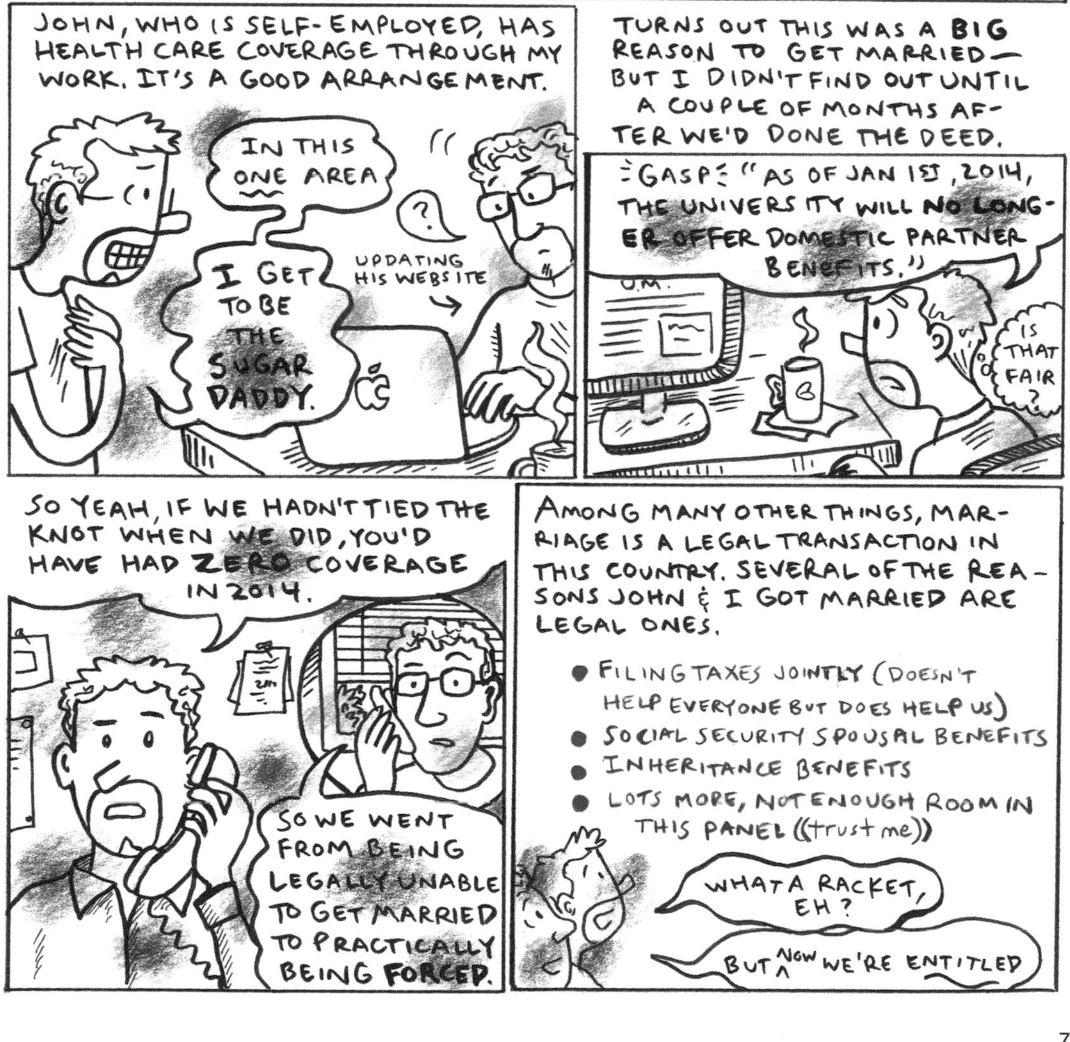

JOHN, WHO IS SELF-EMPLOYED, HAS HEALTH CARE COVERAGE THROUGH MY WORK. IT'S A GOOD ARRANGEMENT.
IN THIS ONE AREA
I GET TO BE THE SUGAR DADDY.
?
UPDATING HIS WEBSITE
TURNS OUT THIS WAS A BIG REASON TO GET MARRIED—BUT I DIDN'T FIND OUT UNTIL A COUPLE OF MONTHS AFTER WE'D DONE THE DEED.
GASP "AS OF JAN 1ST, 2014, THE UNIVERSITY WILL NO LONGER OFFER DOMESTIC PARTNER BENEFITS."
IS THAT FAIR?
SO YEAH, IF WE HADN'T TIED THE KNOT WHEN WE DID, YOU'D HAVE HAD ZERO COVERAGE IN 2014.
SO WE WENT FROM BEING LEGALLY UNABLE TO GET MARRIED TO PRACTICALLY BEING FORCED.
AMONG MANY OTHER THINGS, MARRIAGE IS A LEGAL TRANSACTION IN THIS COUNTRY. SEVERAL OF THE REASONS JOHN & I GOT MARRIED ARE LEGAL ONES.
• FILING TAXES JOINTLY (DOESN'T HELP EVERYONE BUT DOES HELP US)
• SOCIAL SECURITY SPOUSAL BENEFITS
• INHERITANCE BENEFITS
• LOTS MORE, NOT ENOUGH ROOM IN THIS PANEL ((trust me))
WHAT A RACKET, EH?
BUT NOW WE'RE ENTITLED

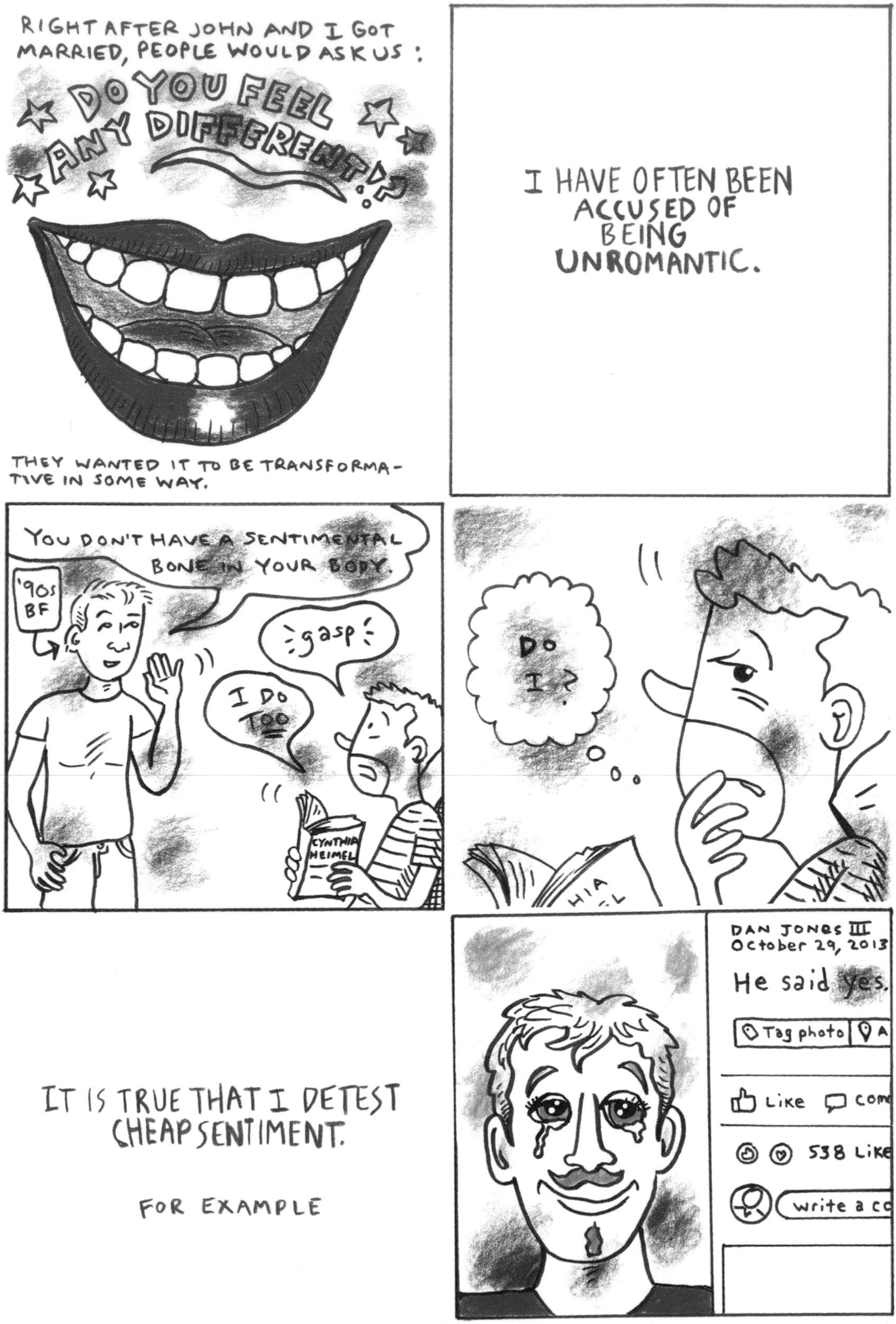
RIGHT AFTER JOHN AND I GOT MARRIED, PEOPLE WOULD ASK US :
DO YOU FEEL ANY DIFFERENT!??
THEY WANTED IT TO BE TRANSFORMATIVE IN SOME WAY.
I HAVE OFTEN BEEN ACCUSED OF BEING UNROMANTIC.
YOU DON'T HAVE A SENTIMENTAL BONE IN YOUR BODY.
'90s BF
gasp
I DO TOO
CYNTHIA HEIMEL
DO I?
IT IS TRUE THAT I DETEST CHEAP SENTIMENT.
FOR EXAMPLE
DAN JONES III
October 29, 2013
He said yes.
Tag photo
Like
538 Like

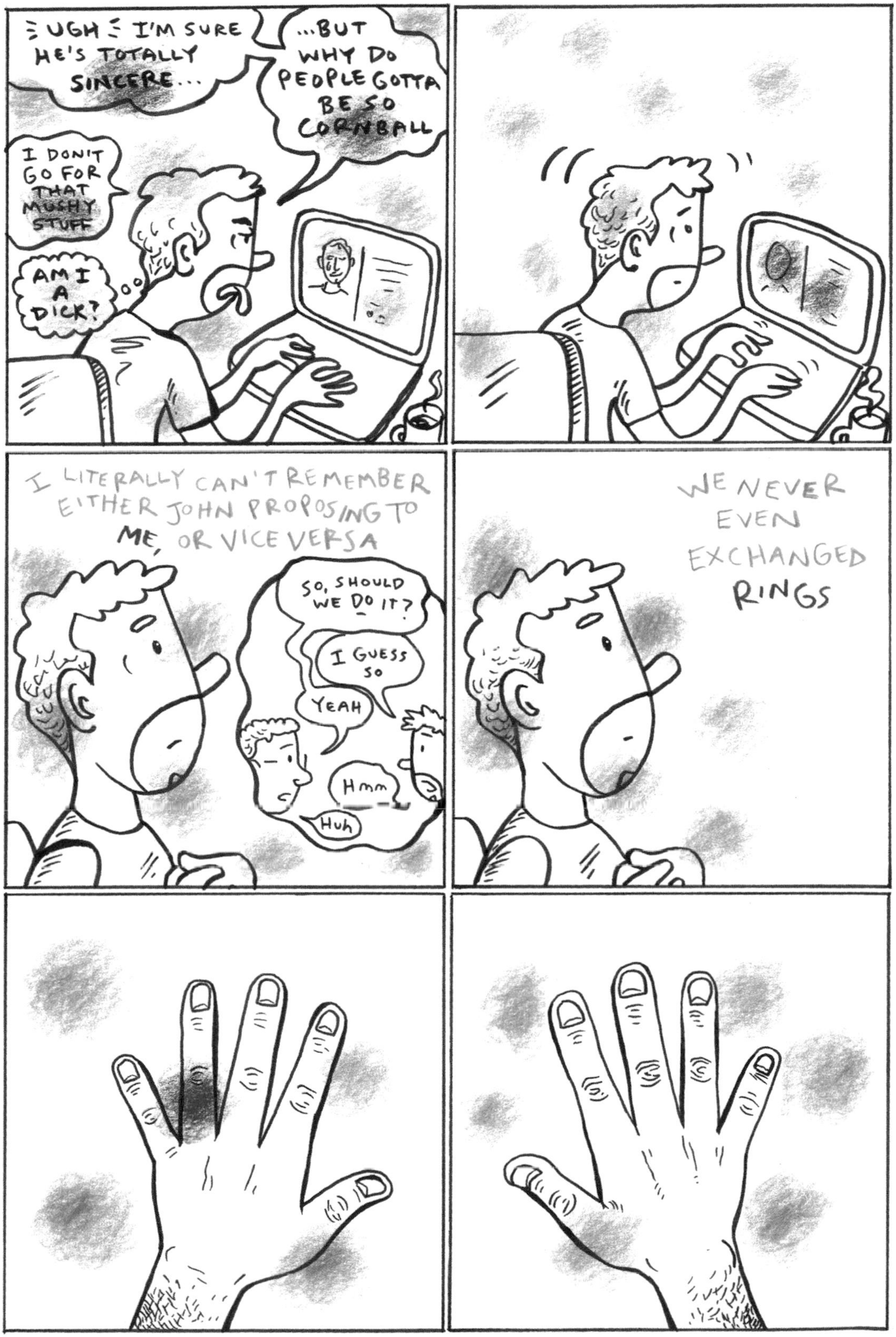
UGH I'M SURE HE'S TOTALLY SINCERE...
...BUT WHY DO PEOPLE GOTTA BE SO CORNBALL
I DON'T GO FOR THAT MUSHY STUFF
AM I A DICK?
I LITERALLY CAN'T REMEMBER EITHER JOHN PROPOSING TO ME, OR VICE VERSA
SO, SHOULD WE DO IT?
I GUESS SO
YEAH
Hmm
Huh
WE NEVER EVEN EXCHANGED RINGS

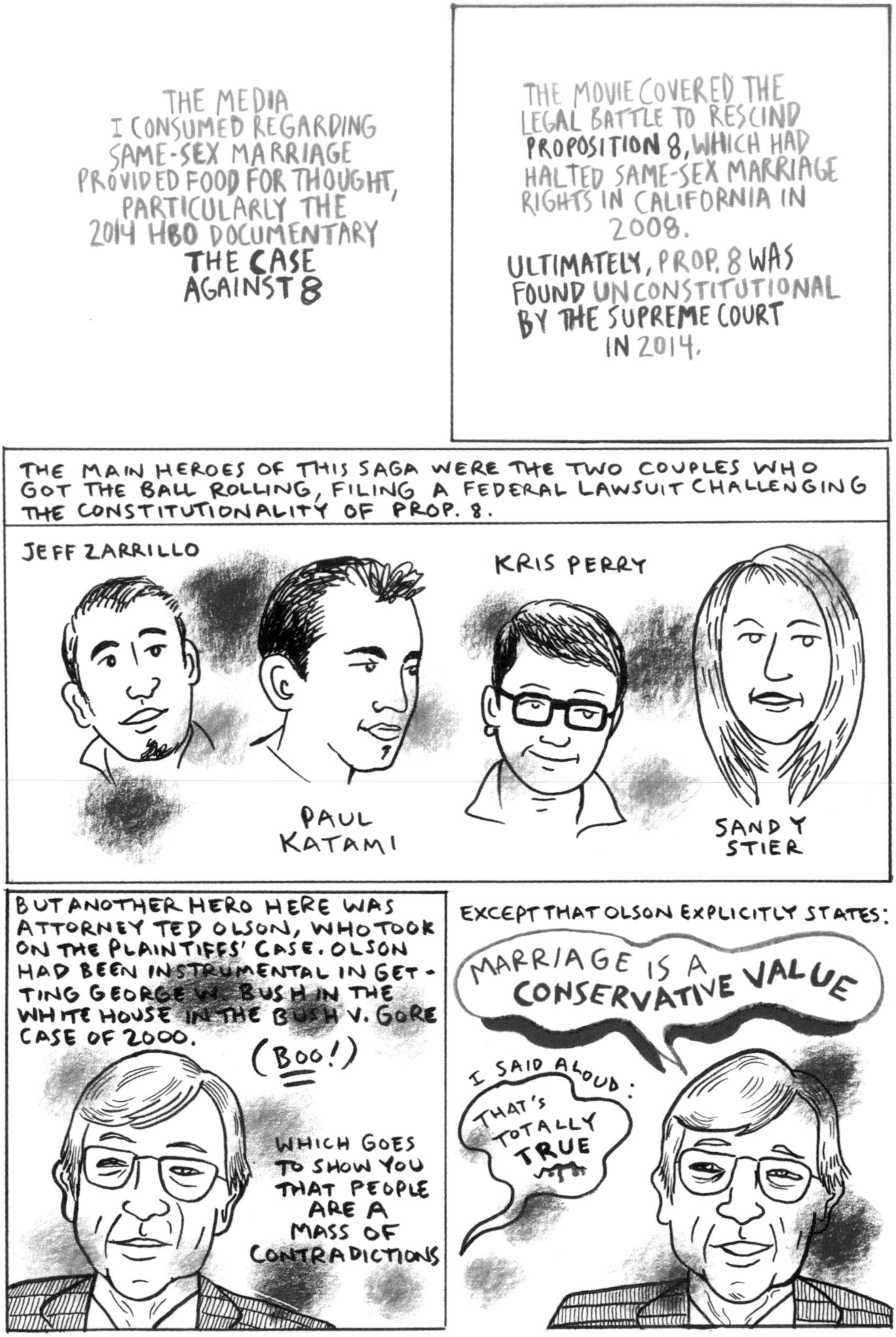
THE MEDIA I CONSUMED REGARDING SAME-SEX MARRIAGE PROVIDED FOOD FOR THOUGHT, PARTICULARLY THE 2014 HBO DOCUMENTARY THE CASE AGAINST 8
THE MOVIE COVERED THE LEGAL BATTLE TO RESCIND PROPOSITION 8, WHICH HAD HALTED SAME-SEX MARRIAGE RIGHTS IN CALIFORNIA IN 2008.
ULTIMATELY, PROP. 8 WAS FOUND UNCONSTITUTIONAL BY THE SUPREME COURT IN 2014.
THE MAIN HEROES OF THIS SAGA WERE THE TWO COUPLES WHO GOT THE BALL ROLLING, FILING A FEDERAL LAWSUIT CHALLENGING THE CONSTITUTIONALITY OF PROP. 8.
JEFF ZARRILLO
PAUL KATAMI
KRIS PERRY
SANDY STIER
BUT ANOTHER HERO HERE WAS ATTORNEY TED OLSON, WHO TOOK ON THE PLAINTIFFS' CASE. OLSON HAD BEEN INSTRUMENTAL IN GETTING GEORGE W. BUSH IN THE WHITE HOUSE IN THE BUSH V. GORE CASE OF 2000.
(BOO!)
WHICH GOES TO SHOW YOU THAT PEOPLE ARE A MASS OF CONTRADICTIONS
EXCEPT THAT OLSON EXPLICITLY STATES:
MARRIAGE IS A CONSERVATIVE VALUE
I SAID ALOUD:
THAT'S TOTALLY TRUE

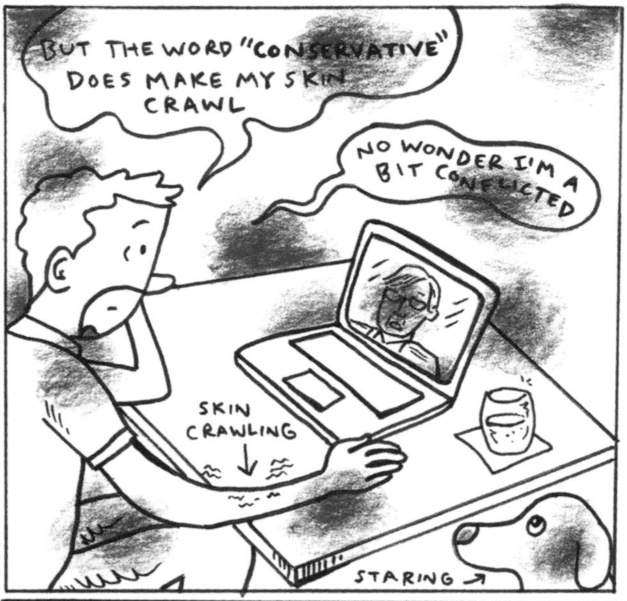
BUT THE WORD "CONSERVATIVE" DOES MAKE MY SKIN CRAWL
NO WONDER I'M A BIT CONFLICTED
SKIN CRAWLING
STARING

FOR ME, THE EMOTIONAL PEAK OF THE FILM IS WHEN KRIS PERRY TALKS ABOUT THE LITTLE WAYS IN WHICH WE DESENSITIZE OURSELVES, JUST TO GET THROUGH. AND WHAT IT FEELS LIKE TO RECOGNIZE THIS.

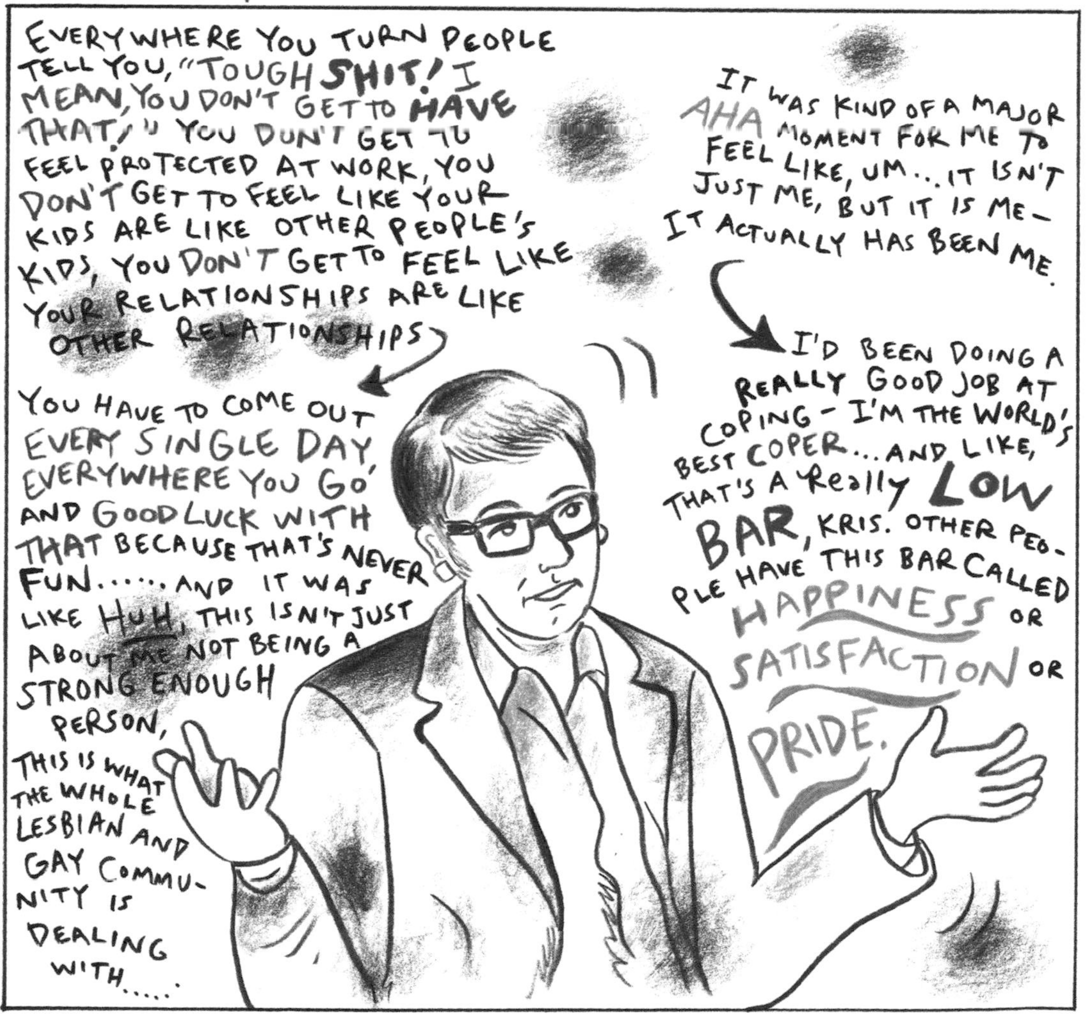
EVERYWHERE YOU TURN PEOPLE TELL YOU, "TOUGH SHIT! I MEAN, YOU DON'T GET TO HAVE THAT!" YOU DON'T GET TO FEEL PROTECTED AT WORK, YOU DON'T GET TO FEEL LIKE YOUR KIDS ARE LIKE OTHER PEOPLE'S KIDS, YOU DON'T GET TO FEEL LIKE YOUR RELATIONSHIPS ARE LIKE OTHER RELATIONSHIPS
YOU HAVE TO COME OUT EVERY SINGLE DAY, EVERYWHERE YOU GO' AND GOOD LUCK WITH THAT BECAUSE THAT'S NEVER FUN..... AND IT WAS LIKE HUH, THIS ISN'T JUST ABOUT ME NOT BEING A STRONG ENOUGH PERSON,
THIS IS WHAT THE WHOLE LESBIAN AND GAY COMMUNITY IS DEALING WITH.....
IT WAS KIND OF A MAJOR AHA MOMENT FOR ME TO FEEL LIKE, UM... IT ISN'T JUST ME, BUT IT IS ME— IT ACTUALLY HAS BEEN ME.
I'D BEEN DOING A REALLY GOOD JOB AT COPING — I'M THE WORLD'S BEST COPER... AND LIKE, THAT'S A REALLY LOW BAR, KRIS. OTHER PEOPLE HAVE THIS BAR CALLED HAPPINESS OR SATISFACTION OR PRIDE.

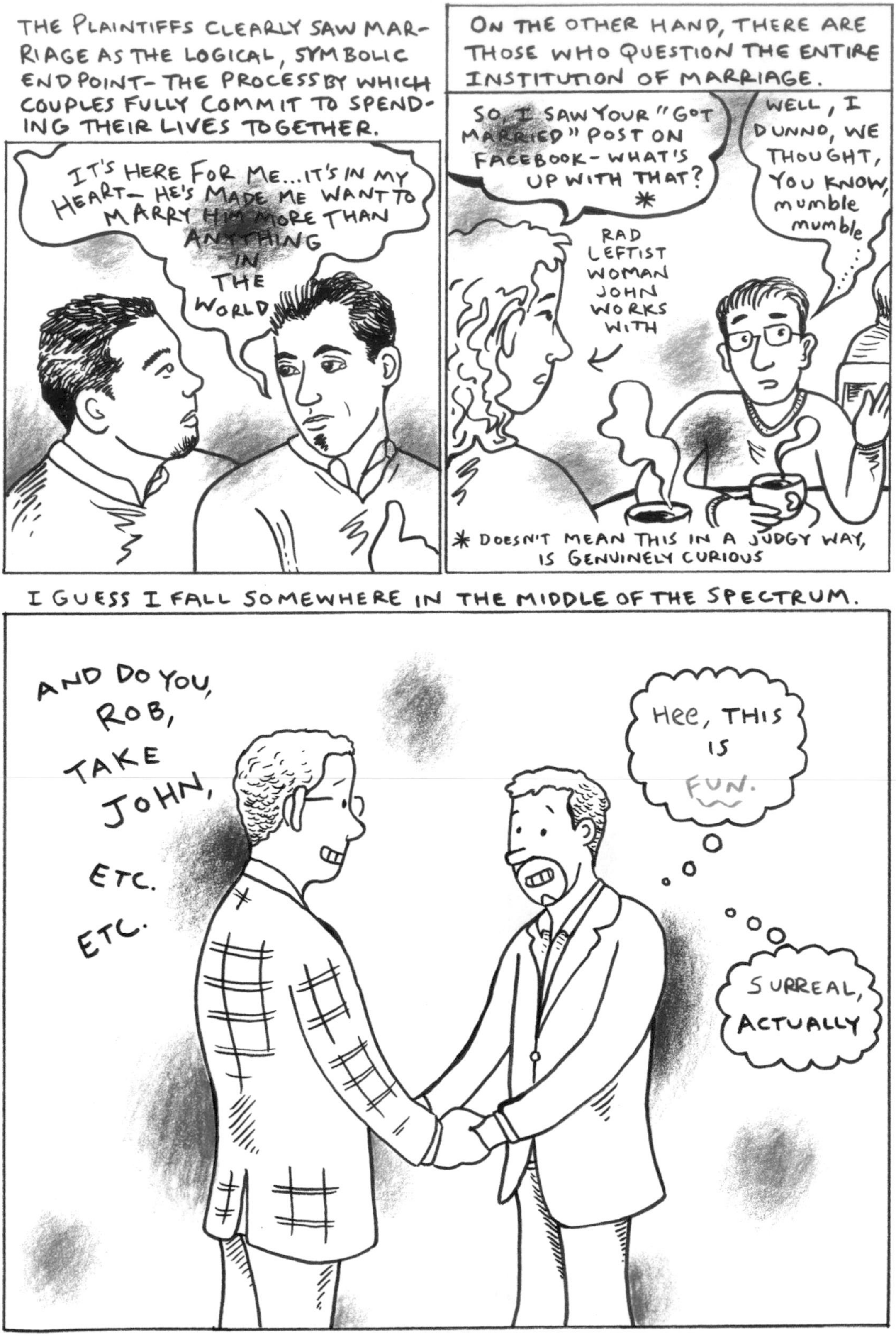
THE PLAINTIFFS CLEARLY SAW MARRIAGE AS THE LOGICAL, SYMBOLIC ENDPOINT- THE PROCESS BY WHICH COUPLES FULLY COMMIT TO SPENDING THEIR LIVES TOGETHER.
IT'S HERE FOR ME...IT'S IN MY HEART- HE'S MADE ME WANT TO MARRY HIM MORE THAN ANYTHING IN THE WORLD
ON THE OTHER HAND, THERE ARE THOSE WHO QUESTION THE ENTIRE INSTITUTION OF MARRIAGE.
SO, I SAW YOUR "GOT MARRIED" POST ON FACEBOOK- WHAT'S UP WITH THAT? *
RAD LEFTIST WOMAN JOHN WORKS WITH
WELL, I DUNNO, WE THOUGHT, YOU KNOW, mumble mumble
* DOESN'T MEAN THIS IN A JUDGY WAY, IS GENUINELY CURIOUS
I GUESS I FALL SOMEWHERE IN THE MIDDLE OF THE SPECTRUM.
AND DO YOU, ROB, TAKE JOHN, ETC. ETC.
Hee, THIS IS FUN.
SURREAL, ACTUALLY

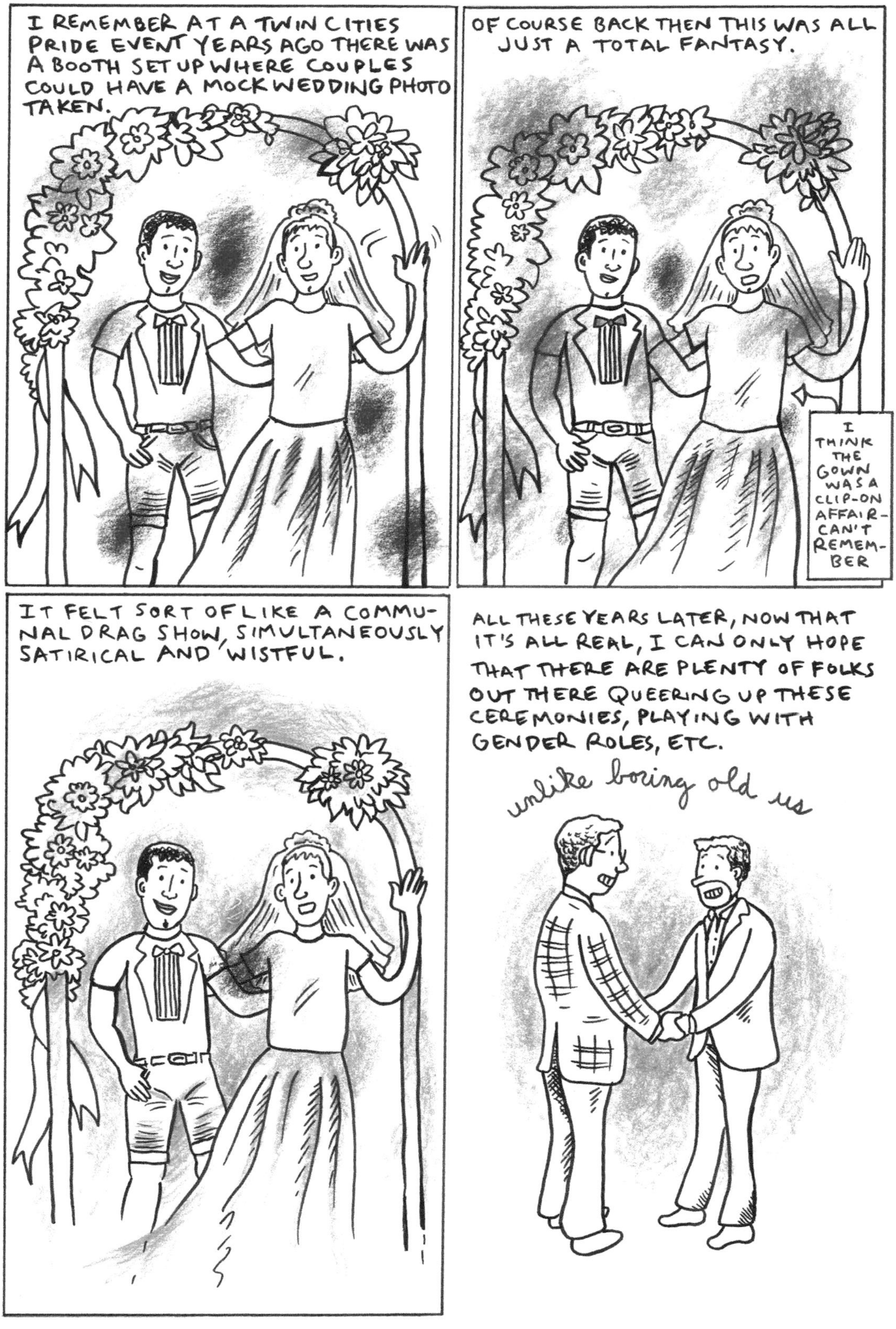
I REMEMBER AT A TWIN CITIES PRIDE EVENT YEARS AGO THERE WAS A BOOTH SET UP WHERE COUPLES COULD HAVE A MOCK WEDDING PHOTO TAKEN.
OF COURSE BACK THEN THIS WAS ALL JUST A TOTAL FANTASY.
I THINK THE GOWN WAS A CLIP-ON AFFAIR-CAN'T REMEMBER
IT FELT SORT OF LIKE A COMMUNAL DRAG SHOW, SIMULTANEOUSLY SATIRICAL AND WISTFUL.
ALL THESE YEARS LATER, NOW THAT IT'S ALL REAL, I CAN ONLY HOPE THAT THERE ARE PLENTY OF FOLKS OUT THERE QUEERING UP THESE CEREMONIES, PLAYING WITH GENDER ROLES, ETC.
unlike boring old us

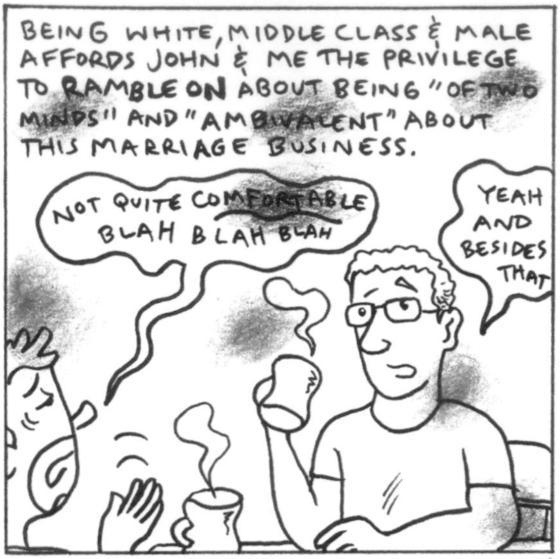
BEING WHITE, MIDDLE CLASS & MALE AFFORDS JOHN & ME THE PRIVILEGE TO RAMBLE ON ABOUT BEING "OF TWO MINDS" AND "AMBIVALENT" ABOUT THIS MARRIAGE BUSINESS.
NOT QUITE COMFORTABLE BLAH BLAH BLAH
YEAH AND BESIDES THAT

I READ THIS GREAT COLUMN* BY WRITER VIKKI REICH, WHERE SHE ADDRESSES THIS AMBIVALENCE. ONE LINE REALLY HIT HOME FOR ME:

> IT'S FRIGHTENING HOW EASY IT IS TO LEARN TO LIVE WITH INEQUALITY, TO ACCEPT LIFE AS AN OUTSIDER.

* MPLS STAR TRIBUNE, 5/21/2015

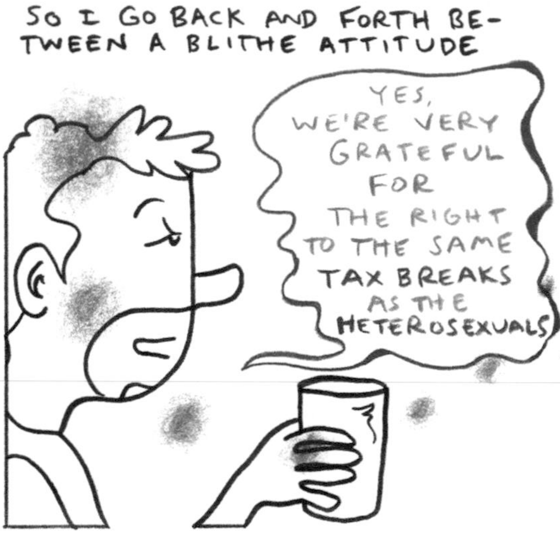
SO I GO BACK AND FORTH BE-TWEEN A BLITHE ATTITUDE
YES, WE'RE VERY GRATEFUL FOR THE RIGHT TO THE SAME TAX BREAKS AS THE HETEROSEXUALS

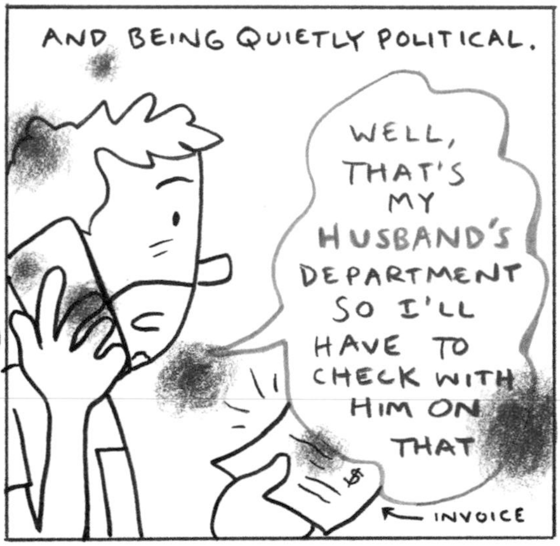
AND BEING QUIETLY POLITICAL.
WELL, THAT'S MY HUSBAND'S DEPARTMENT SO I'LL HAVE TO CHECK WITH HIM ON THAT
INVOICE

"... COME OUT EVERY SINGLE DAY EVERYWHERE YOU GO."

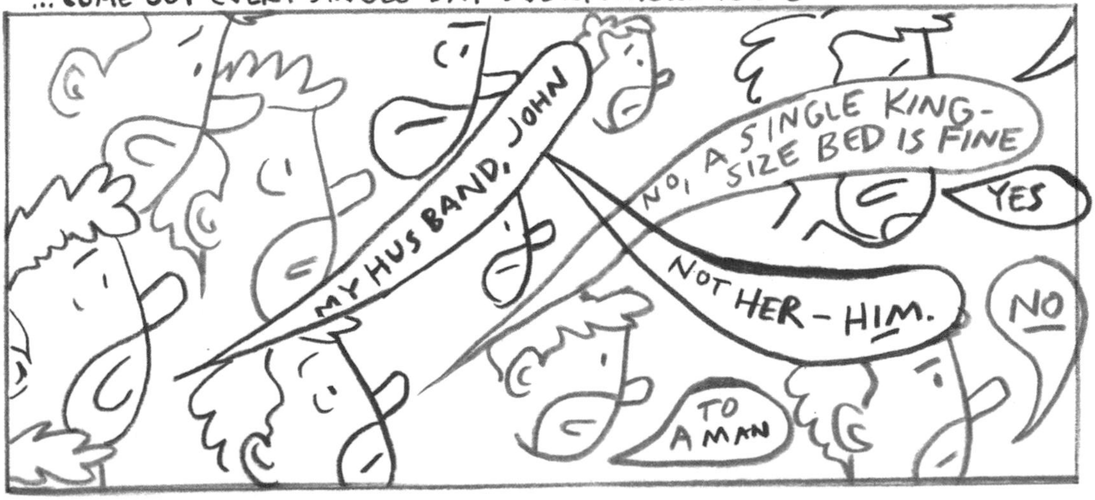
MY HUSBAND, JOHN
NO, A SINGLE KING-SIZE BED IS FINE
YES
NOT HER - HIM.
NO
TO A MAN

JOHN PREFERS "PARTNER" OR "SPOUSE."

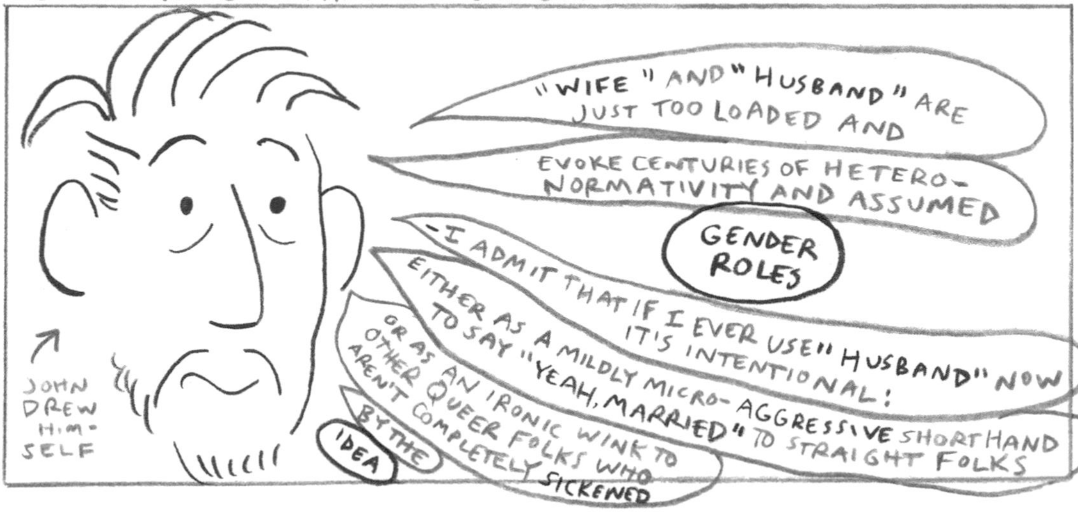

"WIFE" AND "HUSBAND" ARE JUST TOO LOADED AND
EVOKE CENTURIES OF HETERO-NORMATIVITY AND ASSUMED
GENDER ROLES
-I ADMIT THAT IF I EVER USE "HUSBAND" NOW IT'S INTENTIONAL:
EITHER AS A MILDLY MICRO-AGGRESSIVE SHORTHAND TO SAY "YEAH, MARRIED" TO STRAIGHT FOLKS
OR AS AN IRONIC WINK TO OTHER QUEER FOLKS WHO AREN'T COMPLETELY SICKENED
BY THE
IDEA
JOHN DREW HIM-SELF

GROWING UP GAY, LET ME TELL YOU, I WAS TOTALLY DOWN WITH THOSE WHO WANTED TO TEAR DOWN ALL THE TOOLS OF THE PATRIARCHY, INCLUDING MARRIAGE.

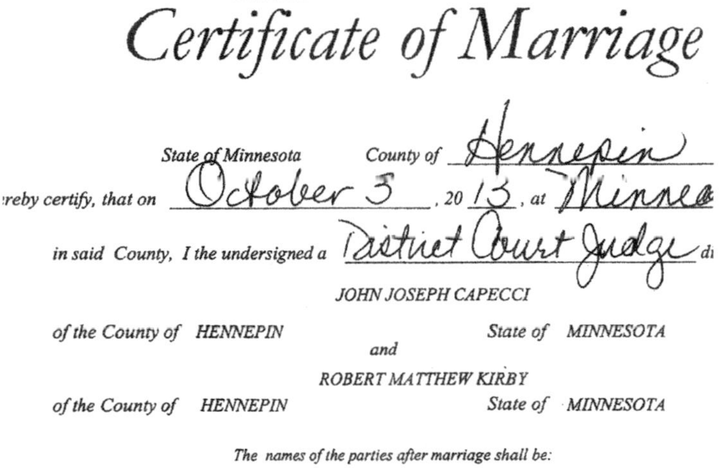

Certificate of Marriage

State of Minnesota County of Hennepin

ereby certify, that on October 3, 2013, at Minnea

in said County, I the undersigned a District Court Judge di

JOHN JOSEPH CAPECCI

of the County of HENNEPIN State of MINNESOTA

and

ROBERT MATTHEW KIRBY

of the County of HENNEPIN State of MINNESOTA

The names of the parties after marriage shall be:

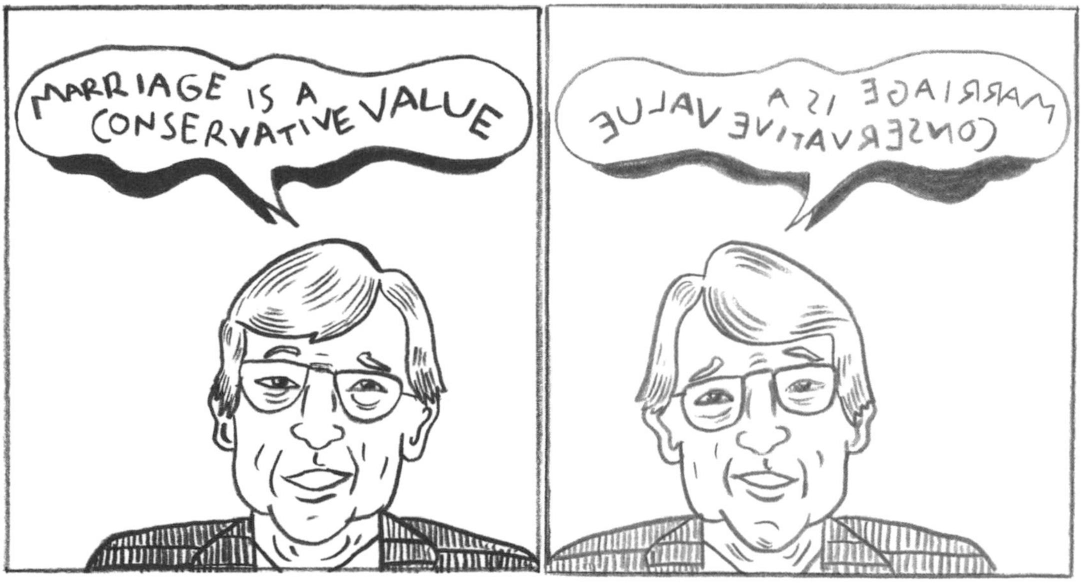

MARRIAGE IS A CONSERVATIVE VALUE
MARRIAGE IS A CONSERVATIVE VALUE

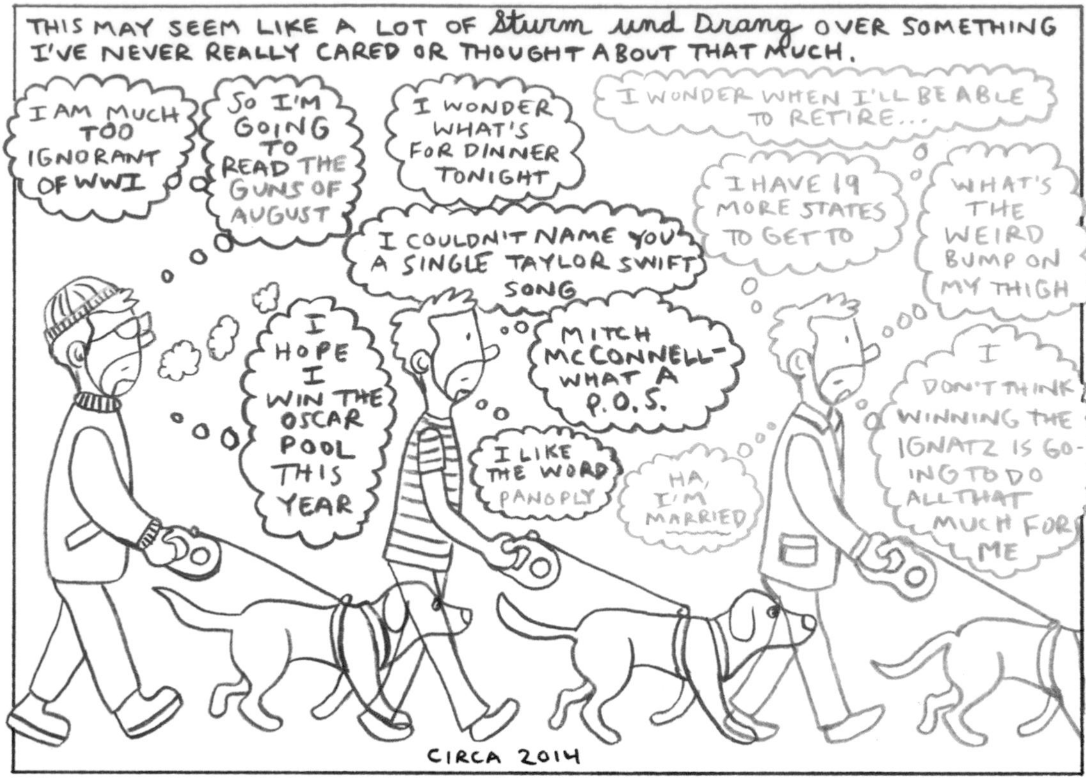
THIS MAY SEEM LIKE A LOT OF *Sturm und Drang* OVER SOMETHING I'VE NEVER REALLY CARED OR THOUGHT ABOUT THAT MUCH.
I AM MUCH TOO IGNORANT OF WWI
SO I'M GOING TO READ THE GUNS OF AUGUST
I WONDER WHAT'S FOR DINNER TONIGHT
I WONDER WHEN I'LL BE ABLE TO RETIRE...
I HAVE 19 MORE STATES TO GET TO
WHAT'S THE WEIRD BUMP ON MY THIGH
I COULDN'T NAME YOU A SINGLE TAYLOR SWIFT SONG
I HOPE I WIN THE OSCAR POOL THIS YEAR
MITCH McCONNELL- WHAT A P.O.S.
I LIKE THE WORD PANOPLY
HA, I'M MARRIED
I DON'T THINK WINNING THE IGNATZ IS GOING TO DO ALL THAT MUCH FOR ME
CIRCA 2014

BUT GET ME GOING

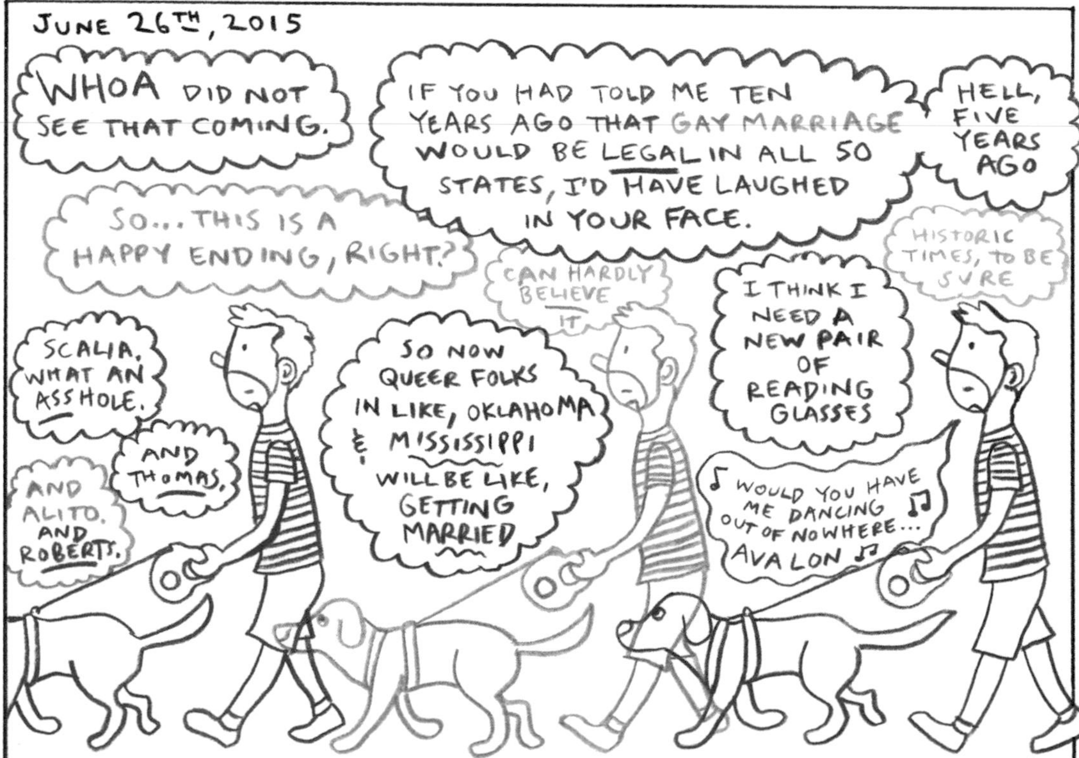
JUNE 26TH, 2015
WHOA DID NOT SEE THAT COMING.
IF YOU HAD TOLD ME TEN YEARS AGO THAT GAY MARRIAGE WOULD BE LEGAL IN ALL 50 STATES, I'D HAVE LAUGHED IN YOUR FACE.
HELL, FIVE YEARS AGO
SO... THIS IS A HAPPY ENDING, RIGHT?
CAN HARDLY BELIEVE IT
HISTORIC TIMES, TO BE SURE
I THINK I NEED A NEW PAIR OF READING GLASSES
SCALIA. WHAT AN ASSHOLE.
AND THOMAS.
AND ALITO. AND ROBERTS.
SO NOW QUEER FOLKS IN LIKE, OKLAHOMA & MISSISSIPPI WILL BE LIKE, GETTING MARRIED
♪ WOULD YOU HAVE ME DANCING ♫ OUT OF NOWHERE... AVALON ♫

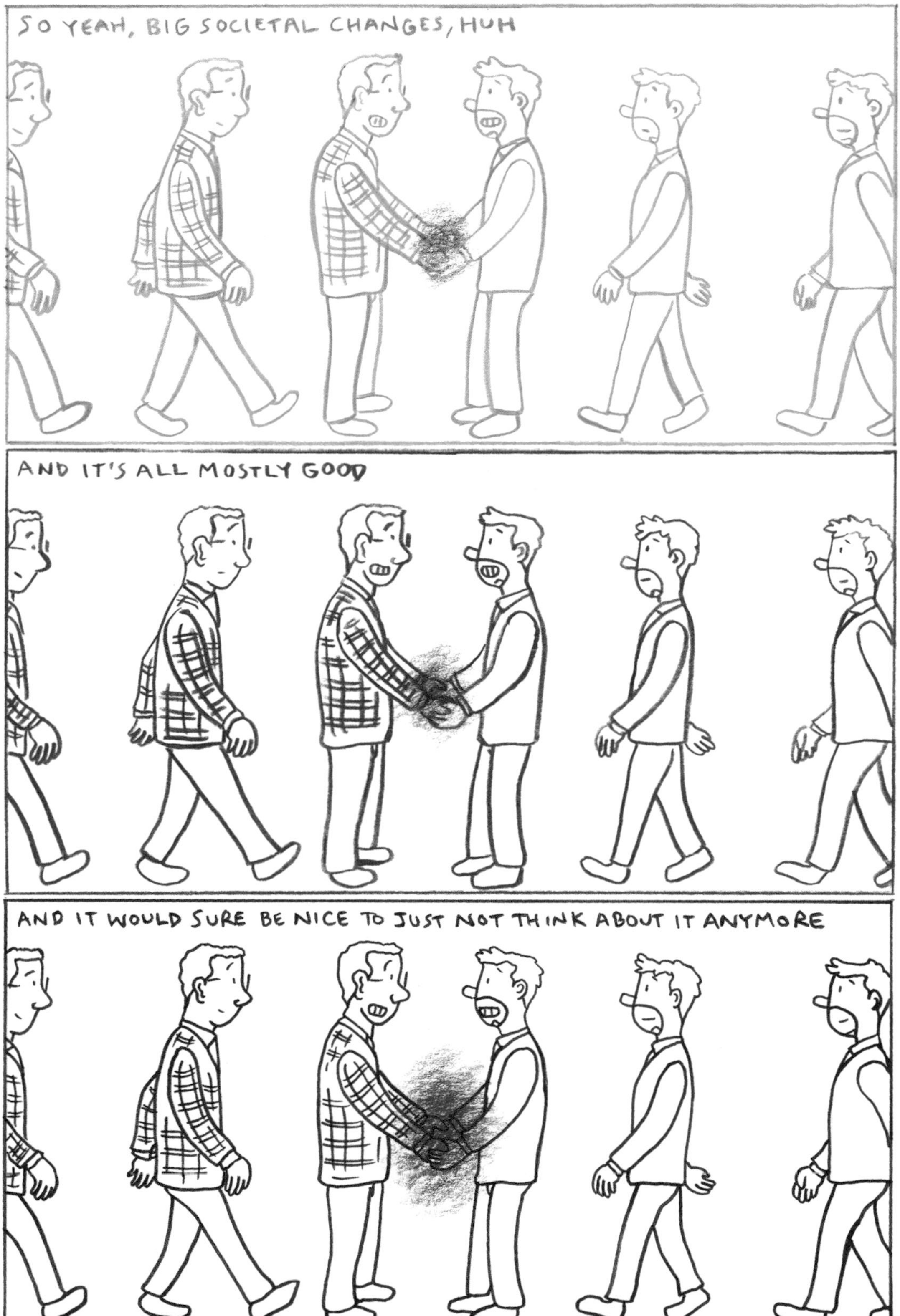

SO YEAH, BIG SOCIETAL CHANGES, HUH
AND IT'S ALL MOSTLY GOOD
AND IT WOULD SURE BE NICE TO JUST NOT THINK ABOUT IT ANYMORE

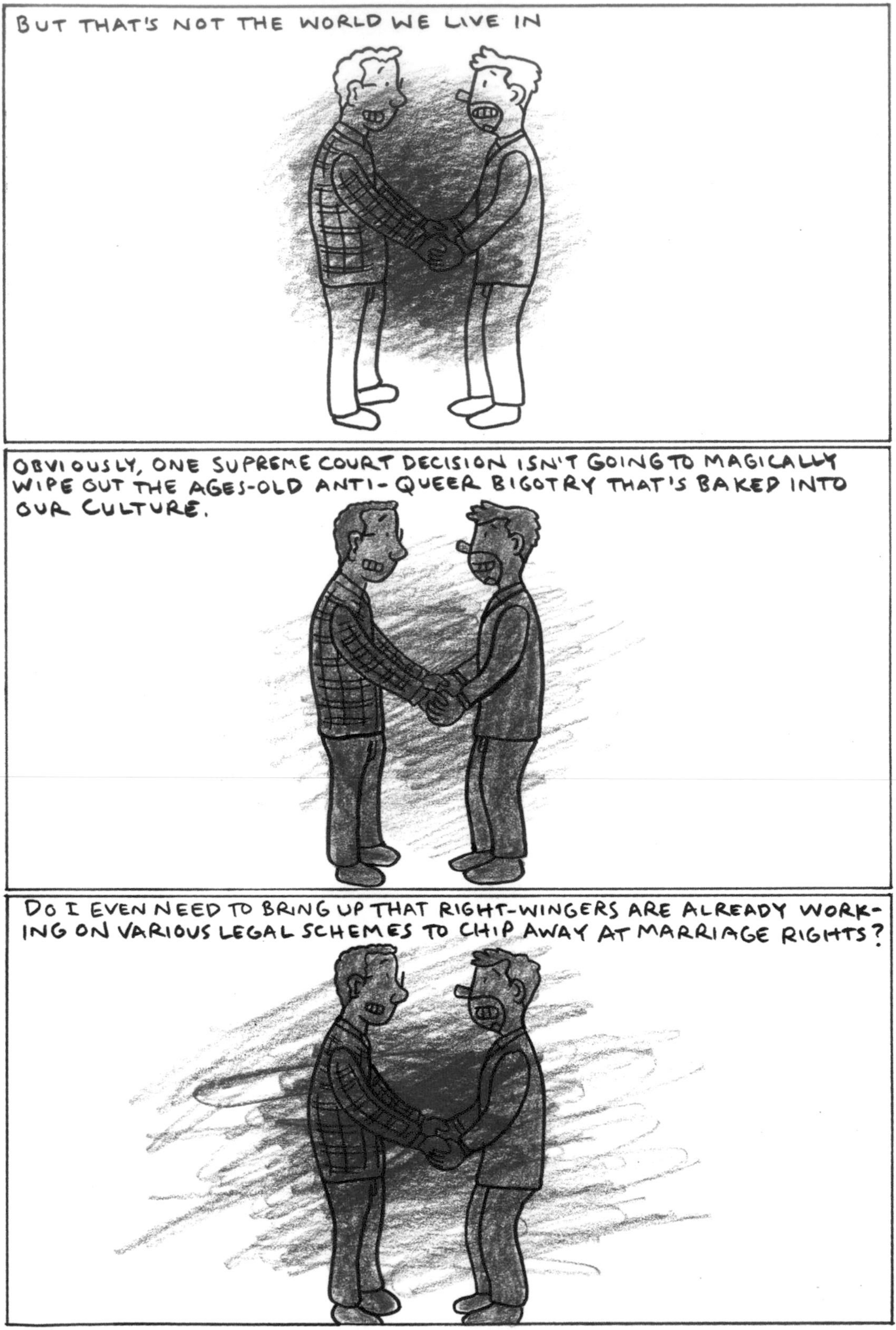
BUT THAT'S NOT THE WORLD WE LIVE IN
OBVIOUSLY, ONE SUPREME COURT DECISION ISN'T GOING TO MAGICALLY WIPE OUT THE AGES-OLD ANTI-QUEER BIGOTRY THAT'S BAKED INTO OUR CULTURE.
DO I EVEN NEED TO BRING UP THAT RIGHT-WINGERS ARE ALREADY WORKING ON VARIOUS LEGAL SCHEMES TO CHIP AWAY AT MARRIAGE RIGHTS?

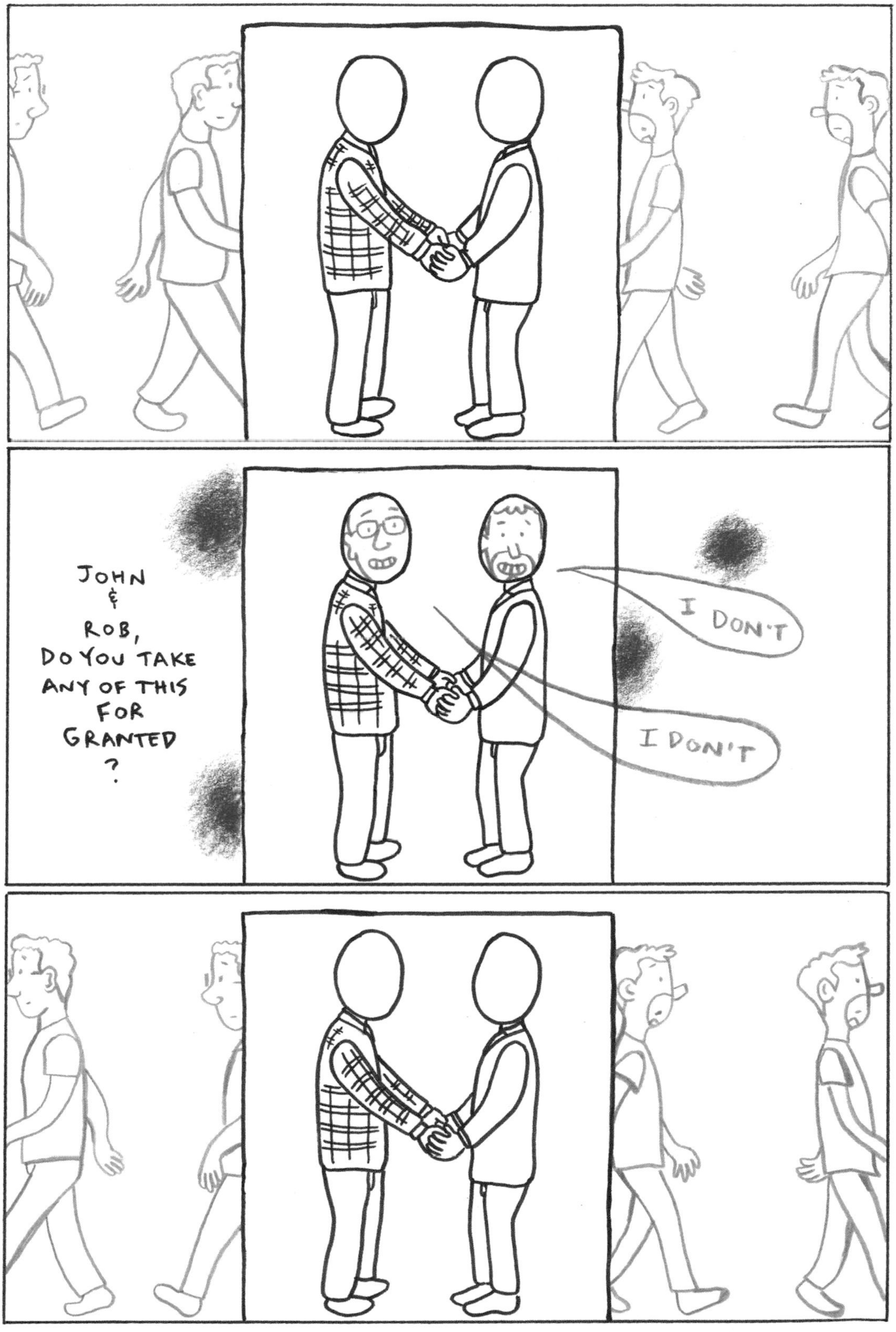
JOHN & ROB, DO YOU TAKE ANY OF THIS FOR GRANTED?
I DON'T
I DON'T

On September 3rd, 1971, Jack Baker & Michael McConnell got married in a friend's apartment in Minneapolis.

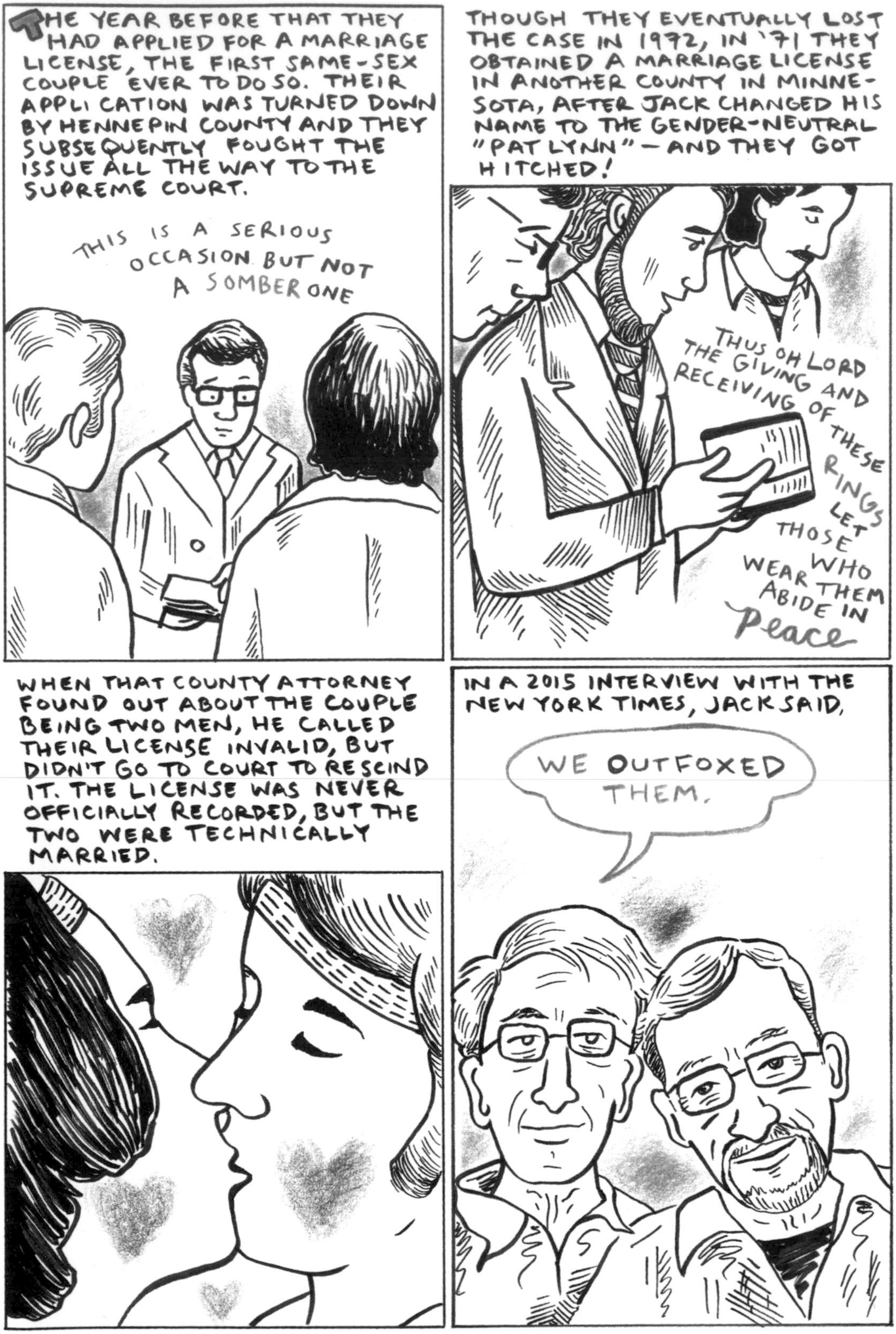
THE YEAR BEFORE THAT THEY HAD APPLIED FOR A MARRIAGE LICENSE, THE FIRST SAME-SEX COUPLE EVER TO DO SO. THEIR APPLICATION WAS TURNED DOWN BY HENNEPIN COUNTY AND THEY SUBSEQUENTLY FOUGHT THE ISSUE ALL THE WAY TO THE SUPREME COURT.
THIS IS A SERIOUS OCCASION. BUT NOT A SOMBER ONE
THOUGH THEY EVENTUALLY LOST THE CASE IN 1972, IN '71 THEY OBTAINED A MARRIAGE LICENSE IN ANOTHER COUNTY IN MINNESOTA, AFTER JACK CHANGED HIS NAME TO THE GENDER-NEUTRAL "PAT LYNN" — AND THEY GOT HITCHED!
THUS OH LORD THE GIVING AND RECEIVING OF THESE RINGS LET THOSE WHO WEAR THEM ABIDE IN Peace
WHEN THAT COUNTY ATTORNEY FOUND OUT ABOUT THE COUPLE BEING TWO MEN, HE CALLED THEIR LICENSE INVALID, BUT DIDN'T GO TO COURT TO RESCIND IT. THE LICENSE WAS NEVER OFFICIALLY RECORDED, BUT THE TWO WERE TECHNICALLY MARRIED.
IN A 2015 INTERVIEW WITH THE NEW YORK TIMES, JACK SAID,
WE OUTFOXED THEM.

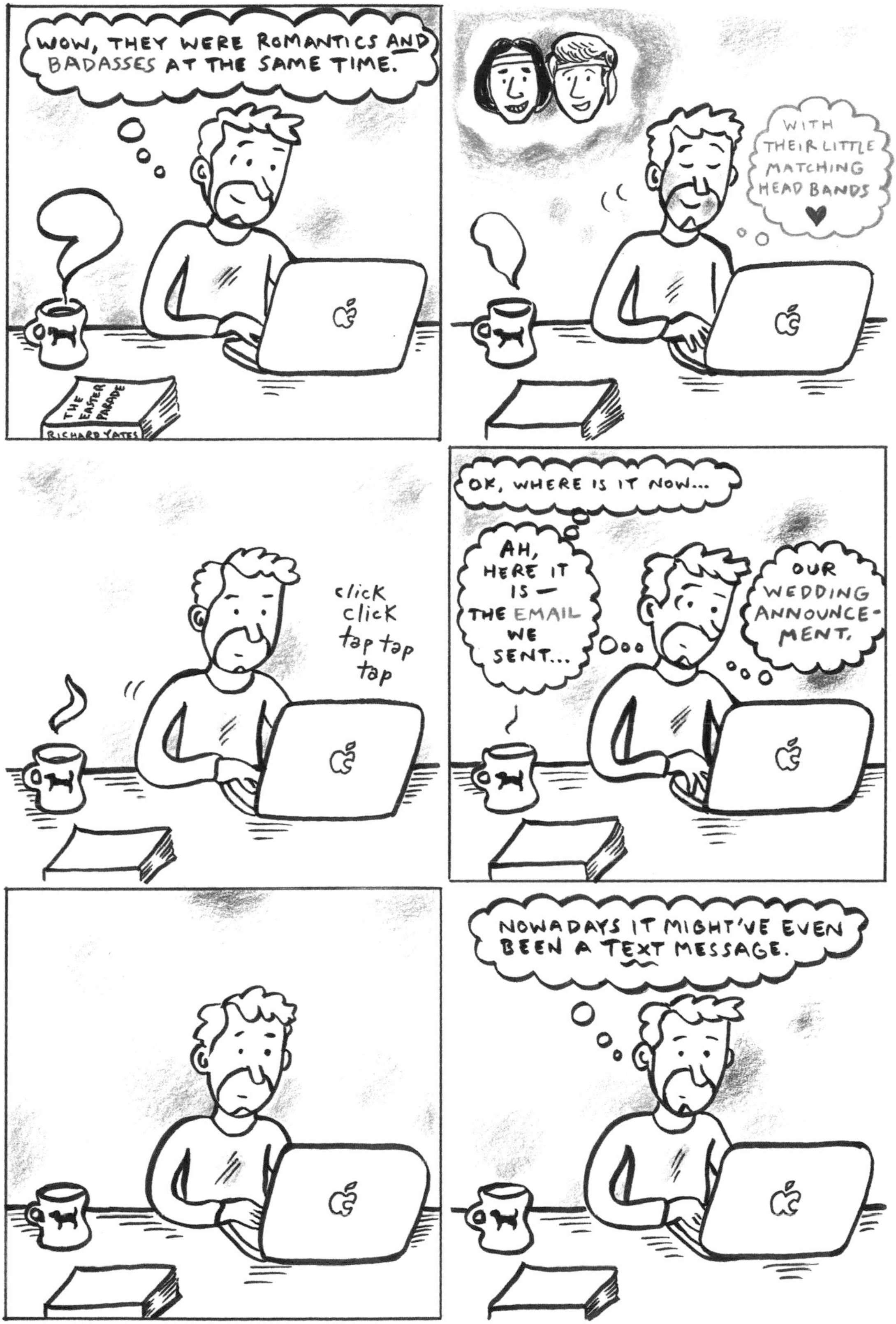
WOW, THEY WERE ROMANTICS AND BADASSES AT THE SAME TIME.
THE EASTER PARADE
RICHARD YATES
WITH THEIR LITTLE MATCHING HEAD BANDS ♥
click click tap tap tap
OK, WHERE IS IT NOW...
AH, HERE IT IS — THE EMAIL WE SENT...
OUR WEDDING ANNOUNCEMENT.
NOWADAYS IT MIGHT'VE EVEN BEEN A TEXT MESSAGE.

From: John Capecci <jcapecci@earthlink.net> Robert Kirby <curbside2@earthlink.net>
To: <everybody>
Sent: Sunday, September 29, 2013 8:54 AM
Subject: news from the midwest

Hello, dears:

Just a quick note to say that this Thursday we'll be stopping off at Judge Elizabeth Cutter's chambers to sign a few papers that will make the State (and gov!) recognize what we've been working on and enjoying for over 10 years. Whoo hoo!

We're doing it "unceremoniously": no big party, no registry, no releasing of doves. Just going out to dinner with some locals afterwards and looking forward to raising glasses with you—hopefully soon—to toast love and long friendships and commitment.

Love,

John and Rob

PS. Being the true romantics that we are, we'll officially announce on Thursday by changing our Facebook statuses. :)

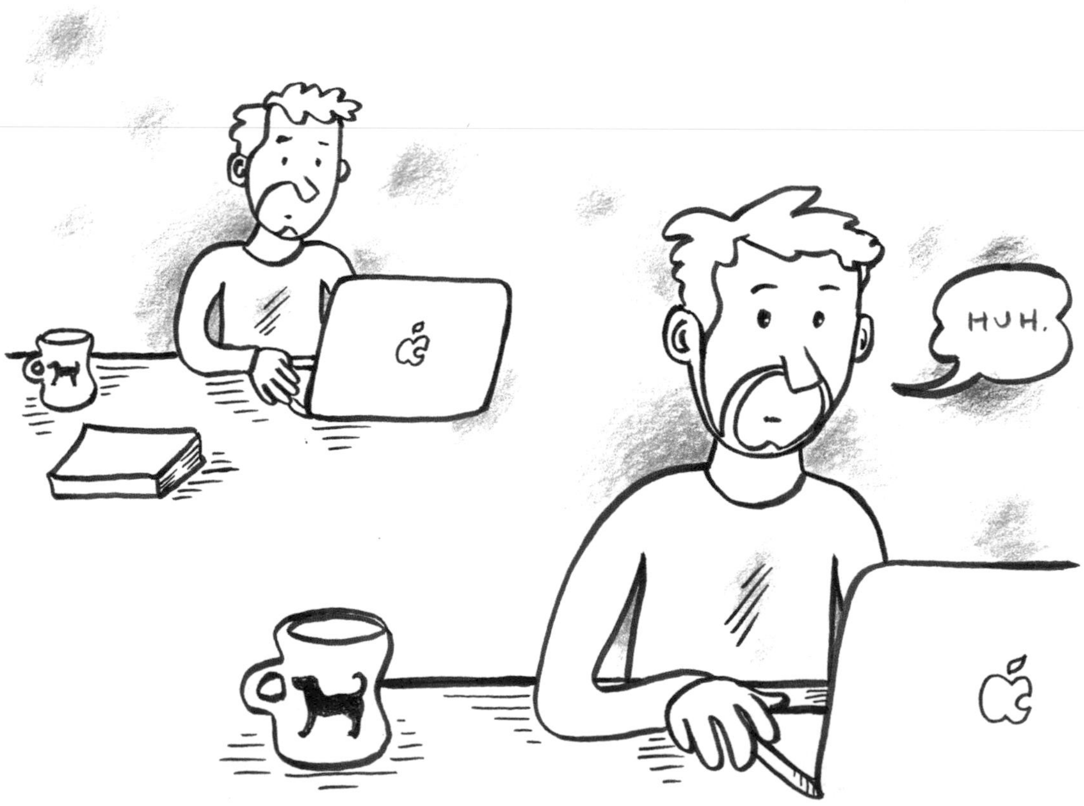
HUH.

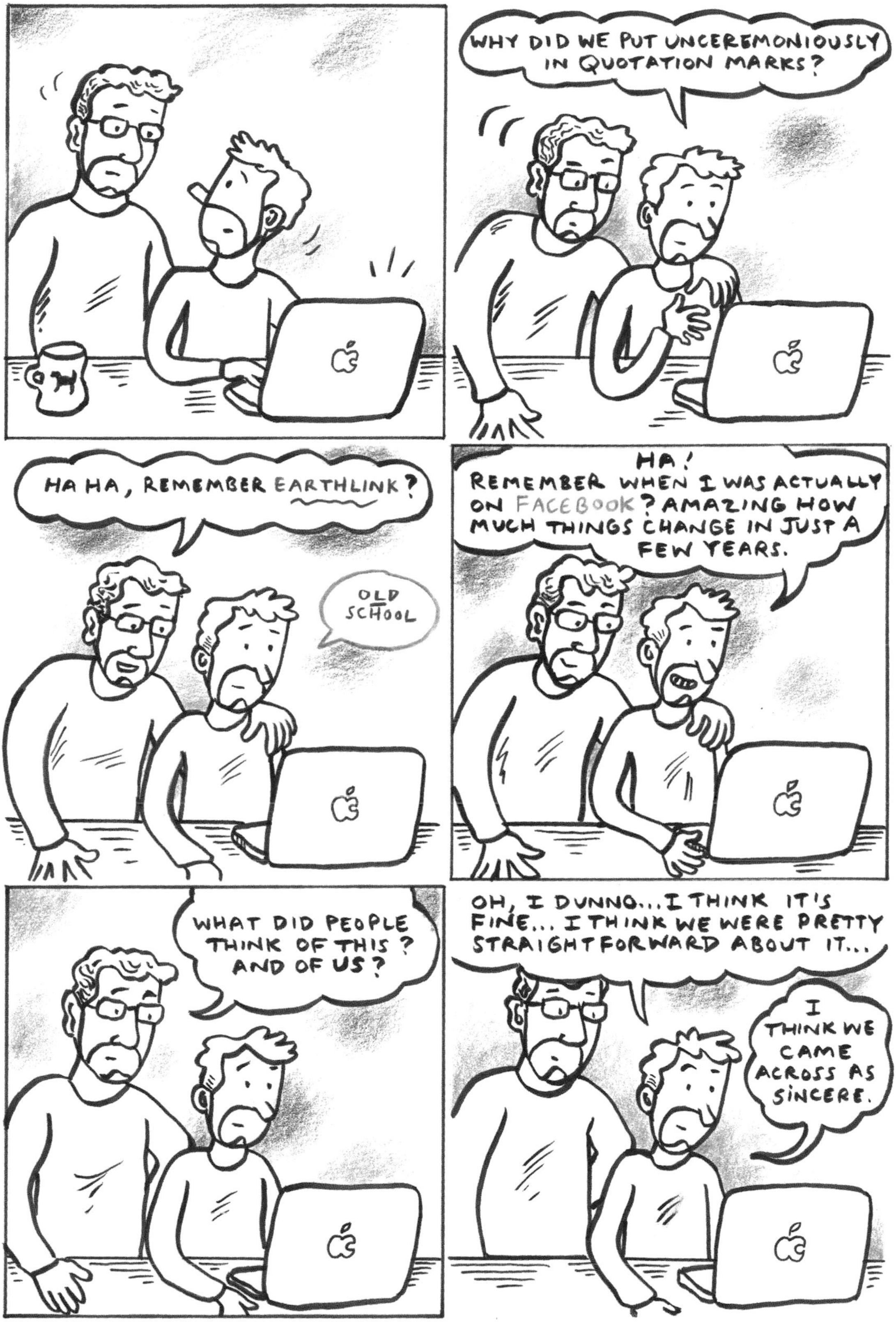
WHY DID WE PUT UNCEREMONIOUSLY IN QUOTATION MARKS?
HA HA, REMEMBER EARTHLINK?
OLD SCHOOL
HA! REMEMBER WHEN I WAS ACTUALLY ON FACEBOOK? AMAZING HOW MUCH THINGS CHANGE IN JUST A FEW YEARS.
WHAT DID PEOPLE THINK OF THIS? AND OF US?
OH, I DUNNO... I THINK IT'S FINE... I THINK WE WERE PRETTY STRAIGHTFORWARD ABOUT IT...
I THINK WE CAME ACROSS AS SINCERE.

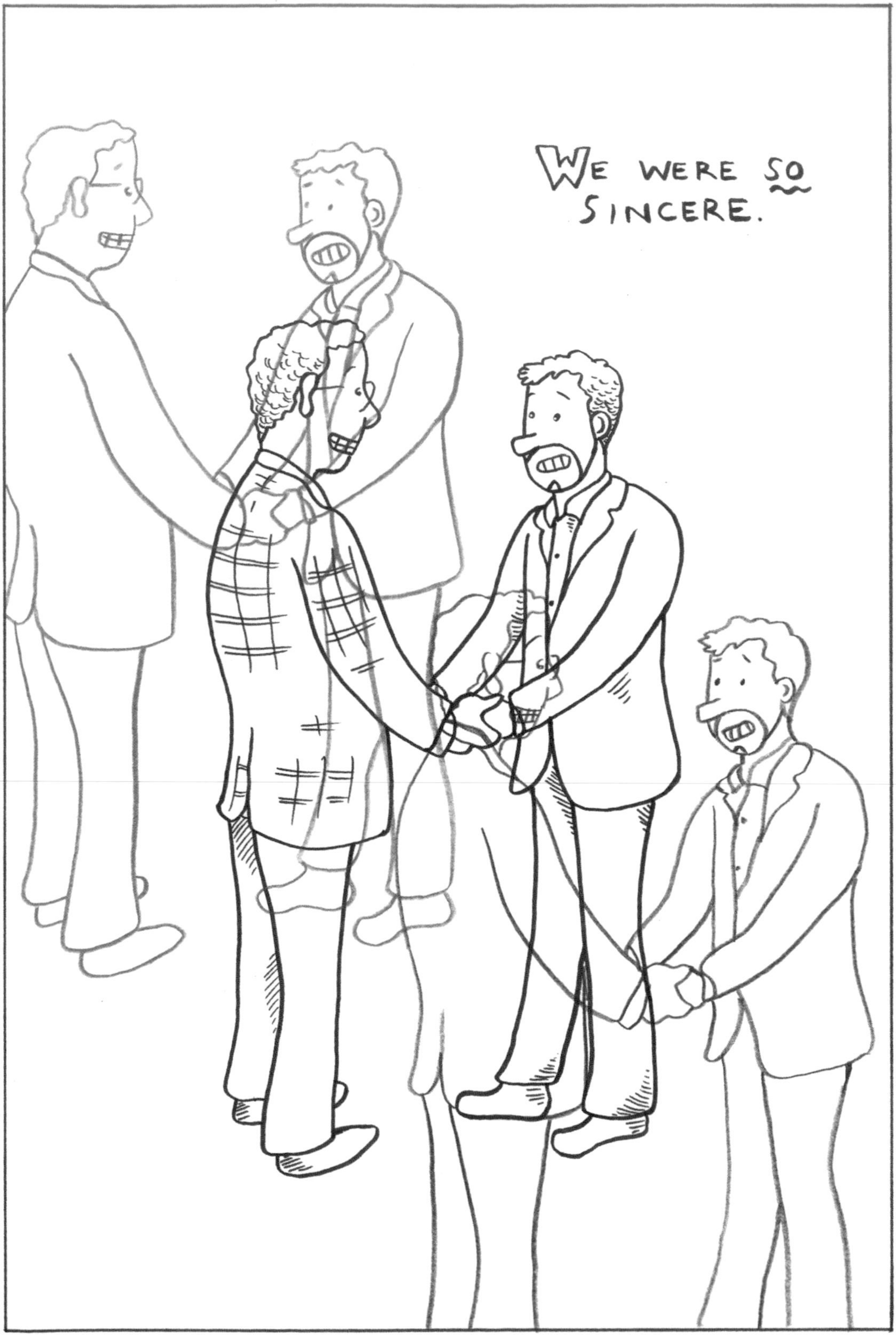
WE WERE SO SINCERE.

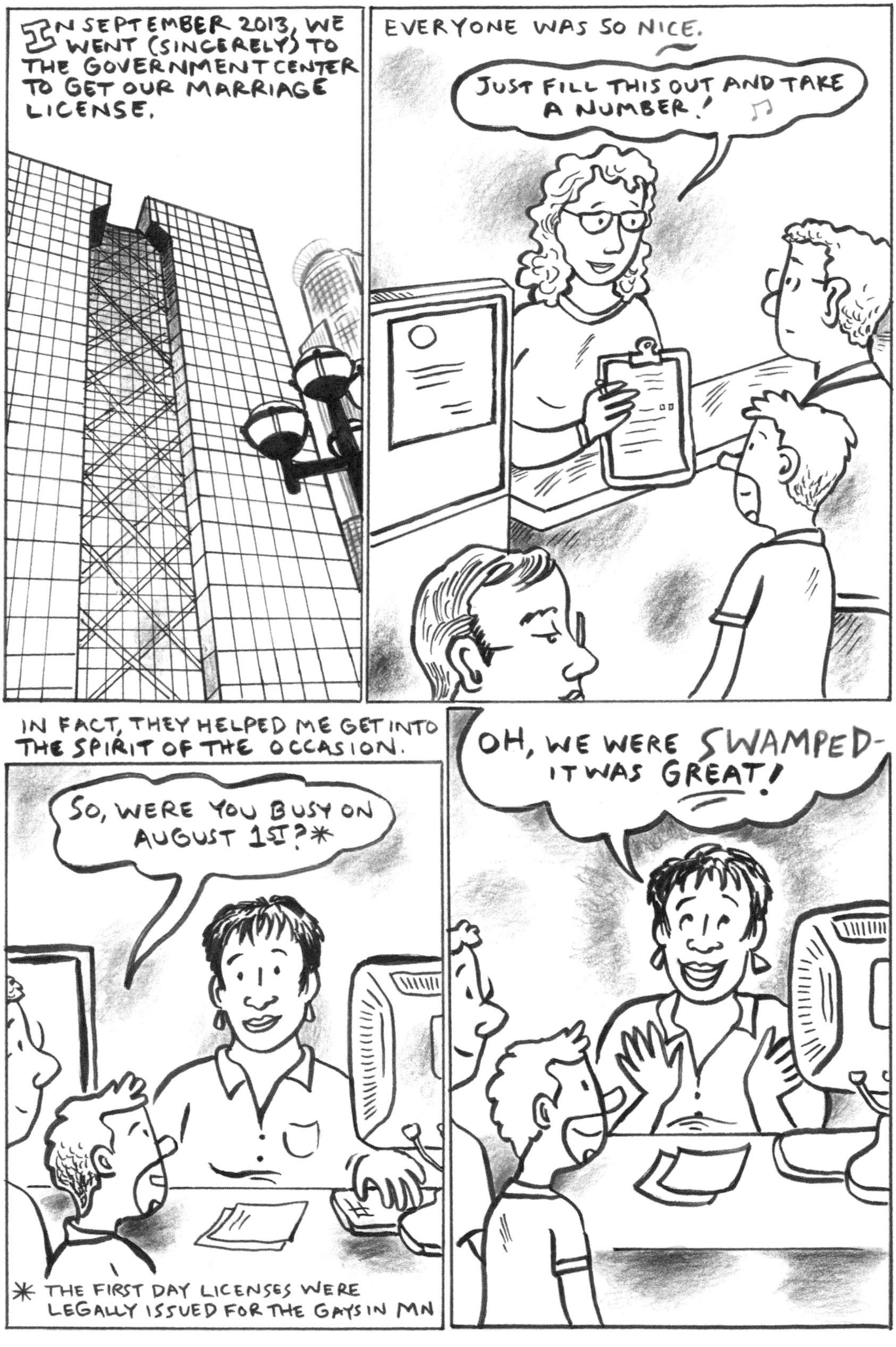

IN SEPTEMBER 2013, WE WENT (SINCERELY) TO THE GOVERNMENT CENTER TO GET OUR MARRIAGE LICENSE.
EVERYONE WAS SO NICE.
JUST FILL THIS OUT AND TAKE A NUMBER!
IN FACT, THEY HELPED ME GET INTO THE SPIRIT OF THE OCCASION.
SO, WERE YOU BUSY ON AUGUST 1ST?*
* THE FIRST DAY LICENSES WERE LEGALLY ISSUED FOR THE GAYS IN MN
OH, WE WERE SWAMPED- IT WAS GREAT!

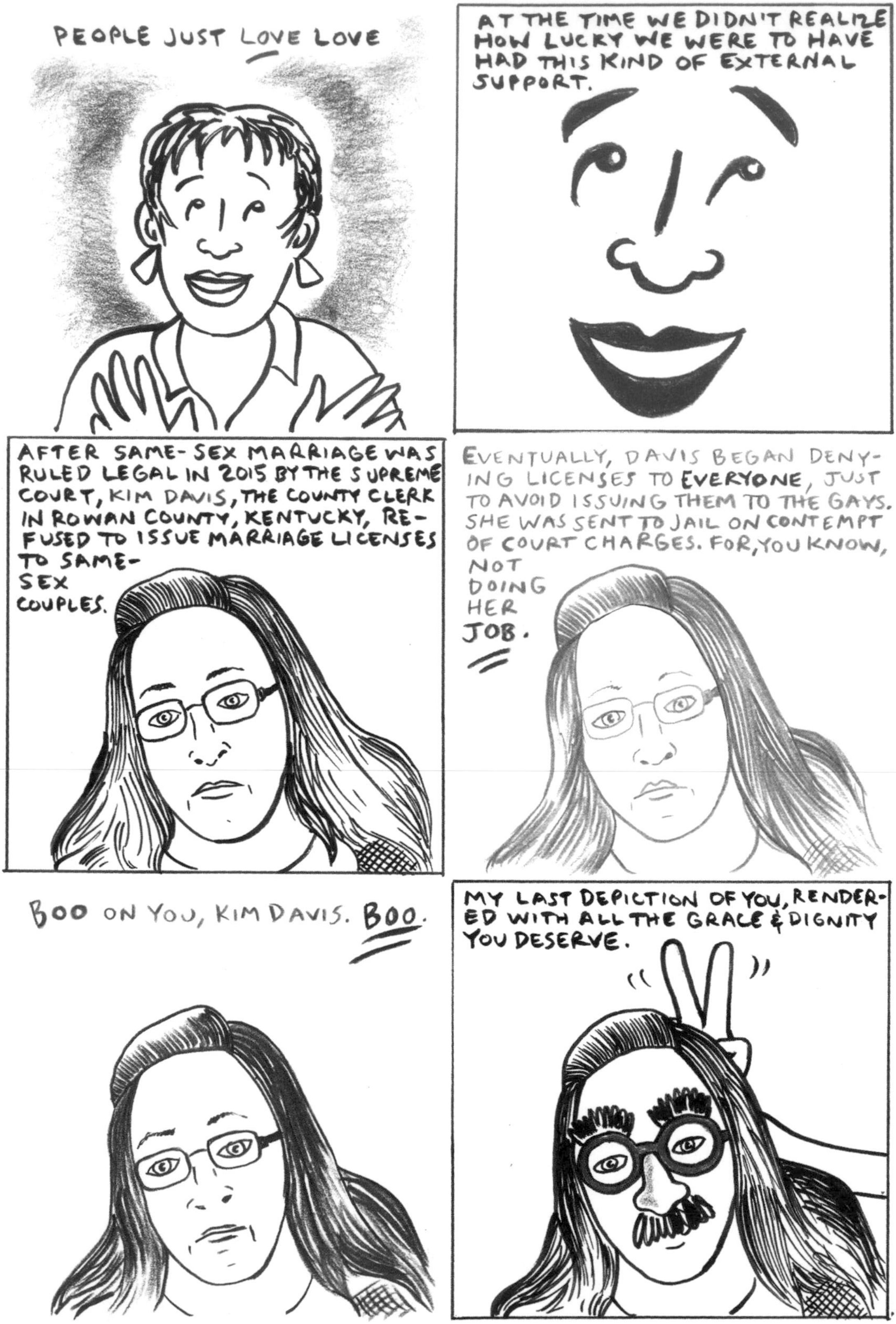
PEOPLE JUST LOVE LOVE
AT THE TIME WE DIDN'T REALIZE HOW LUCKY WE WERE TO HAVE HAD THIS KIND OF EXTERNAL SUPPORT.
AFTER SAME-SEX MARRIAGE WAS RULED LEGAL IN 2015 BY THE SUPREME COURT, KIM DAVIS, THE COUNTY CLERK IN ROWAN COUNTY, KENTUCKY, REFUSED TO ISSUE MARRIAGE LICENSES TO SAME-SEX COUPLES.
EVENTUALLY, DAVIS BEGAN DENYING LICENSES TO EVERYONE, JUST TO AVOID ISSUING THEM TO THE GAYS. SHE WAS SENT TO JAIL ON CONTEMPT OF COURT CHARGES. FOR, YOU KNOW, NOT DOING HER JOB.
BOO ON YOU, KIM DAVIS. BOO.
MY LAST DEPICTION OF YOU, RENDERED WITH ALL THE GRACE & DIGNITY YOU DESERVE.

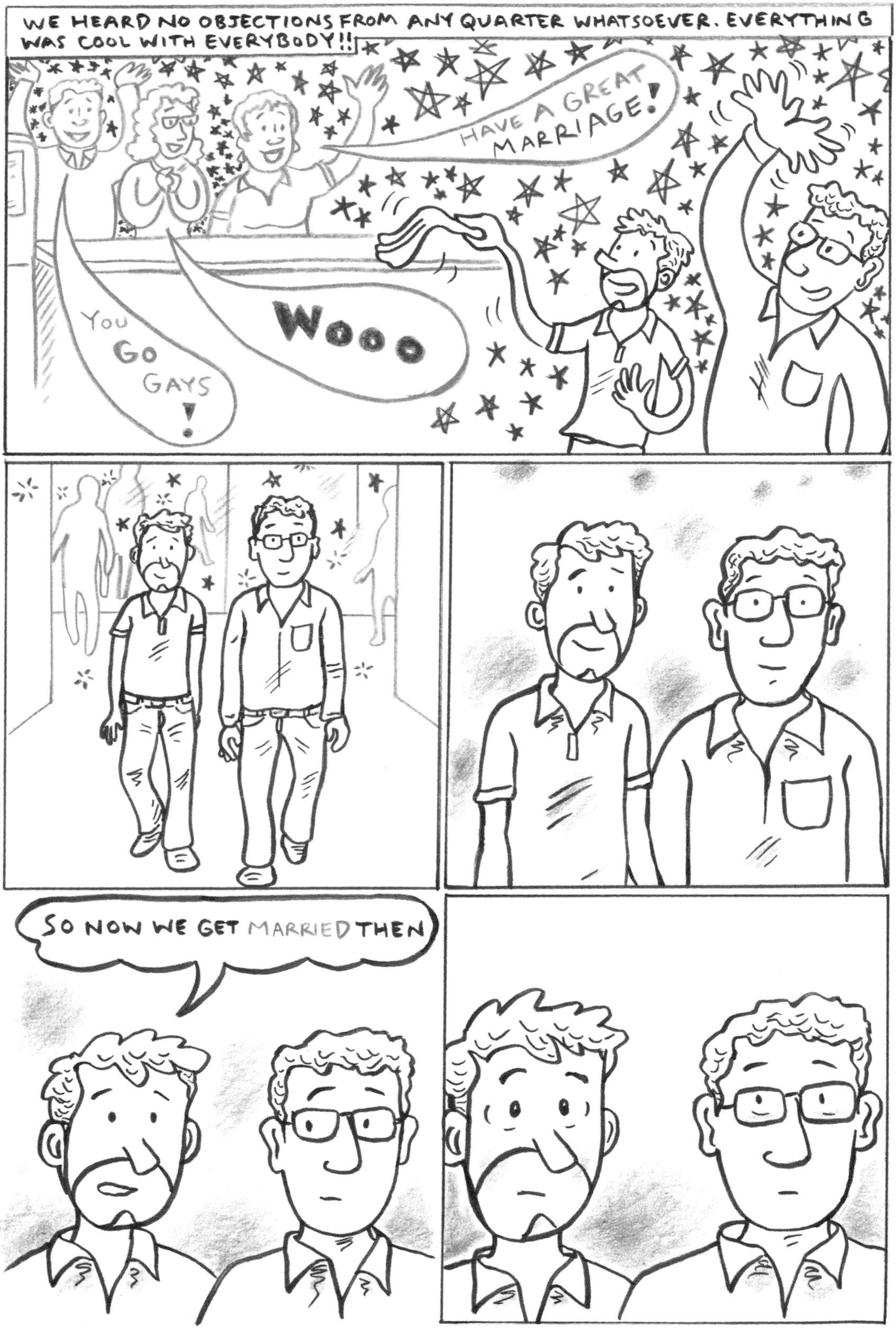
WE HEARD NO OBJECTIONS FROM ANY QUARTER WHATSOEVER. EVERYTHING WAS COOL WITH EVERYBODY!!
HAVE A GREAT MARRIAGE!
YOU GO GAYS!
WOOO
SO NOW WE GET MARRIED THEN

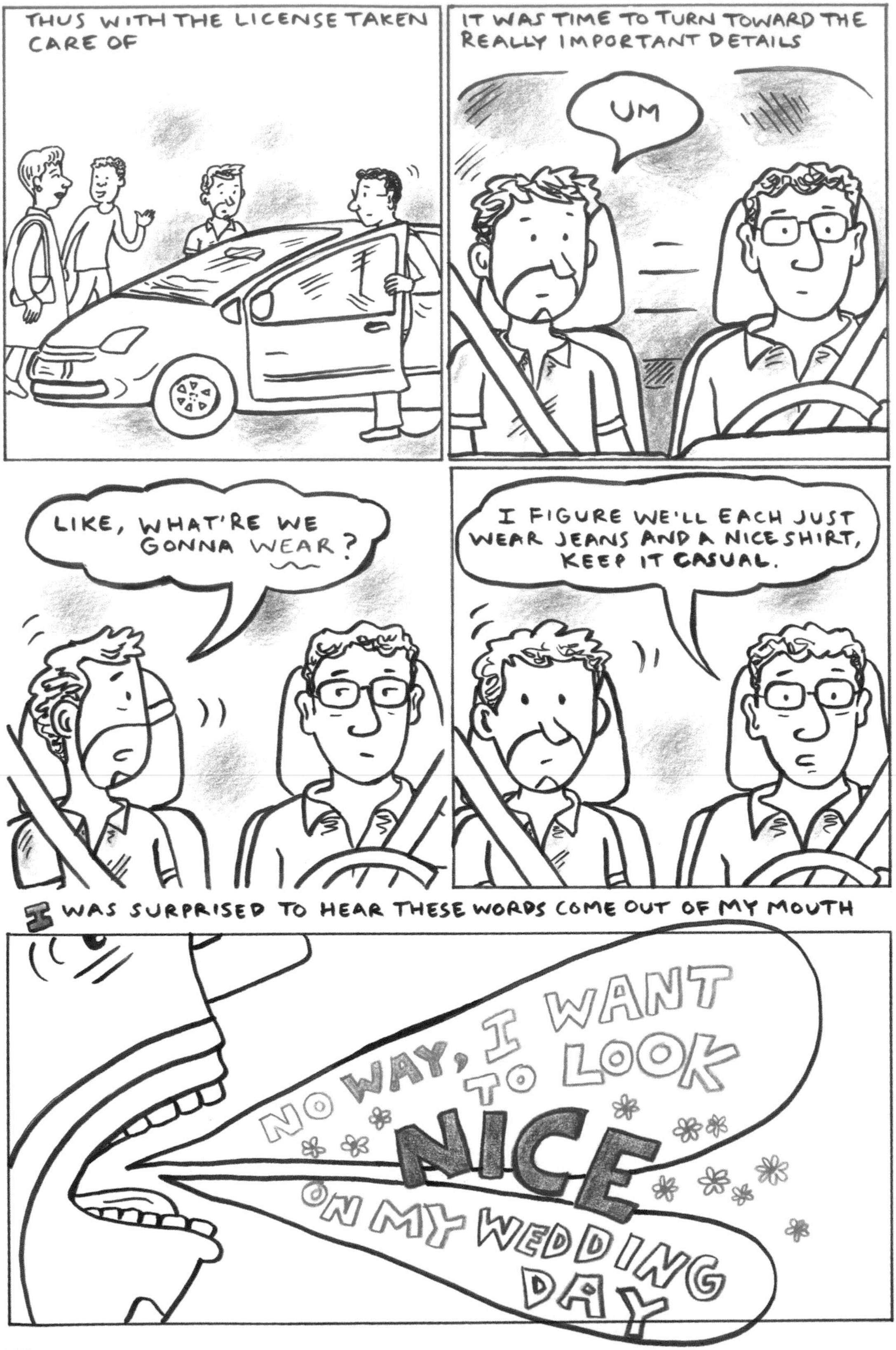

THUS WITH THE LICENSE TAKEN CARE OF
IT WAS TIME TO TURN TOWARD THE REALLY IMPORTANT DETAILS
UM
LIKE, WHAT'RE WE GONNA WEAR?
I FIGURE WE'LL EACH JUST WEAR JEANS AND A NICE SHIRT, KEEP IT CASUAL.
I WAS SURPRISED TO HEAR THESE WORDS COME OUT OF MY MOUTH
NO WAY, I WANT TO LOOK NICE ON MY WEDDING DAY

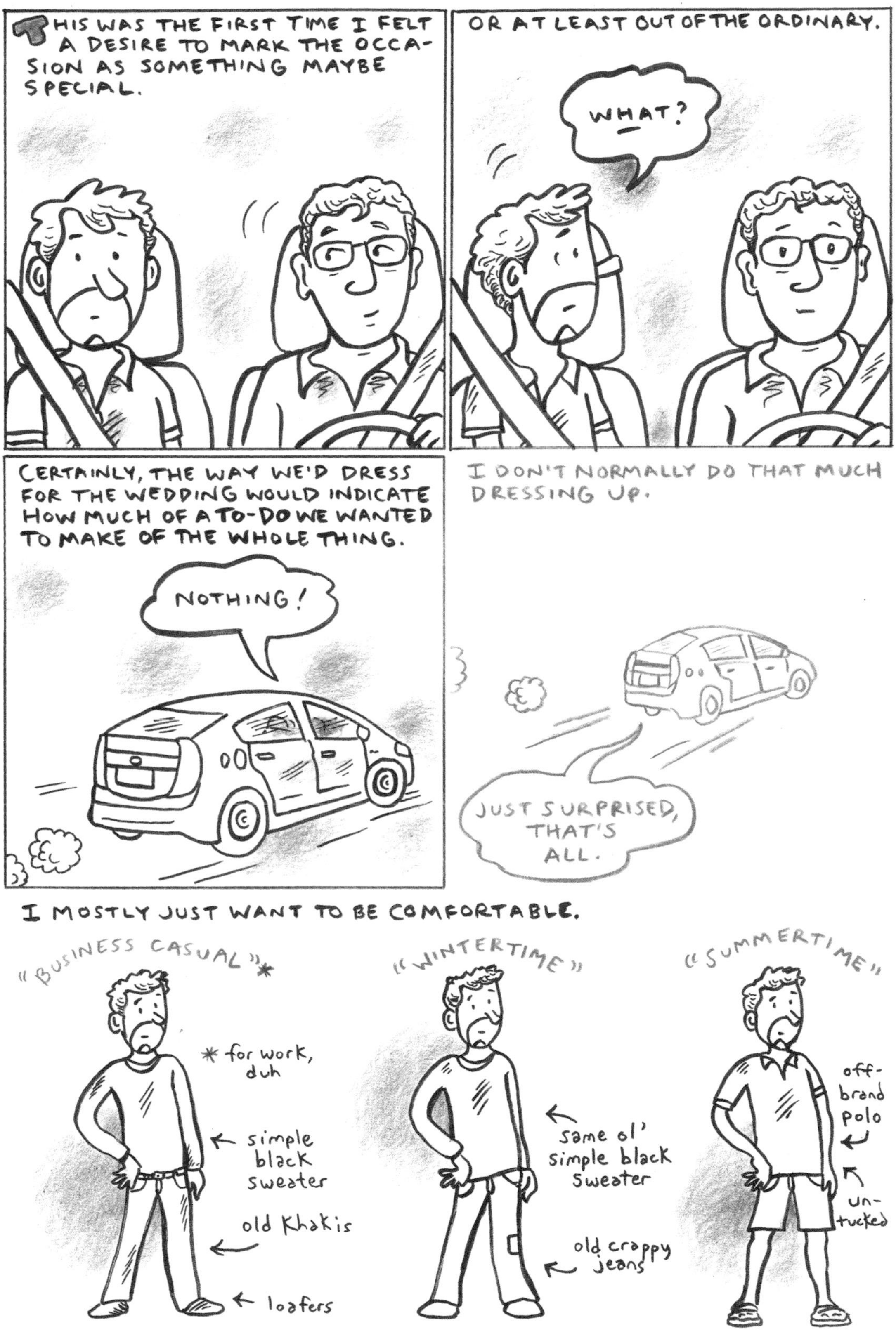
THIS WAS THE FIRST TIME I FELT A DESIRE TO MARK THE OCCASION AS SOMETHING MAYBE SPECIAL.
OR AT LEAST OUT OF THE ORDINARY.
WHAT?
CERTAINLY, THE WAY WE'D DRESS FOR THE WEDDING WOULD INDICATE HOW MUCH OF A TO-DO WE WANTED TO MAKE OF THE WHOLE THING.
NOTHING!
I DON'T NORMALLY DO THAT MUCH DRESSING UP.
JUST SURPRISED, THAT'S ALL.
I MOSTLY JUST WANT TO BE COMFORTABLE.
"BUSINESS CASUAL"*
* for work, duh
simple black sweater
old khakis
loafers
"WINTERTIME"
same ol' simple black sweater
old crappy jeans
"SUMMERTIME"
off-brand polo
un-tucked

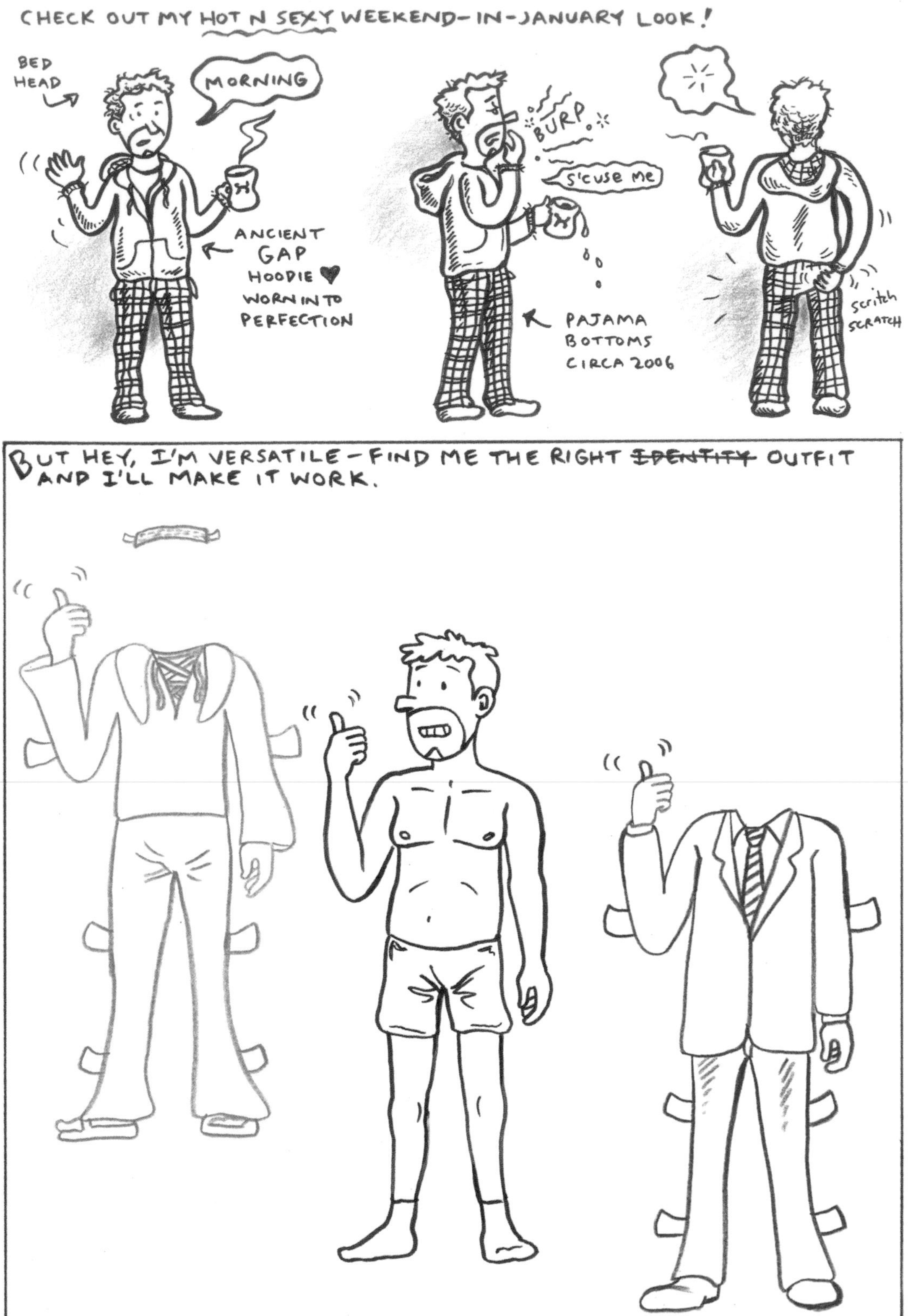
CHECK OUT MY HOT N SEXY WEEKEND-IN-JANUARY LOOK!
BED HEAD
MORNING
ANCIENT GAP HOODIE ♥ WORN IN TO PERFECTION
BURP
S'CUSE ME
PAJAMA BOTTOMS CIRCA 2006
SCRITCH SCRATCH
BUT HEY, I'M VERSATILE—FIND ME THE RIGHT ~~IDENTITY~~ OUTFIT AND I'LL MAKE IT WORK.

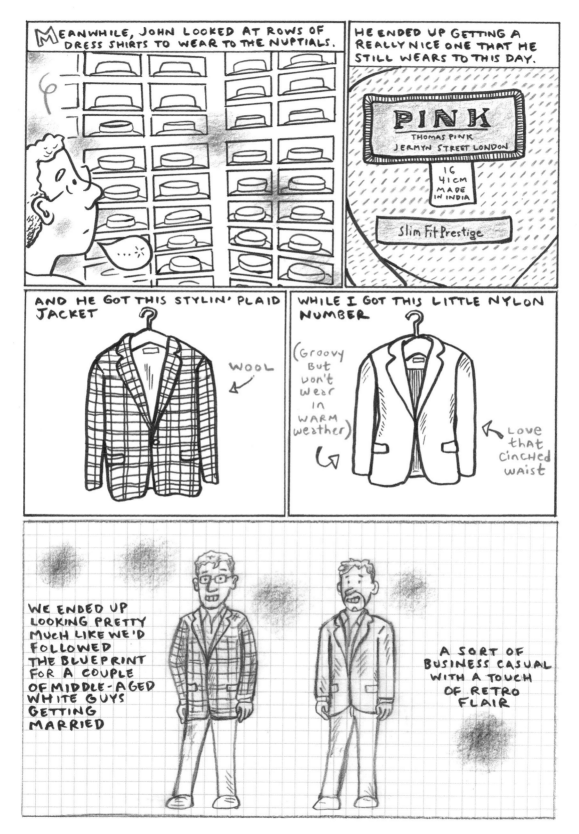

MEANWHILE, JOHN LOOKED AT ROWS OF DRESS SHIRTS TO WEAR TO THE NUPTIALS.

HE ENDED UP GETTING A REALLY NICE ONE THAT HE STILL WEARS TO THIS DAY.

PINK
THOMAS PINK
JERMYN STREET LONDON

16
41CM
MADE IN INDIA

Slim Fit Prestige

AND HE GOT THIS STYLIN' PLAID JACKET

WOOL

WHILE I GOT THIS LITTLE NYLON NUMBER

(Groovy but Don't wear in WARM weather)

Love that cinched waist

WE ENDED UP LOOKING PRETTY MUCH LIKE WE'D FOLLOWED THE BLUEPRINT FOR A COUPLE OF MIDDLE-AGED WHITE GUYS GETTING MARRIED

A SORT OF BUSINESS CASUAL WITH A TOUCH OF RETRO FLAIR

33

MEANWHILE, TWO MONTHS EARLIER, ON 7/13/13, JOHN'S BROTHER LOU AND HIS PARTNER, GARY, GOT MARRIED.

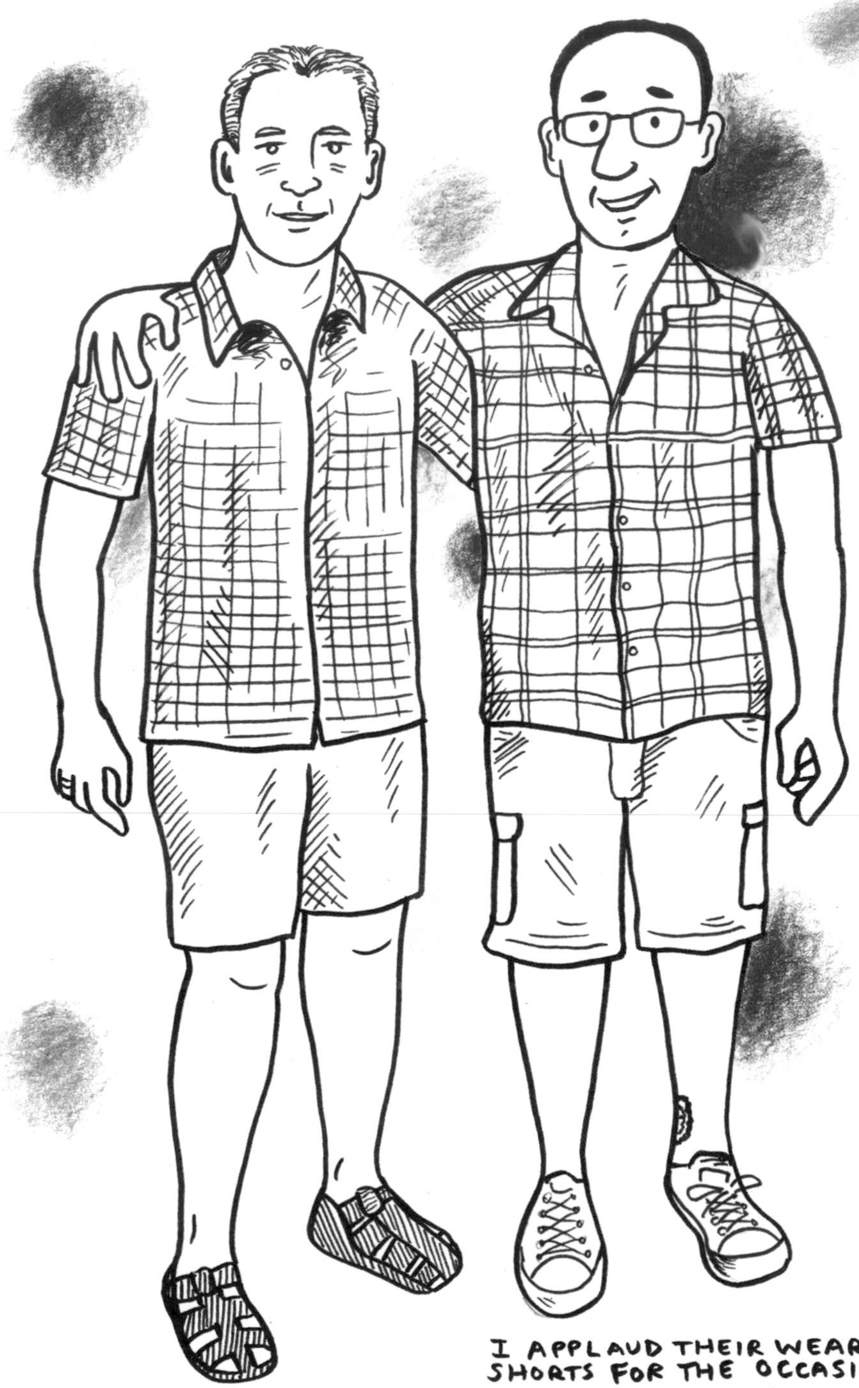

I APPLAUD THEIR WEARING SHORTS FOR THE OCCASION.

THEY LIVE IN PALM SPRINGS, WHERE THINGS ARE MORE CASŹH.

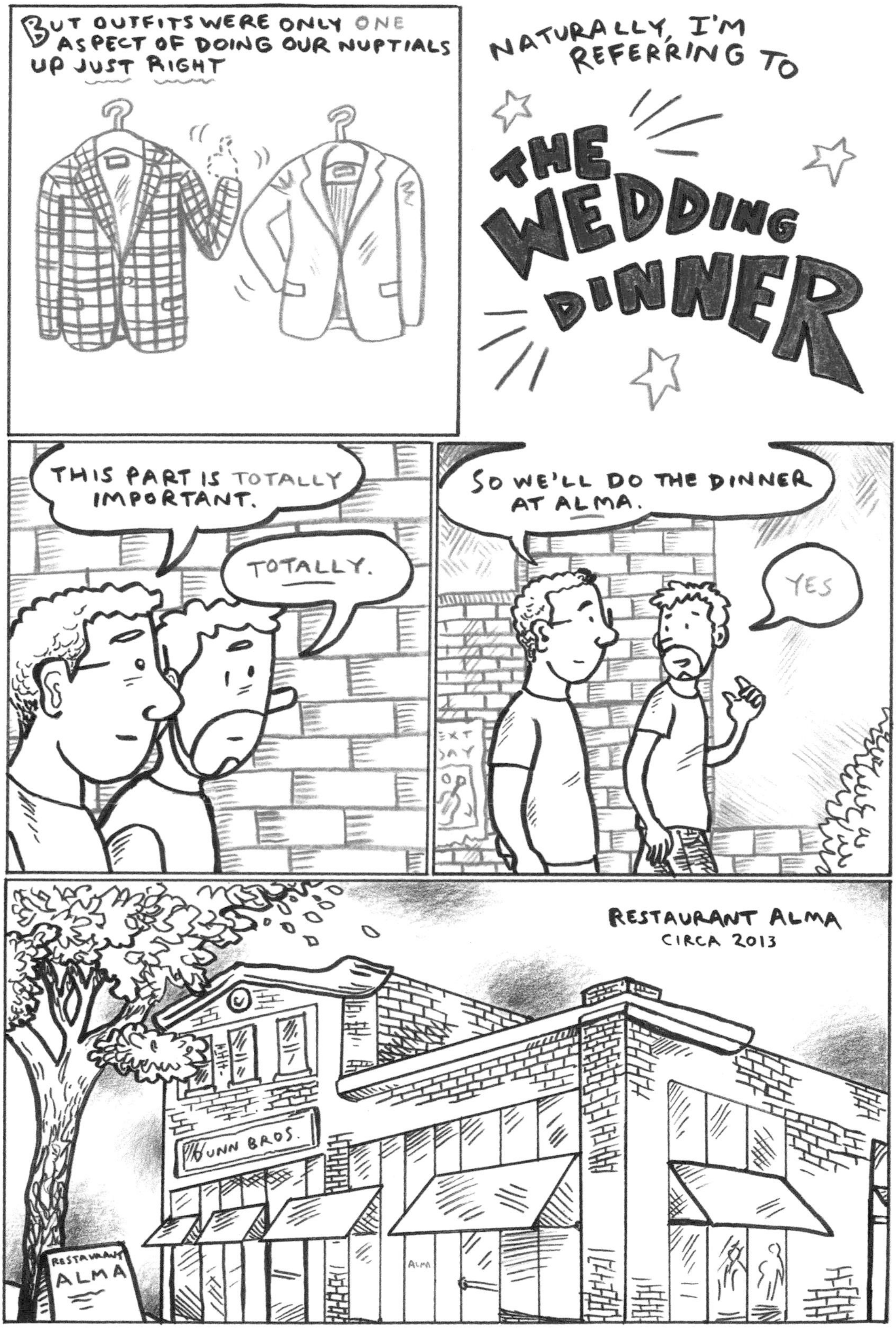
BUT OUTFITS WERE ONLY ONE ASPECT OF DOING OUR NUPTIALS UP JUST RIGHT
NATURALLY, I'M REFERRING TO
THE WEDDING DINNER
THIS PART IS TOTALLY IMPORTANT.
TOTALLY.
SO WE'LL DO THE DINNER AT ALMA.
YES
RESTAURANT ALMA
CIRCA 2013
DUNN BROS.
RESTAURANT ALMA
ALMA

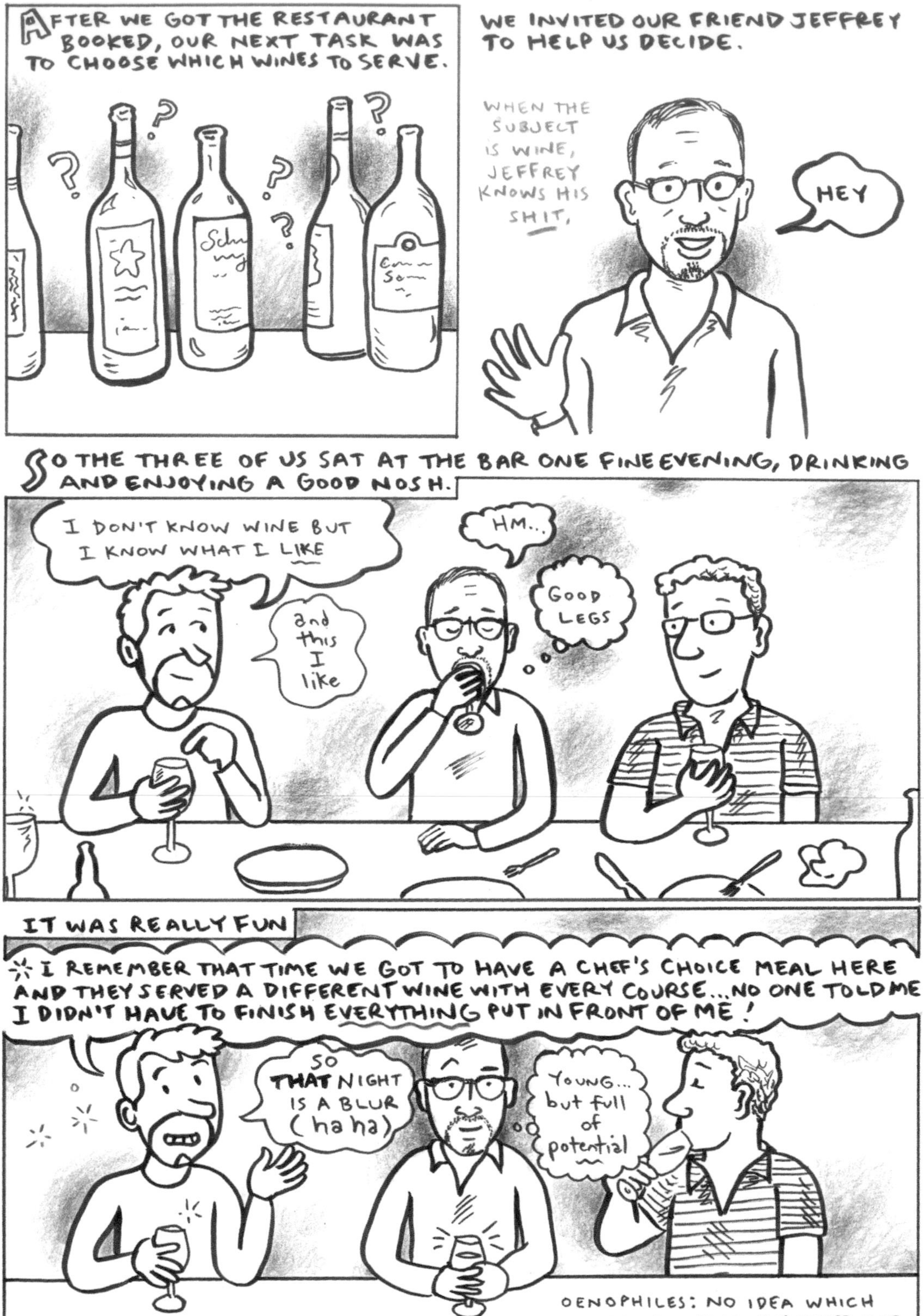
AFTER WE GOT THE RESTAURANT BOOKED, OUR NEXT TASK WAS TO CHOOSE WHICH WINES TO SERVE.
WE INVITED OUR FRIEND JEFFREY TO HELP US DECIDE.
WHEN THE SUBJECT IS WINE, JEFFREY KNOWS HIS SHIT.
HEY
SO THE THREE OF US SAT AT THE BAR ONE FINE EVENING, DRINKING AND ENJOYING A GOOD NOSH.
I DON'T KNOW WINE BUT I KNOW WHAT I LIKE
and this I like
HM...
GOOD LEGS
IT WAS REALLY FUN
I REMEMBER THAT TIME WE GOT TO HAVE A CHEF'S CHOICE MEAL HERE AND THEY SERVED A DIFFERENT WINE WITH EVERY COURSE... NO ONE TOLD ME I DIDN'T HAVE TO FINISH EVERYTHING PUT IN FRONT OF ME!
SO THAT NIGHT IS A BLUR (ha ha)
YOUNG... but full of potential
OENOPHILES: NO IDEA WHICH WINES WE ULTIMATELY CHOSE, BUT I'M SURE THEY WERE STELLAR.

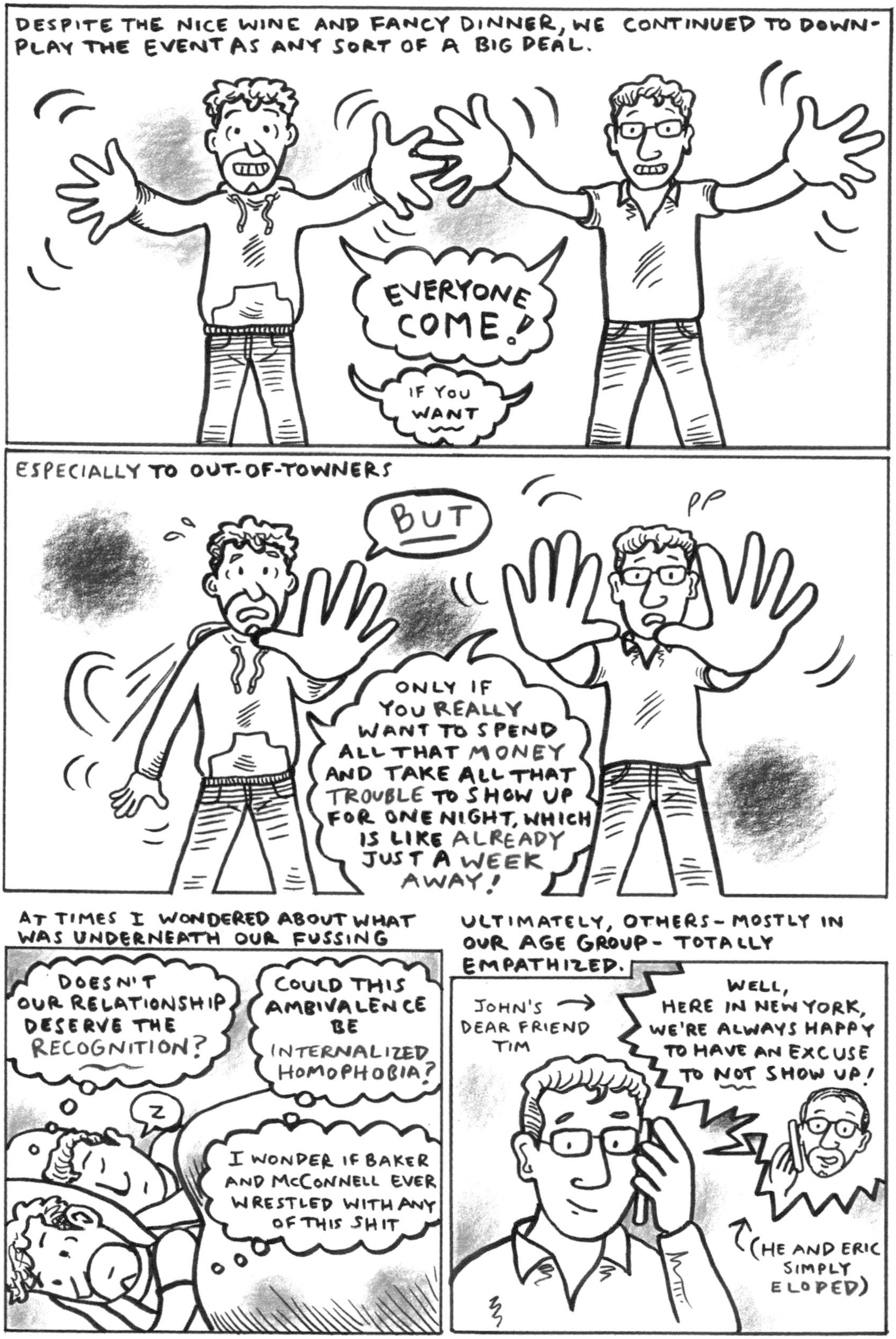
DESPITE THE NICE WINE AND FANCY DINNER, WE CONTINUED TO DOWN-PLAY THE EVENT AS ANY SORT OF A BIG DEAL.
EVERYONE COME!
IF YOU WANT
ESPECIALLY TO OUT-OF-TOWNERS
BUT
ONLY IF YOU REALLY WANT TO SPEND ALL THAT MONEY AND TAKE ALL THAT TROUBLE TO SHOW UP FOR ONE NIGHT, WHICH IS LIKE ALREADY JUST A WEEK AWAY!
AT TIMES I WONDERED ABOUT WHAT WAS UNDERNEATH OUR FUSSING
DOESN'T OUR RELATIONSHIP DESERVE THE RECOGNITION?
COULD THIS AMBIVALENCE BE INTERNALIZED HOMOPHOBIA?
Z
I WONDER IF BAKER AND McCONNELL EVER WRESTLED WITH ANY OF THIS SHIT
ULTIMATELY, OTHERS - MOSTLY IN OUR AGE GROUP - TOTALLY EMPATHIZED.
JOHN'S DEAR FRIEND TIM
WELL, HERE IN NEW YORK, WE'RE ALWAYS HAPPY TO HAVE AN EXCUSE TO NOT SHOW UP!
(HE AND ERIC SIMPLY ELOPED)

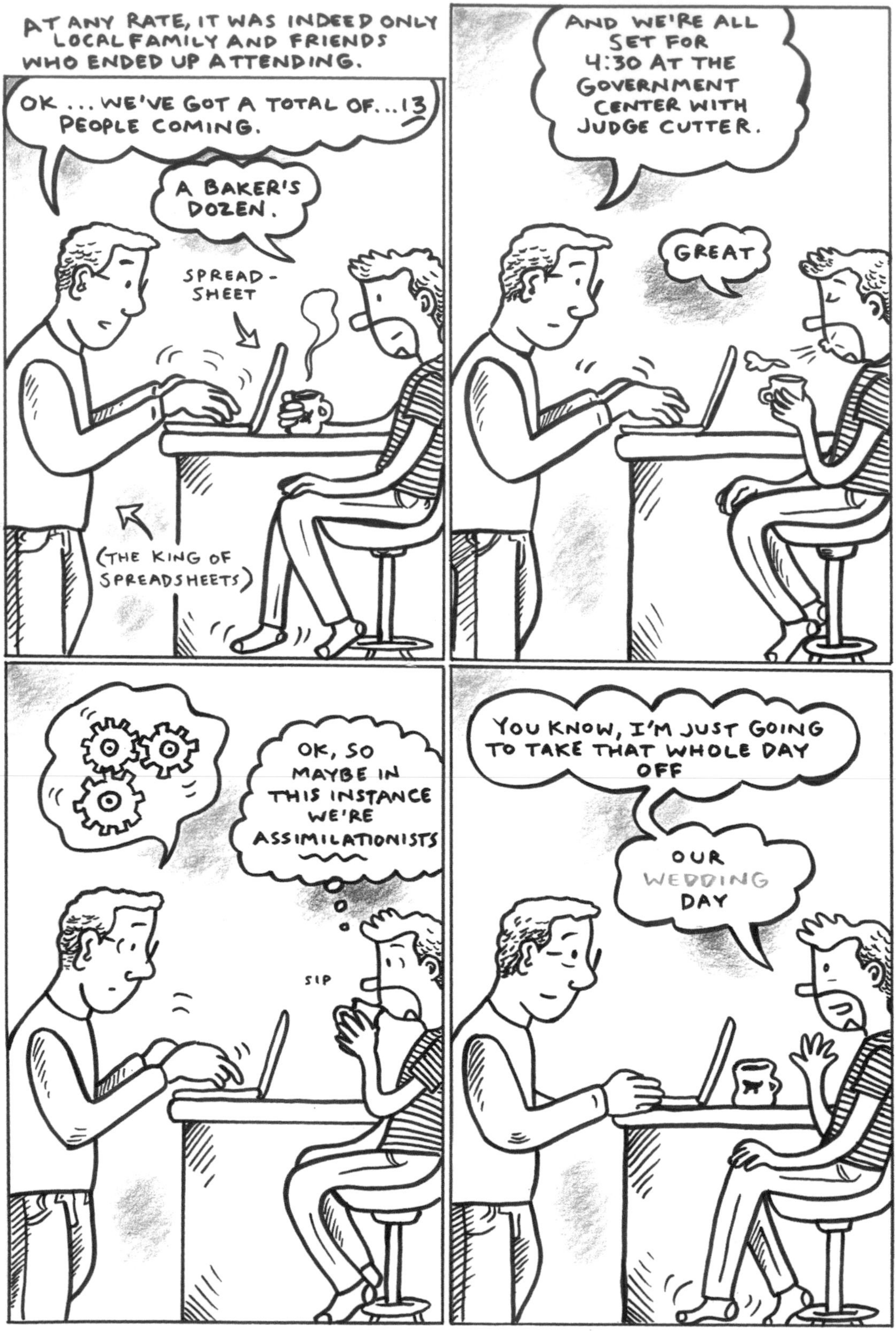
AT ANY RATE, IT WAS INDEED ONLY LOCAL FAMILY AND FRIENDS WHO ENDED UP ATTENDING.
OK ... WE'VE GOT A TOTAL OF...13 PEOPLE COMING.
A BAKER'S DOZEN.
SPREAD-SHEET
(THE KING OF SPREADSHEETS)
AND WE'RE ALL SET FOR 4:30 AT THE GOVERNMENT CENTER WITH JUDGE CUTTER.
GREAT
OK, SO MAYBE IN THIS INSTANCE WE'RE ASSIMILATIONISTS
SIP
YOU KNOW, I'M JUST GOING TO TAKE THAT WHOLE DAY OFF
OUR WEDDING DAY

WEDDING SONGS

YOUR GUIDE TO THE BEST TUNES ABOUT GETTIN' HITCHED

hosted by
ROB KIRBY

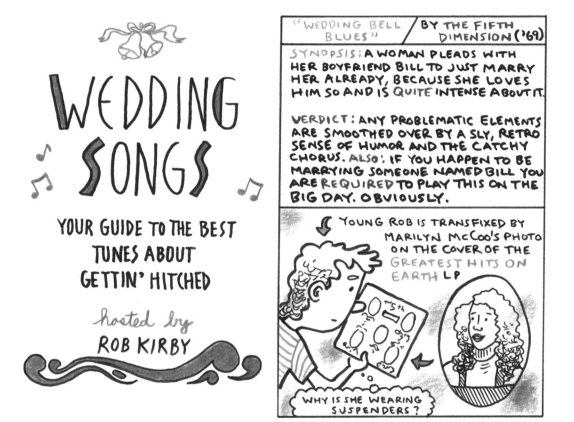

"WEDDING BELL BLUES"	BY THE FIFTH DIMENSION ('69)

SYNOPSIS: A WOMAN PLEADS WITH HER BOYFRIEND BILL TO JUST MARRY HER ALREADY, BECAUSE SHE LOVES HIM SO AND IS QUITE INTENSE ABOUT IT.

VERDICT: ANY PROBLEMATIC ELEMENTS ARE SMOOTHED OVER BY A SLY, RETRO SENSE OF HUMOR AND THE CATCHY CHORUS. ALSO: IF YOU HAPPEN TO BE MARRYING SOMEONE NAMED BILL YOU ARE REQUIRED TO PLAY THIS ON THE BIG DAY. OBVIOUSLY.

YOUNG ROB IS TRANSFIXED BY MARILYN McCOO'S PHOTO ON THE COVER OF THE GREATEST HITS ON EARTH LP

WHY IS SHE WEARING SUSPENDERS?

"THIRD FINGER LEFT HAND"	BY MARTHA & THE VANDELLAS ('67)

SYNOPSIS: THIS LYRIC SUMS IT ALL UP: "THAT'S WHERE HE PLACED THE WEDDING BAND"

VERDICT: YES, THIS IS ANOTHER SONG THAT POSITS ROMANTIC LOVE AND MARRIAGE AS PANACEAS FOR ALL OF LIFE'S ILLS, BUT IT'S GOT THAT GREAT MOTOWN SOUND AND YOU CAN DANCE TO IT.

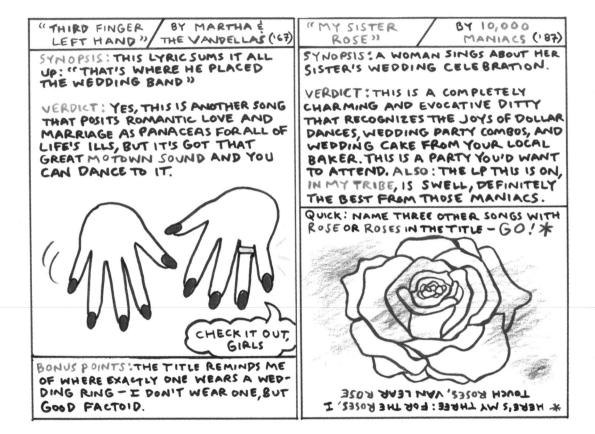

CHECK IT OUT, GIRLS

BONUS POINTS: THE TITLE REMINDS ME OF WHERE EXACTLY ONE WEARS A WEDDING RING — I DON'T WEAR ONE, BUT GOOD FACTOID.

"MY SISTER ROSE"	BY 10,000 MANIACS ('87)

SYNOPSIS: A WOMAN SINGS ABOUT HER SISTER'S WEDDING CELEBRATION.

VERDICT: THIS IS A COMPLETELY CHARMING AND EVOCATIVE DITTY THAT RECOGNIZES THE JOYS OF DOLLAR DANCES, WEDDING PARTY COMBOS, AND WEDDING CAKE FROM YOUR LOCAL BAKER. THIS IS A PARTY YOU'D WANT TO ATTEND. ALSO: THE LP THIS IS ON, IN MY TRIBE, IS SWELL, DEFINITELY THE BEST FROM THOSE MANIACS.

QUICK: NAME THREE OTHER SONGS WITH ROSE OR ROSES IN THE TITLE — GO! *

* HERE'S MY THREE: FOR THE ROSES, I TOUCH ROSES, VAN LEAR ROSE

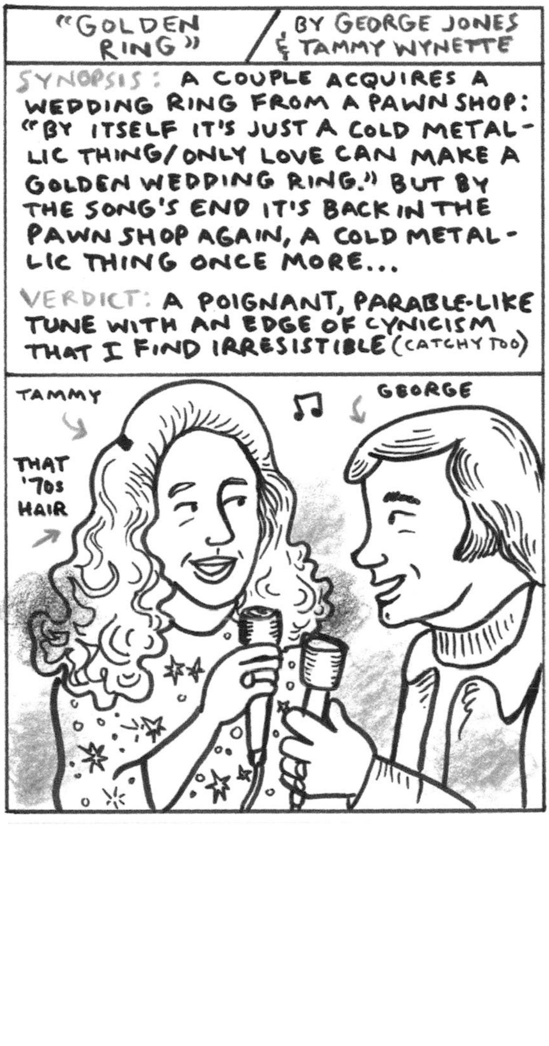
"GOLDEN RING" / BY GEORGE JONES & TAMMY WYNETTE
SYNOPSIS: A COUPLE ACQUIRES A WEDDING RING FROM A PAWN SHOP: "BY ITSELF IT'S JUST A COLD METALLIC THING/ONLY LOVE CAN MAKE A GOLDEN WEDDING RING." BUT BY THE SONG'S END IT'S BACK IN THE PAWN SHOP AGAIN, A COLD METALLIC THING ONCE MORE...
VERDICT: A POIGNANT, PARABLE-LIKE TUNE WITH AN EDGE OF CYNICISM THAT I FIND IRRESISTIBLE (CATCHY TOO)
TAMMY
THAT '70S HAIR
GEORGE

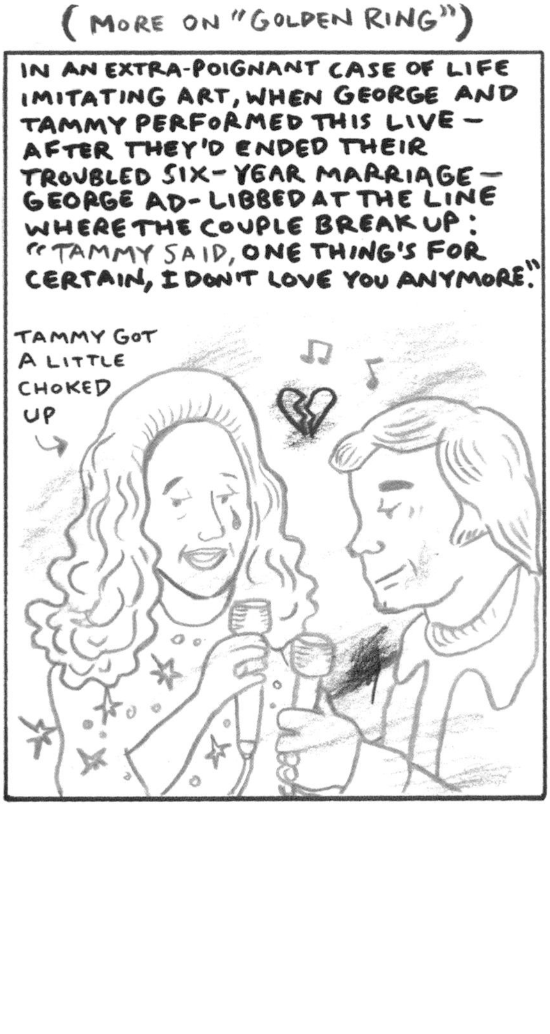
(MORE ON "GOLDEN RING")
IN AN EXTRA-POIGNANT CASE OF LIFE IMITATING ART, WHEN GEORGE AND TAMMY PERFORMED THIS LIVE — AFTER THEY'D ENDED THEIR TROUBLED SIX-YEAR MARRIAGE — GEORGE AD-LIBBED AT THE LINE WHERE THE COUPLE BREAK UP: "TAMMY SAID, ONE THING'S FOR CERTAIN, I DON'T LOVE YOU ANYMORE."
TAMMY GOT A LITTLE CHOKED UP

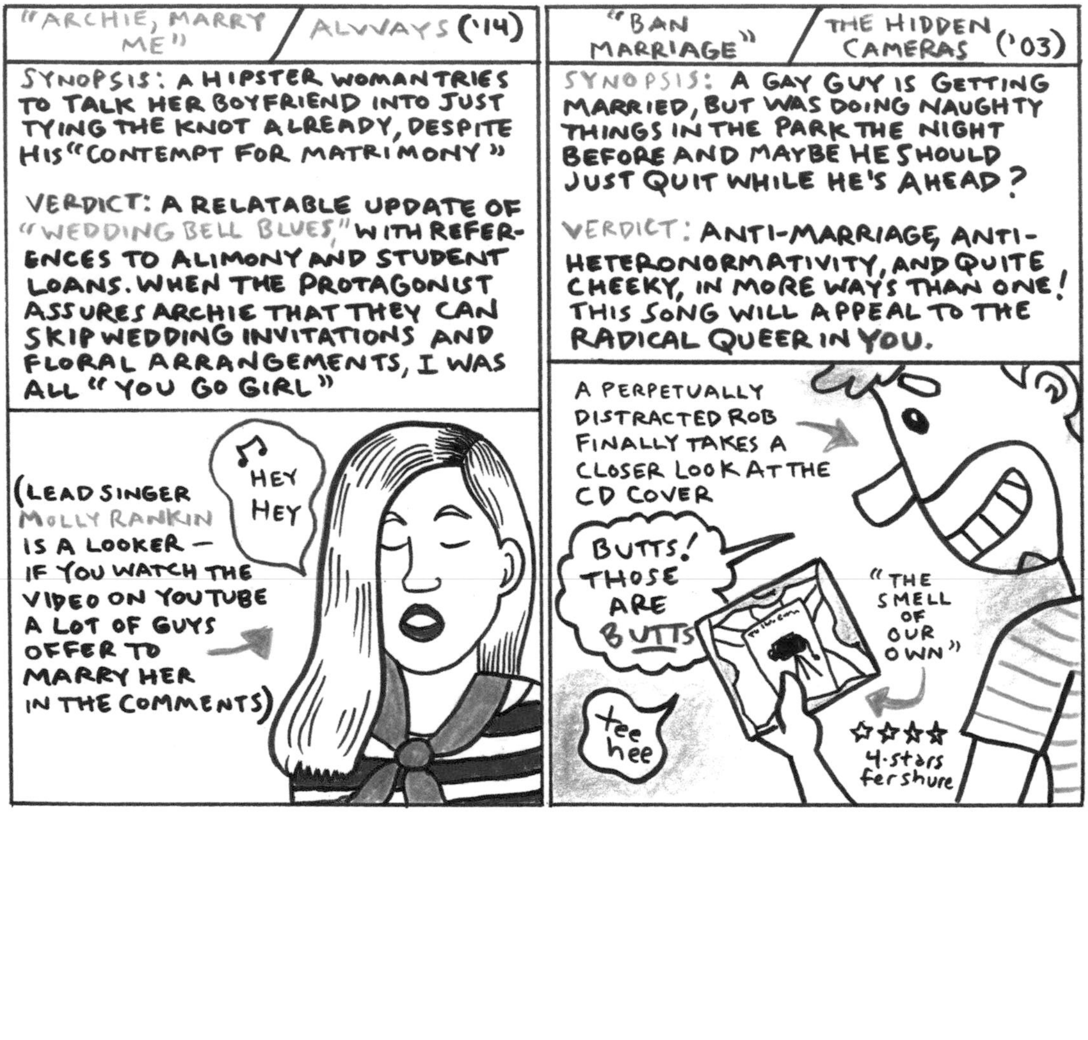
"ARCHIE, MARRY ME"
ALVVAYS ('14)
SYNOPSIS: A HIPSTER WOMAN TRIES TO TALK HER BOYFRIEND INTO JUST TYING THE KNOT ALREADY, DESPITE HIS "CONTEMPT FOR MATRIMONY"
VERDICT: A RELATABLE UPDATE OF "WEDDING BELL BLUES," WITH REFERENCES TO ALIMONY AND STUDENT LOANS. WHEN THE PROTAGONIST ASSURES ARCHIE THAT THEY CAN SKIP WEDDING INVITATIONS AND FLORAL ARRANGEMENTS, I WAS ALL "YOU GO GIRL"
(LEAD SINGER MOLLY RANKIN IS A LOOKER — IF YOU WATCH THE VIDEO ON YOUTUBE A LOT OF GUYS OFFER TO MARRY HER IN THE COMMENTS)
HEY HEY
"BAN MARRIAGE"
THE HIDDEN CAMERAS ('03)
SYNOPSIS: A GAY GUY IS GETTING MARRIED, BUT WAS DOING NAUGHTY THINGS IN THE PARK THE NIGHT BEFORE AND MAYBE HE SHOULD JUST QUIT WHILE HE'S AHEAD?
VERDICT: ANTI-MARRIAGE, ANTI-HETERONORMATIVITY, AND QUITE CHEEKY, IN MORE WAYS THAN ONE! THIS SONG WILL APPEAL TO THE RADICAL QUEER IN YOU.
A PERPETUALLY DISTRACTED ROB FINALLY TAKES A CLOSER LOOK AT THE CD COVER
BUTTS! THOSE ARE BUTTS
"THE SMELL OF OUR OWN"
tee hee
4-stars fer shure

WEDDINGS ON TV SHOWS AND IN MOVIES ARE ALMOST ALWAYS HIGHLY FRAUGHT AFFAIRS.

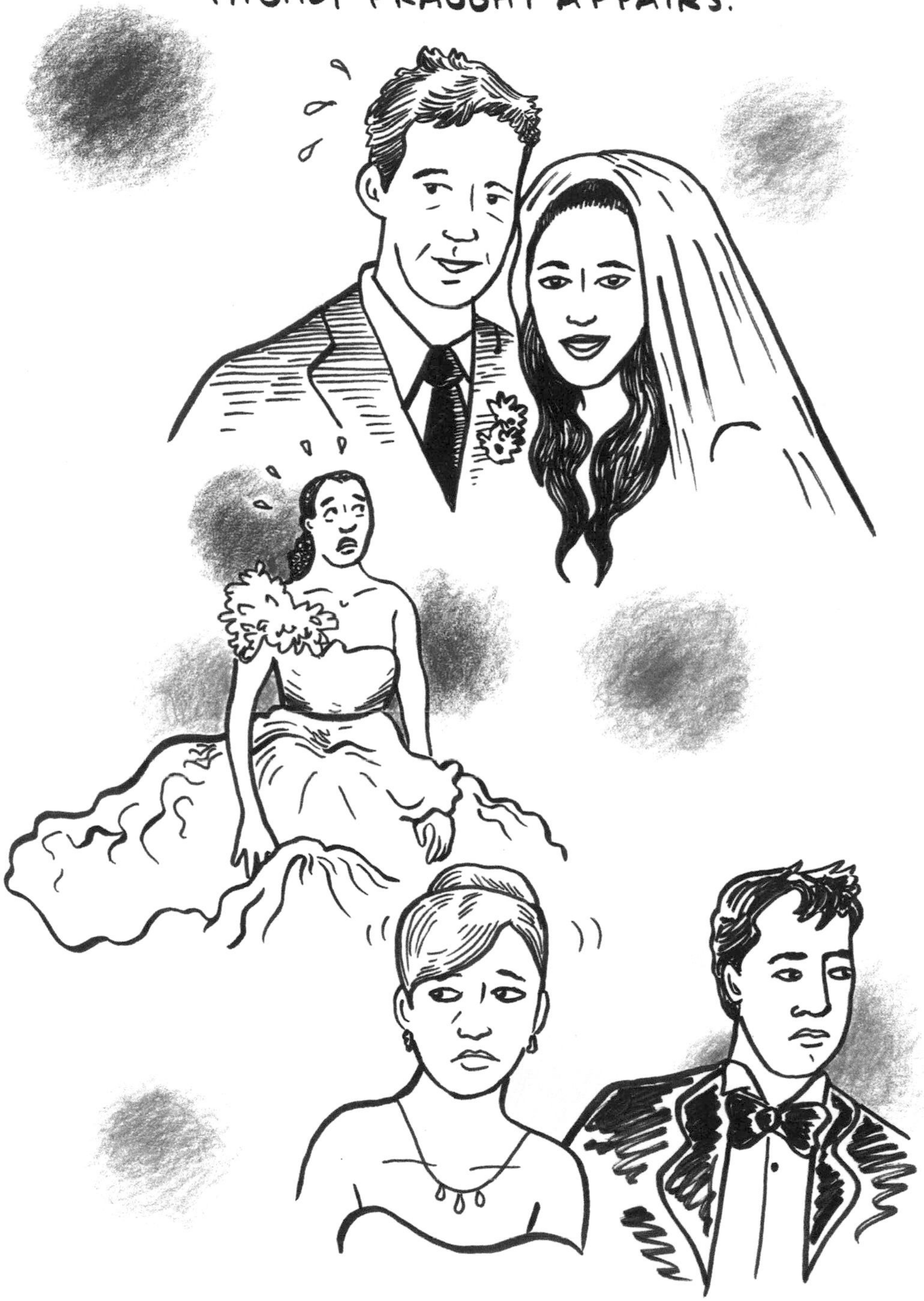

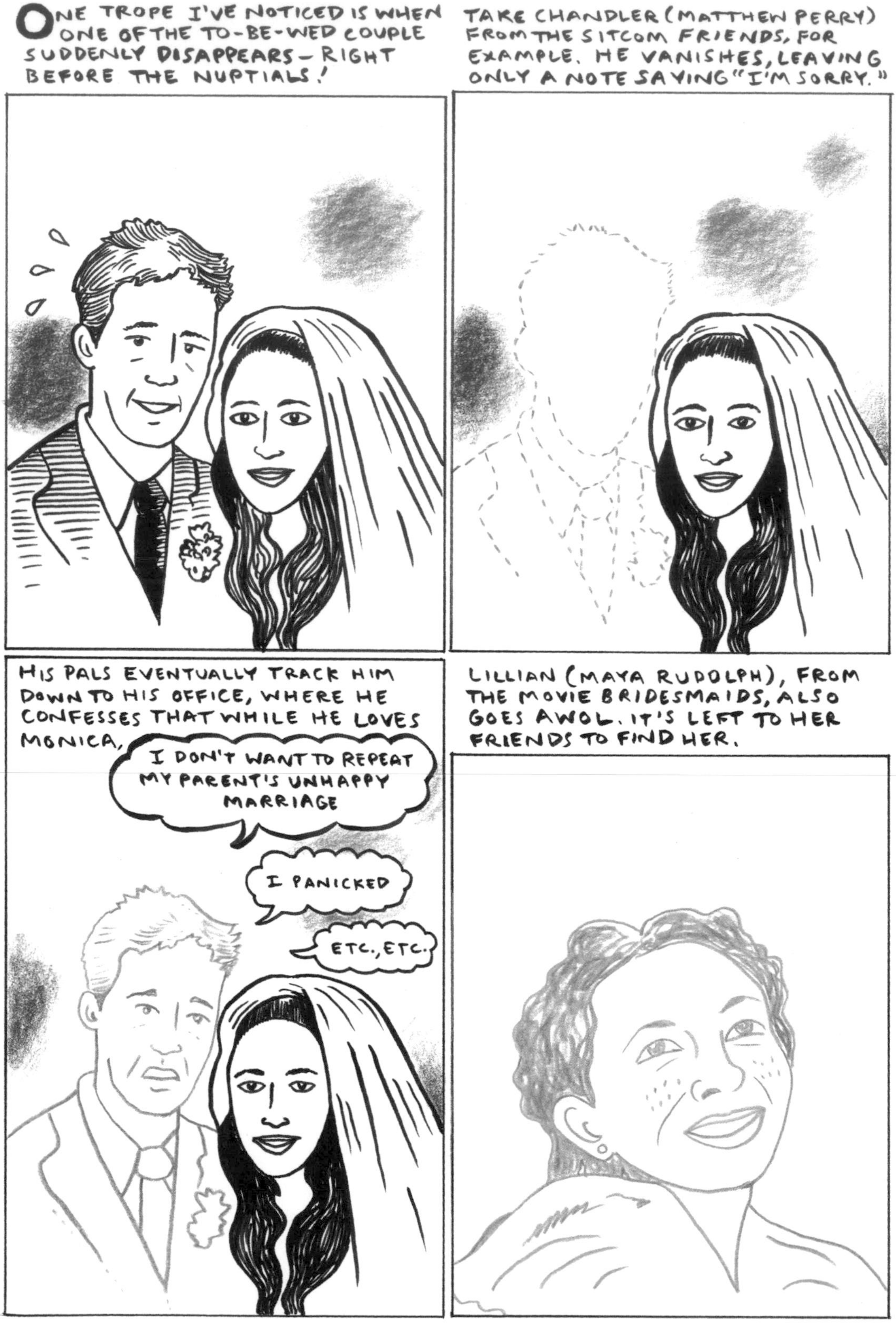
ONE TROPE I'VE NOTICED IS WHEN ONE OF THE TO-BE-WED COUPLE SUDDENLY DISAPPEARS – RIGHT BEFORE THE NUPTIALS!
TAKE CHANDLER (MATTHEW PERRY) FROM THE SITCOM FRIENDS, FOR EXAMPLE. HE VANISHES, LEAVING ONLY A NOTE SAYING "I'M SORRY."
HIS PALS EVENTUALLY TRACK HIM DOWN TO HIS OFFICE, WHERE HE CONFESSES THAT WHILE HE LOVES MONICA,
I DON'T WANT TO REPEAT MY PARENT'S UNHAPPY MARRIAGE
I PANICKED
ETC., ETC.
LILLIAN (MAYA RUDOLPH), FROM THE MOVIE BRIDESMAIDS, ALSO GOES AWOL. IT'S LEFT TO HER FRIENDS TO FIND HER.

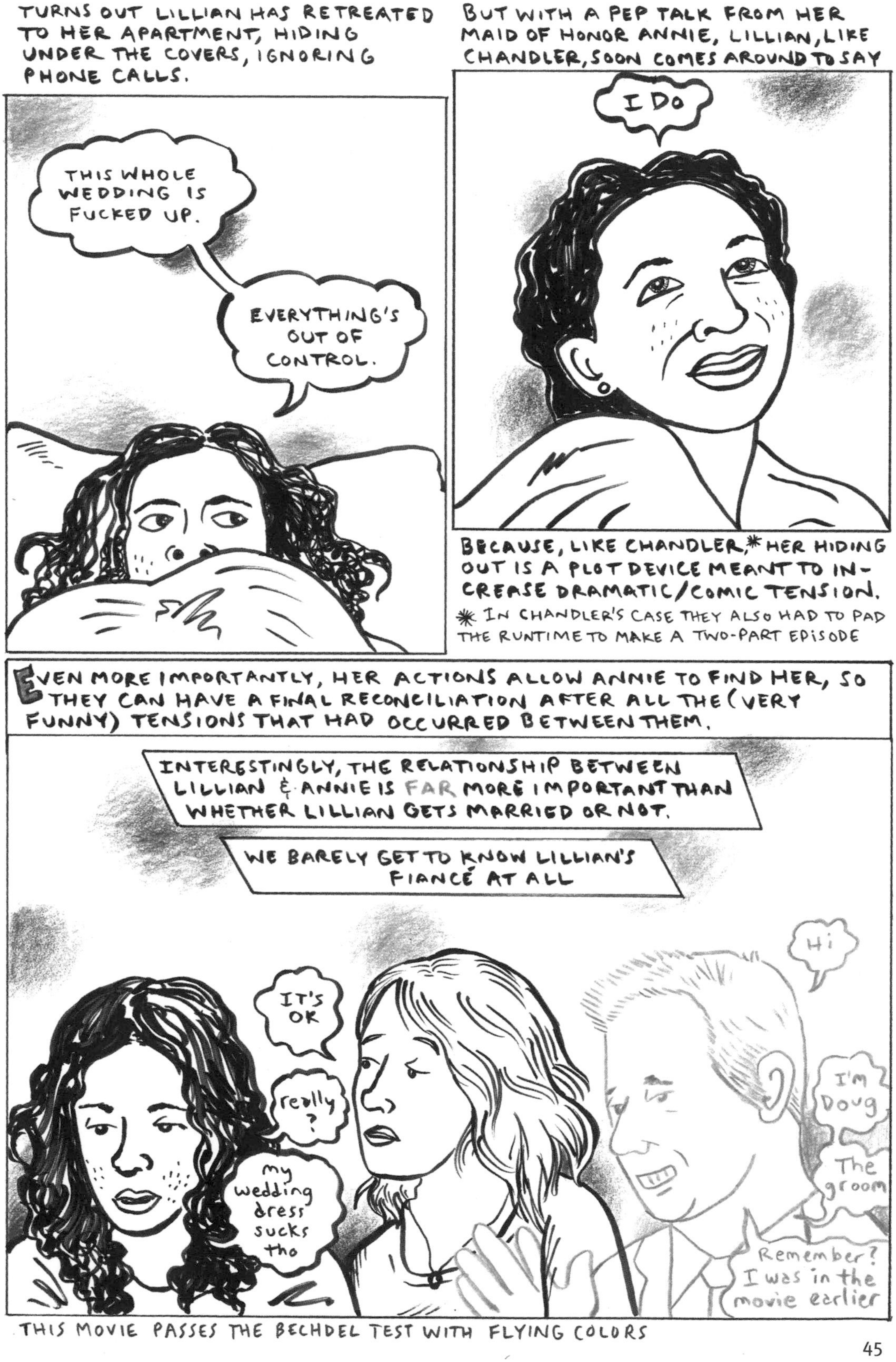
TURNS OUT LILLIAN HAS RETREATED TO HER APARTMENT, HIDING UNDER THE COVERS, IGNORING PHONE CALLS.
THIS WHOLE WEDDING IS FUCKED UP.
EVERYTHING'S OUT OF CONTROL.
BUT WITH A PEP TALK FROM HER MAID OF HONOR ANNIE, LILLIAN, LIKE CHANDLER, SOON COMES AROUND TO SAY
I DO
BECAUSE, LIKE CHANDLER,* HER HIDING OUT IS A PLOT DEVICE MEANT TO INCREASE DRAMATIC/COMIC TENSION.
* IN CHANDLER'S CASE THEY ALSO HAD TO PAD THE RUNTIME TO MAKE A TWO-PART EPISODE
EVEN MORE IMPORTANTLY, HER ACTIONS ALLOW ANNIE TO FIND HER, SO THEY CAN HAVE A FINAL RECONCILIATION AFTER ALL THE (VERY FUNNY) TENSIONS THAT HAD OCCURRED BETWEEN THEM.
INTERESTINGLY, THE RELATIONSHIP BETWEEN LILLIAN & ANNIE IS FAR MORE IMPORTANT THAN WHETHER LILLIAN GETS MARRIED OR NOT.
WE BARELY GET TO KNOW LILLIAN'S FIANCÉ AT ALL
IT'S OK
really?
my wedding dress sucks tho
Hi
I'm Doug
The groom
Remember? I was in the movie earlier
THIS MOVIE PASSES THE BECHDEL TEST WITH FLYING COLORS

IN MY BEST FRIEND'S WEDDING, BRIDE-TO-BE KIMMY (CAMERON DIAZ) IS SHOCKED TO SEE HER GROOM, MICHAEL, KISSING HIS FORMER-GIRLFRIEND-NOW-BFF, JULIANNE (JULIA ROBERTS).

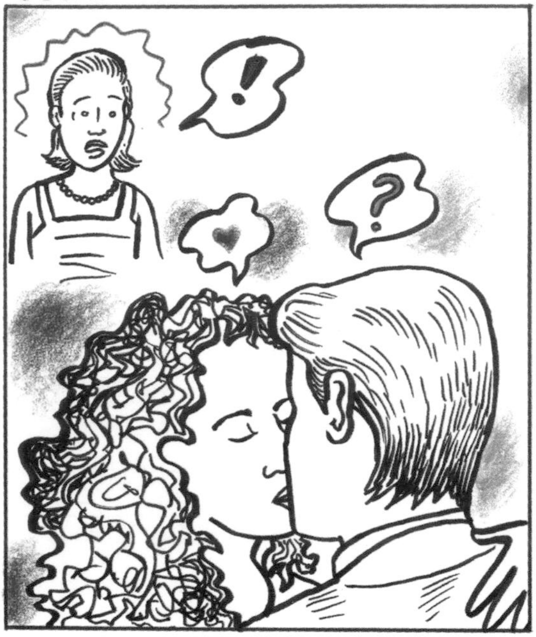
!
?

UNDERSTANDABLY UPSET (THOUGH MISINTERPRETING THE SITUATION), KIMMY MAKES A RAPID EXIT.

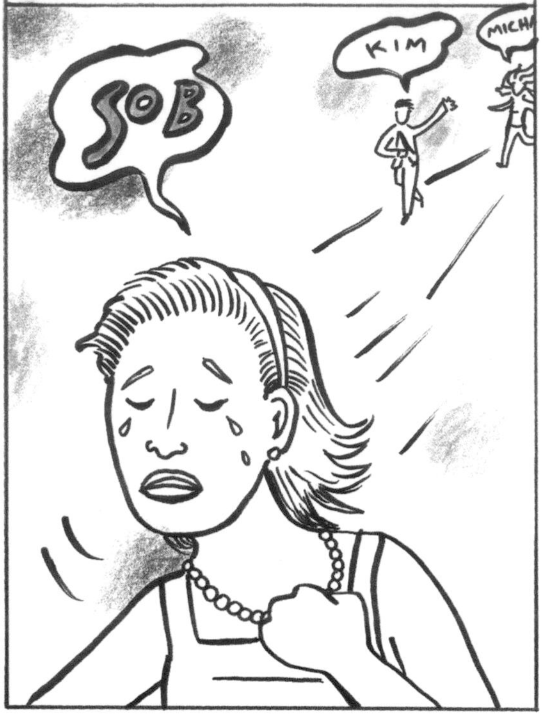
SOB
KIM

LESS UNDERSTANDABLY, SHE ENDS UP HIDING IN THE WOMEN'S ROOM AT COMISKEY PARK (UM... OK). BUT JULIANNE FINDS HER, EXPLAINS HERSELF, AND AFTER A HEATED ARGUMENT ALL IS FORGIVEN AND THE WEDDING PROCEEDS THAT NIGHT AS PLANNED.

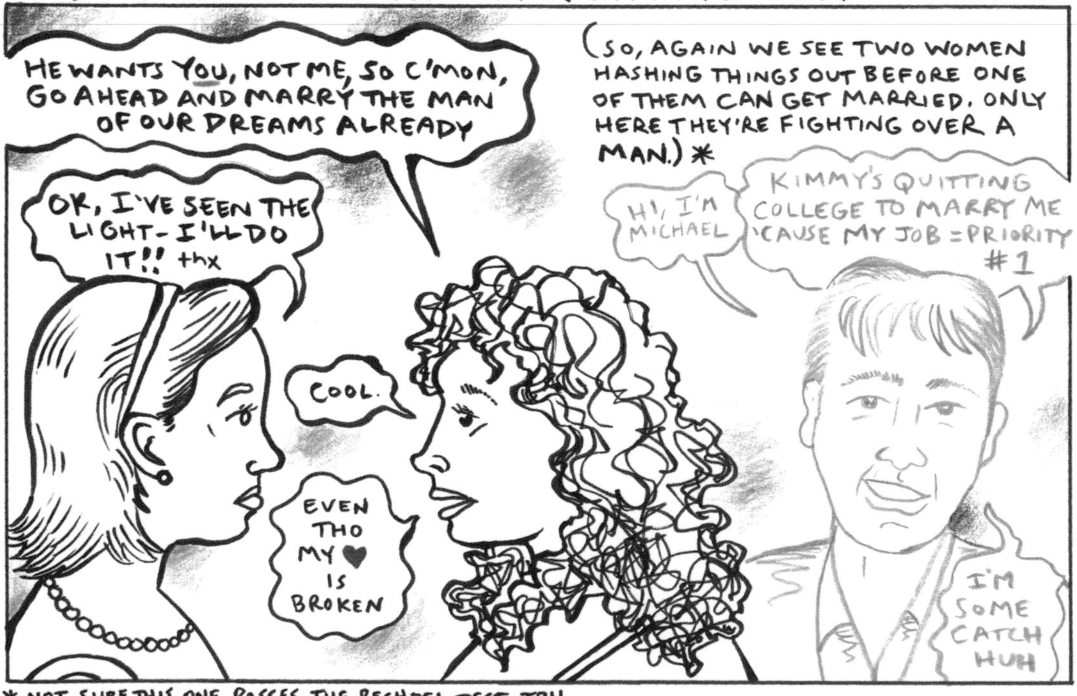
HE WANTS YOU, NOT ME, SO C'MON, GO AHEAD AND MARRY THE MAN OF OUR DREAMS ALREADY
OK, I'VE SEEN THE LIGHT- I'LL DO IT!! thx
COOL.
EVEN THO MY ♥ IS BROKEN
(SO, AGAIN WE SEE TWO WOMEN HASHING THINGS OUT BEFORE ONE OF THEM CAN GET MARRIED. ONLY HERE THEY'RE FIGHTING OVER A MAN.) *
HI, I'M MICHAEL
KIMMY'S QUITTING COLLEGE TO MARRY ME 'CAUSE MY JOB = PRIORITY #1
I'M SOME CATCH HUH

* NOT SURE THIS ONE PASSES THE BECHDEL TEST, TBH

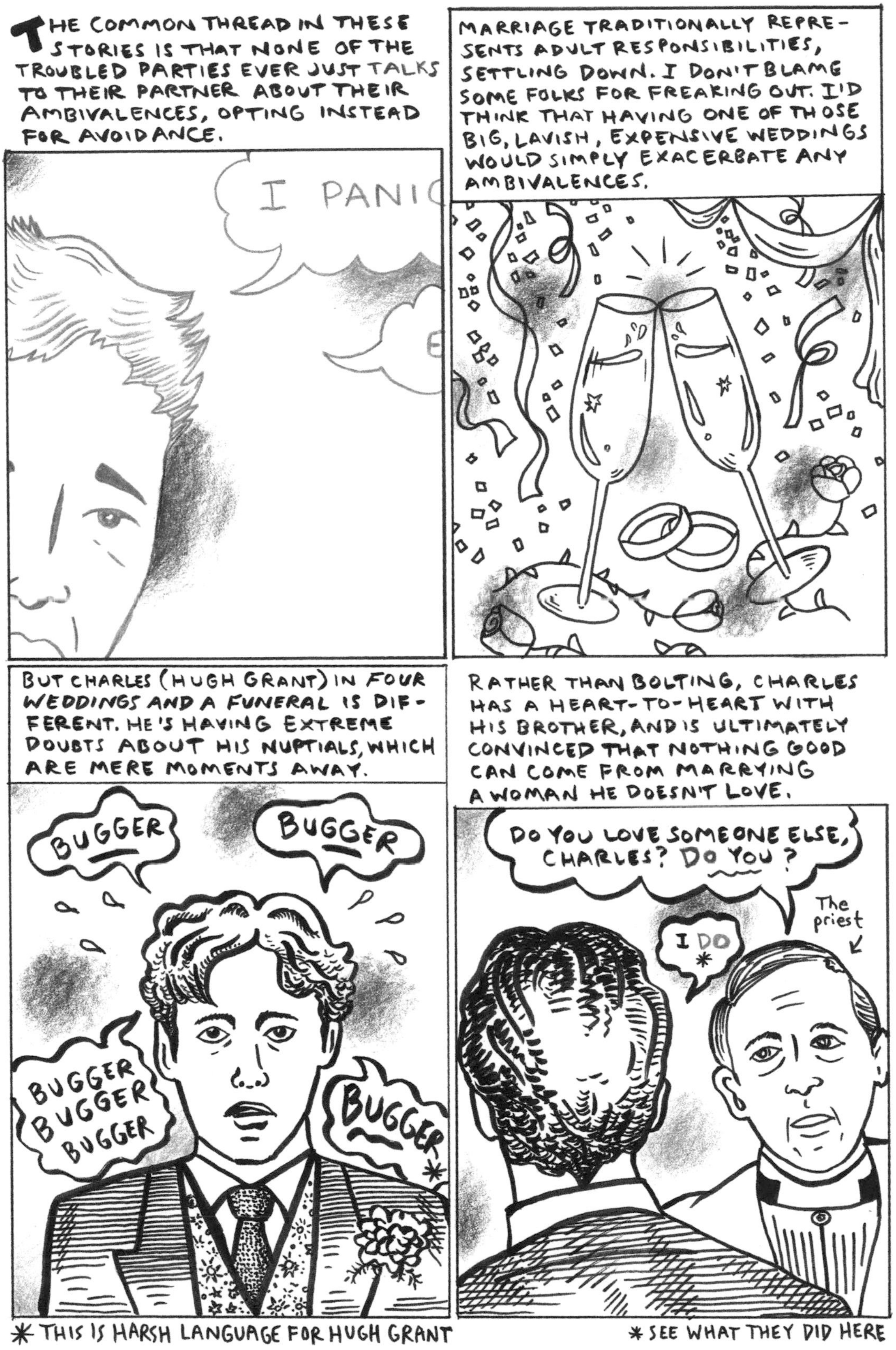
THE COMMON THREAD IN THESE STORIES IS THAT NONE OF THE TROUBLED PARTIES EVER JUST TALKS TO THEIR PARTNER ABOUT THEIR AMBIVALENCES, OPTING INSTEAD FOR AVOIDANCE.
MARRIAGE TRADITIONALLY REPRESENTS ADULT RESPONSIBILITIES, SETTLING DOWN. I DON'T BLAME SOME FOLKS FOR FREAKING OUT. I'D THINK THAT HAVING ONE OF THOSE BIG, LAVISH, EXPENSIVE WEDDINGS WOULD SIMPLY EXACERBATE ANY AMBIVALENCES.
BUT CHARLES (HUGH GRANT) IN *FOUR WEDDINGS AND A FUNERAL* IS DIFFERENT. HE'S HAVING EXTREME DOUBTS ABOUT HIS NUPTIALS, WHICH ARE MERE MOMENTS AWAY.
BUGGER
BUGGER
BUGGER BUGGER BUGGER
BUGGER*
RATHER THAN BOLTING, CHARLES HAS A HEART-TO-HEART WITH HIS BROTHER, AND IS ULTIMATELY CONVINCED THAT NOTHING GOOD CAN COME FROM MARRYING A WOMAN HE DOESN'T LOVE.
DO YOU LOVE SOMEONE ELSE, CHARLES? DO YOU?
I DO*
The priest

* THIS IS HARSH LANGUAGE FOR HUGH GRANT

* SEE WHAT THEY DID HERE

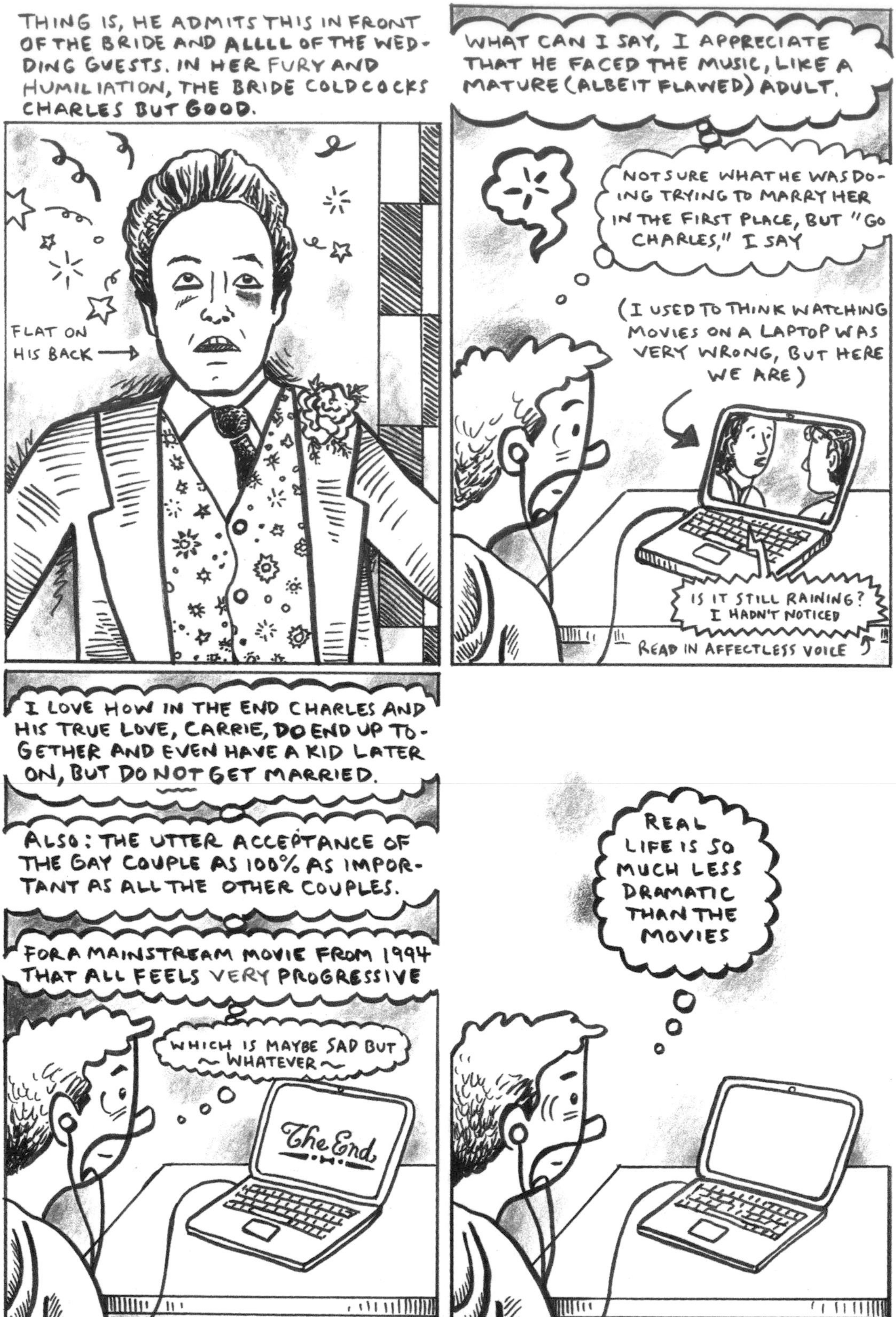
THING IS, HE ADMITS THIS IN FRONT OF THE BRIDE AND ALLLL OF THE WEDDING GUESTS. IN HER FURY AND HUMILIATION, THE BRIDE COLDCOCKS CHARLES BUT GOOD.
FLAT ON HIS BACK
WHAT CAN I SAY, I APPRECIATE THAT HE FACED THE MUSIC, LIKE A MATURE (ALBEIT FLAWED) ADULT.
NOT SURE WHAT HE WAS DOING TRYING TO MARRY HER IN THE FIRST PLACE, BUT "GO CHARLES," I SAY
(I USED TO THINK WATCHING MOVIES ON A LAPTOP WAS VERY WRONG, BUT HERE WE ARE)
IS IT STILL RAINING? I HADN'T NOTICED
READ IN AFFECTLESS VOICE
I LOVE HOW IN THE END CHARLES AND HIS TRUE LOVE, CARRIE, DO END UP TOGETHER AND EVEN HAVE A KID LATER ON, BUT DO NOT GET MARRIED.
ALSO: THE UTTER ACCEPTANCE OF THE GAY COUPLE AS 100% AS IMPORTANT AS ALL THE OTHER COUPLES.
FOR A MAINSTREAM MOVIE FROM 1994 THAT ALL FEELS VERY PROGRESSIVE
WHICH IS MAYBE SAD BUT ~WHATEVER~
The End
REAL LIFE IS SO MUCH LESS DRAMATIC THAN THE MOVIES

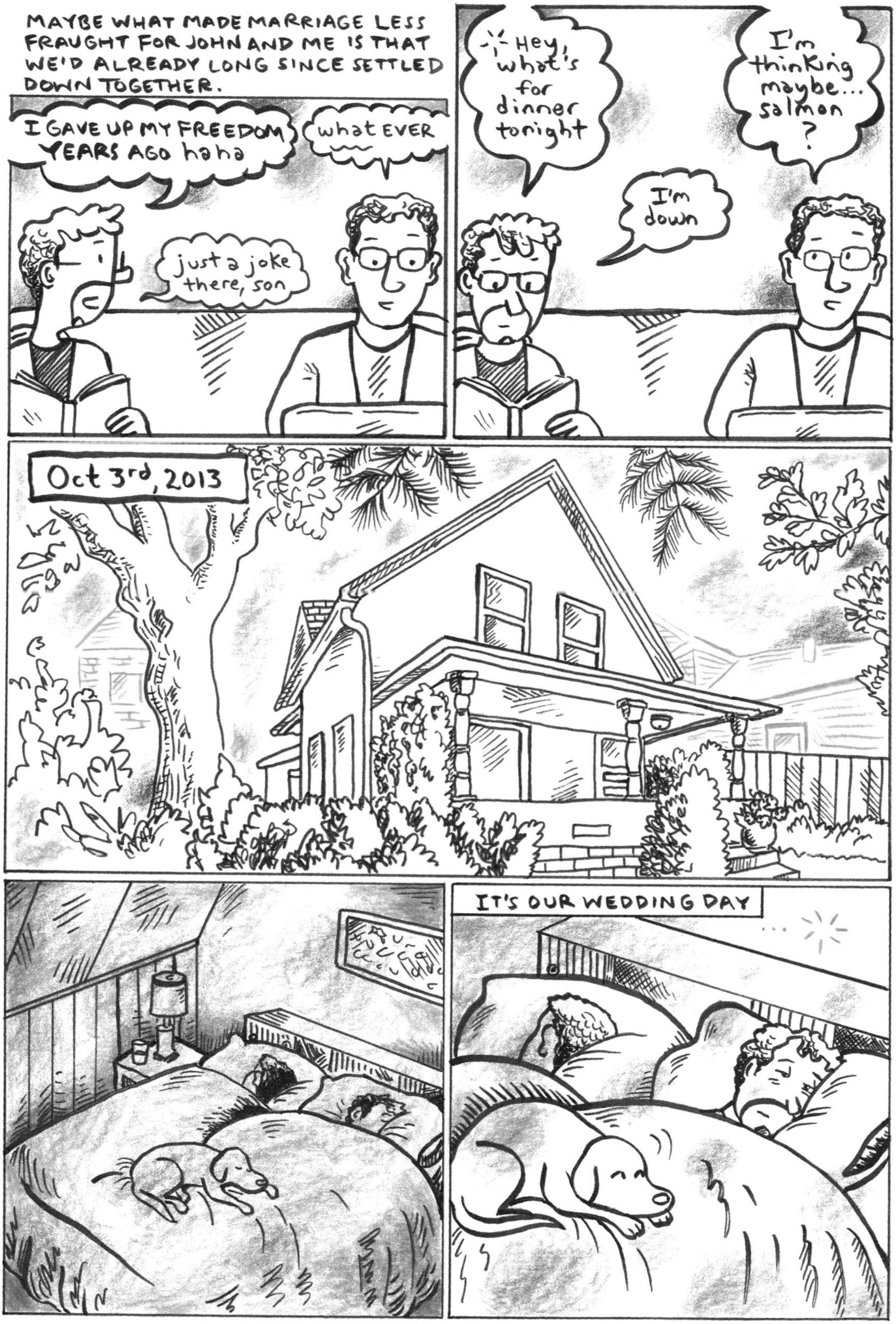
MAYBE WHAT MADE MARRIAGE LESS FRAUGHT FOR JOHN AND ME IS THAT WE'D ALREADY LONG SINCE SETTLED DOWN TOGETHER.
I GAVE UP MY FREEDOM YEARS AGO haha
whatever
just a joke there, son
Hey, what's for dinner tonight
I'm down
I'm thinking maybe... salmon ?
Oct 3rd, 2013
IT'S OUR WEDDING DAY

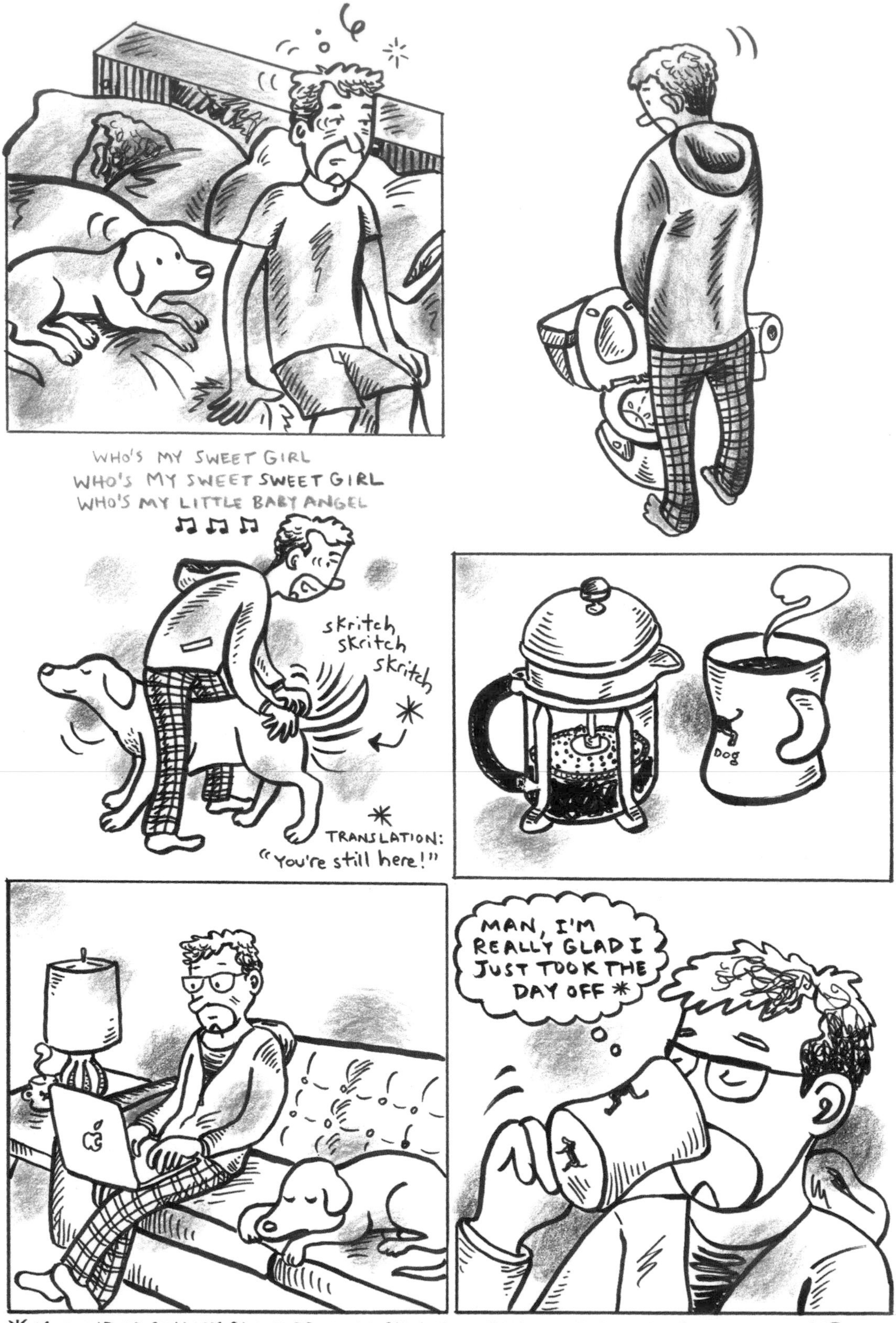
WHO'S MY SWEET GIRL
WHO'S MY SWEET SWEET GIRL
WHO'S MY LITTLE BABY ANGEL
skritch skritch skritch
*
* TRANSLATION: "You're still here!"
Dog
MAN, I'M REALLY GLAD I JUST TOOK THE DAY OFF *

* YEP, I'D ORIGINALLY PLANNED TO WORK A HALF DAY, SINCE THE WEDDING WAS AT 4:30 PM

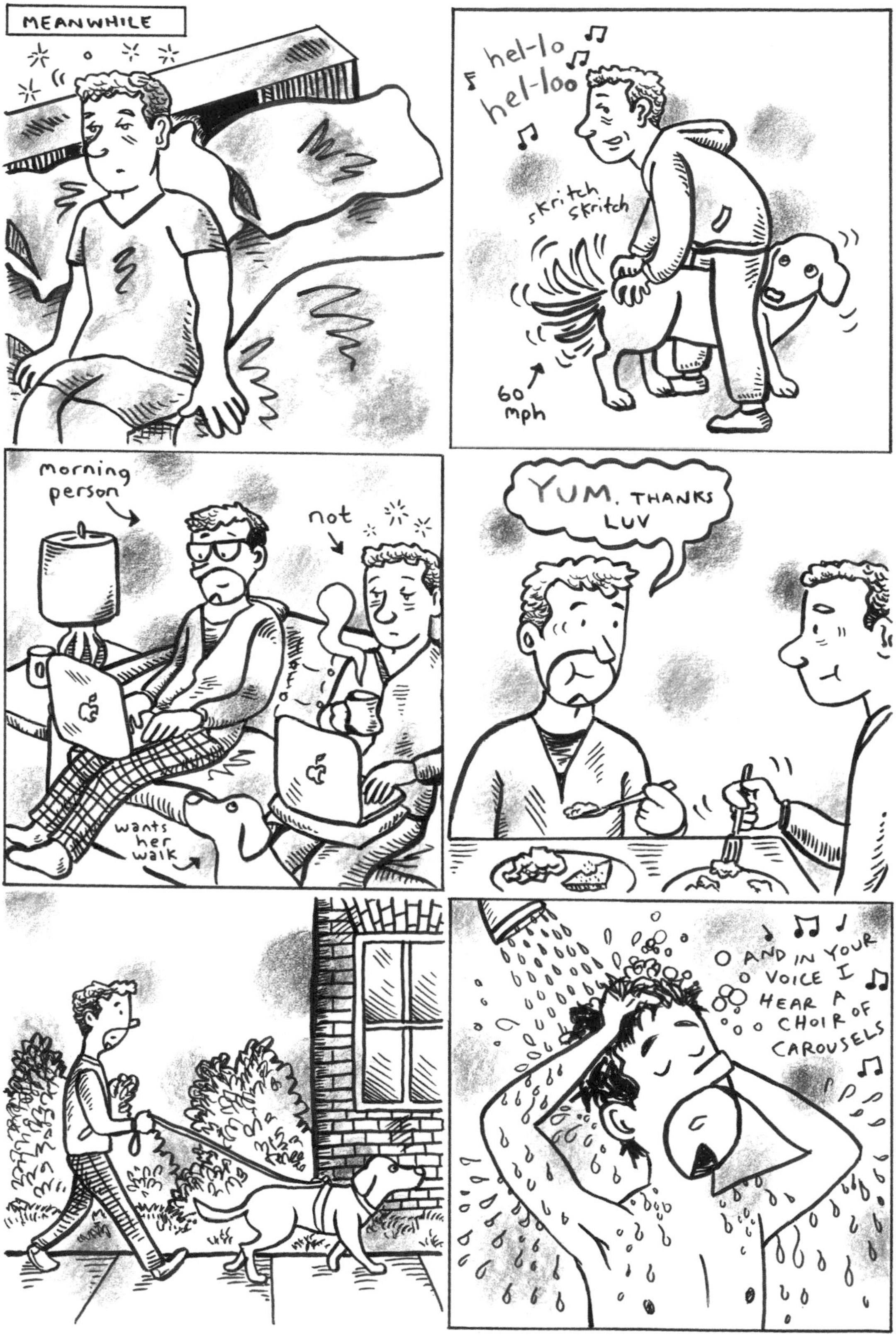

MEANWHILE
hel-lo
hel-loo
skritch skritch
60 mph
morning person
not
wants her walk
YUM. THANKS LUV
AND IN YOUR VOICE I HEAR A CHOIR OF CAROUSELS

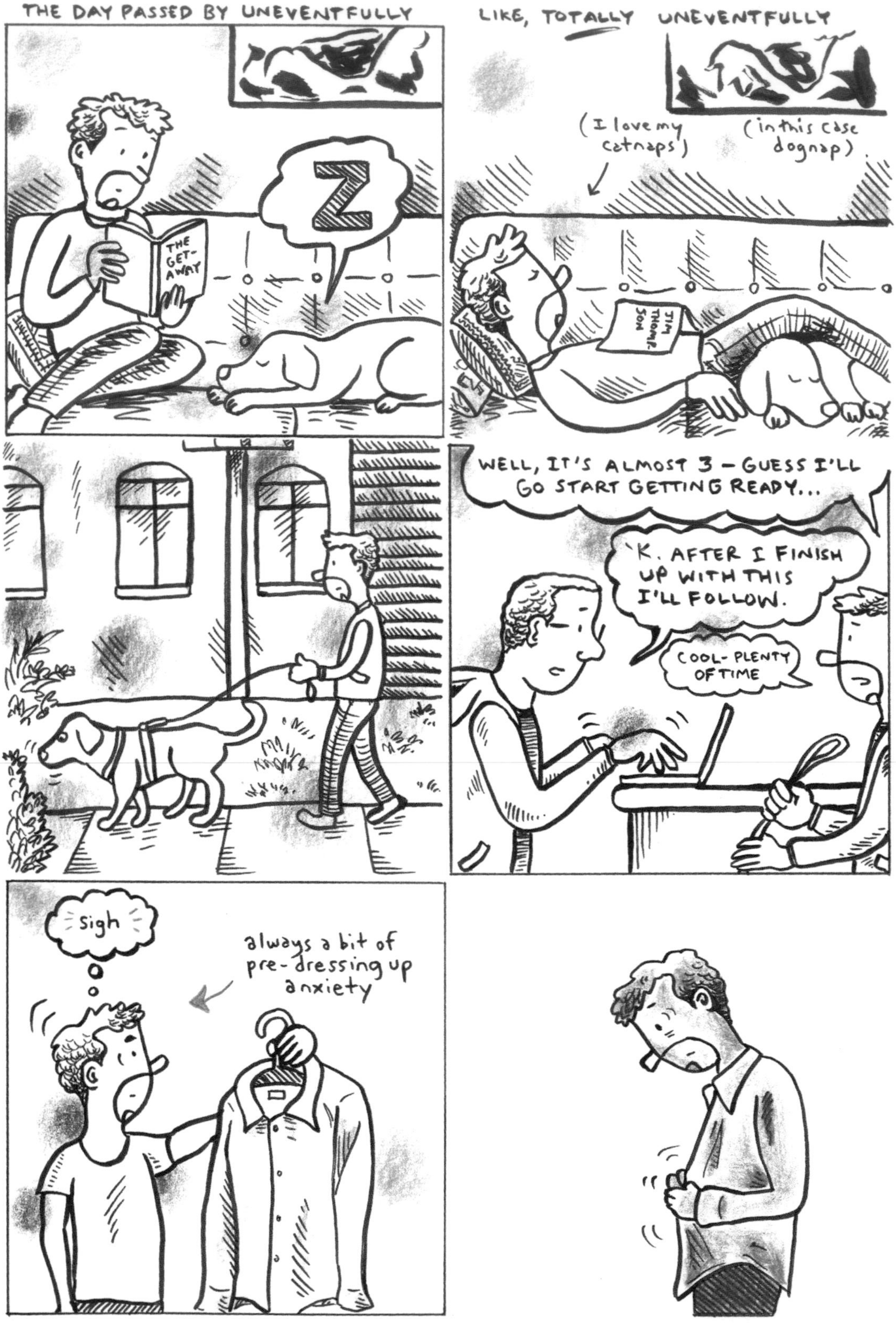
THE DAY PASSED BY UNEVENTFULLY
THE GET-AWAY
Z
LIKE, TOTALLY UNEVENTFULLY
(I love my catnaps)
(in this case dognap)
JIM THOMPSON
WELL, IT'S ALMOST 3 — GUESS I'LL GO START GETTING READY...
'K. AFTER I FINISH UP WITH THIS I'LL FOLLOW.
COOL- PLENTY OF TIME
Sigh
always a bit of pre-dressing up anxiety

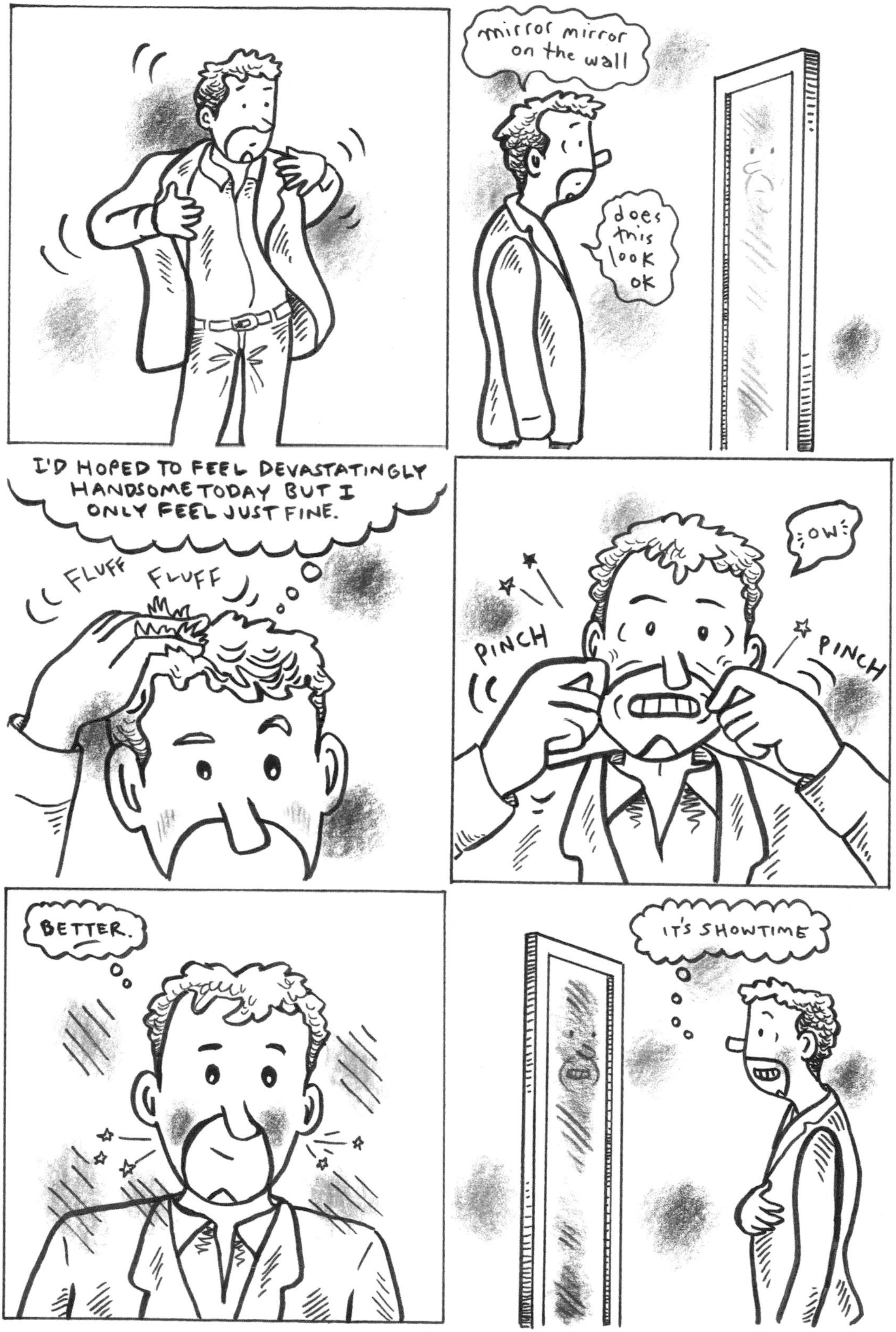
mirror mirror on the wall
does this look ok
I'D HOPED TO FEEL DEVASTATINGLY HANDSOME TODAY BUT I ONLY FEEL JUST FINE.
FLUFF
FLUFF
OW
PINCH
PINCH
BETTER.
IT'S SHOWTIME

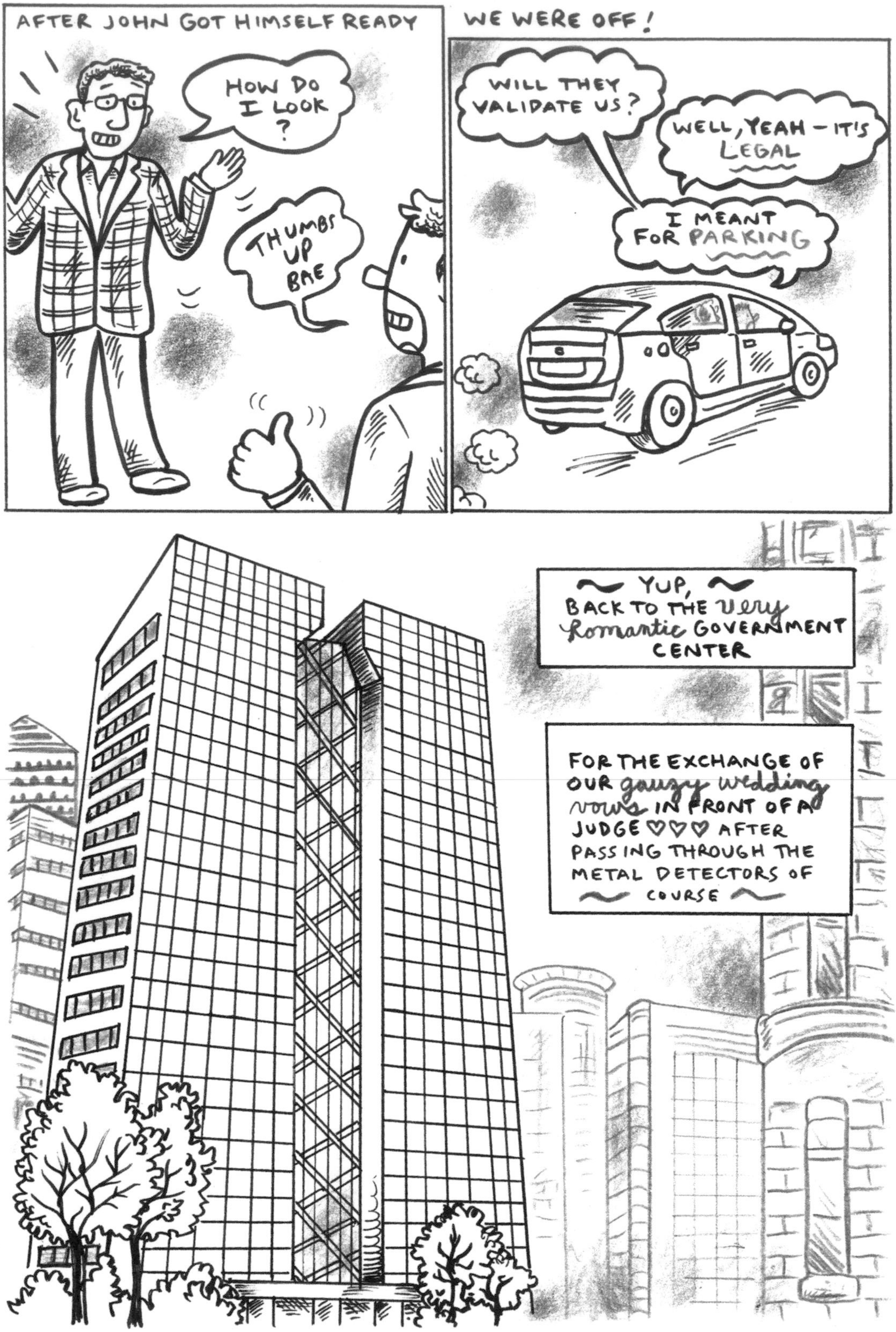
AFTER JOHN GOT HIMSELF READY
HOW DO I LOOK ?
THUMBS UP BAE
WE WERE OFF !
WILL THEY VALIDATE US ?
WELL, YEAH - IT'S LEGAL
I MEANT FOR PARKING
~ YUP, ~ BACK TO THE very Romantic GOVERNMENT CENTER
FOR THE EXCHANGE OF OUR gauzy wedding vows IN FRONT OF A JUDGE ♡♡♡ AFTER PASSING THROUGH THE METAL DETECTORS OF ~ COURSE ~

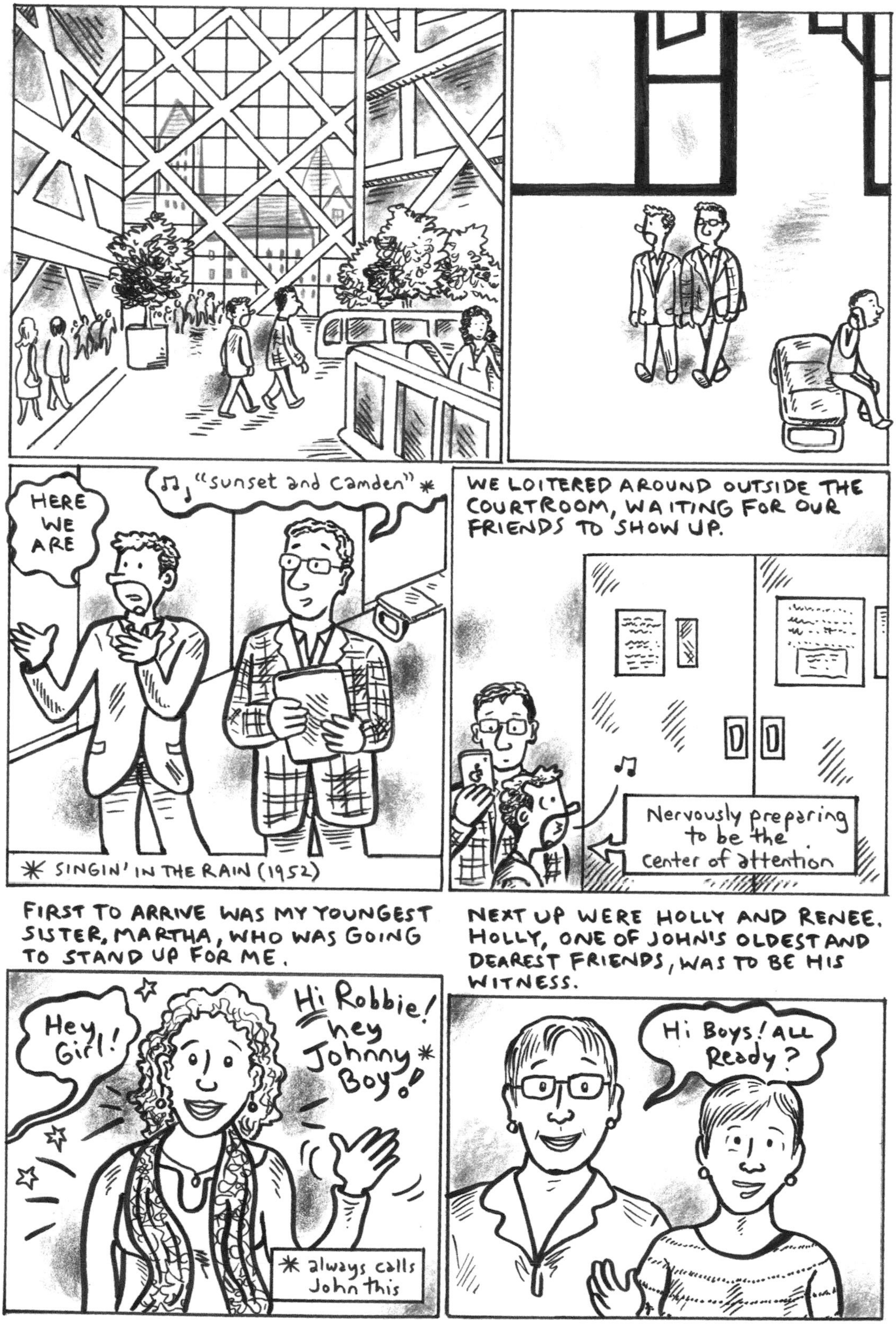
HERE WE ARE
"sunset and camden" *
* SINGIN' IN THE RAIN (1952)
WE LOITERED AROUND OUTSIDE THE COURTROOM, WAITING FOR OUR FRIENDS TO SHOW UP.
Nervously preparing to be the center of attention
FIRST TO ARRIVE WAS MY YOUNGEST SISTER, MARTHA, WHO WAS GOING TO STAND UP FOR ME.
Hey Girl!
Hi Robbie! hey Johnny Boy*!
* always calls John this
NEXT UP WERE HOLLY AND RENEE. HOLLY, ONE OF JOHN'S OLDEST AND DEAREST FRIENDS, WAS TO BE HIS WITNESS.
Hi Boys! ALL Ready?

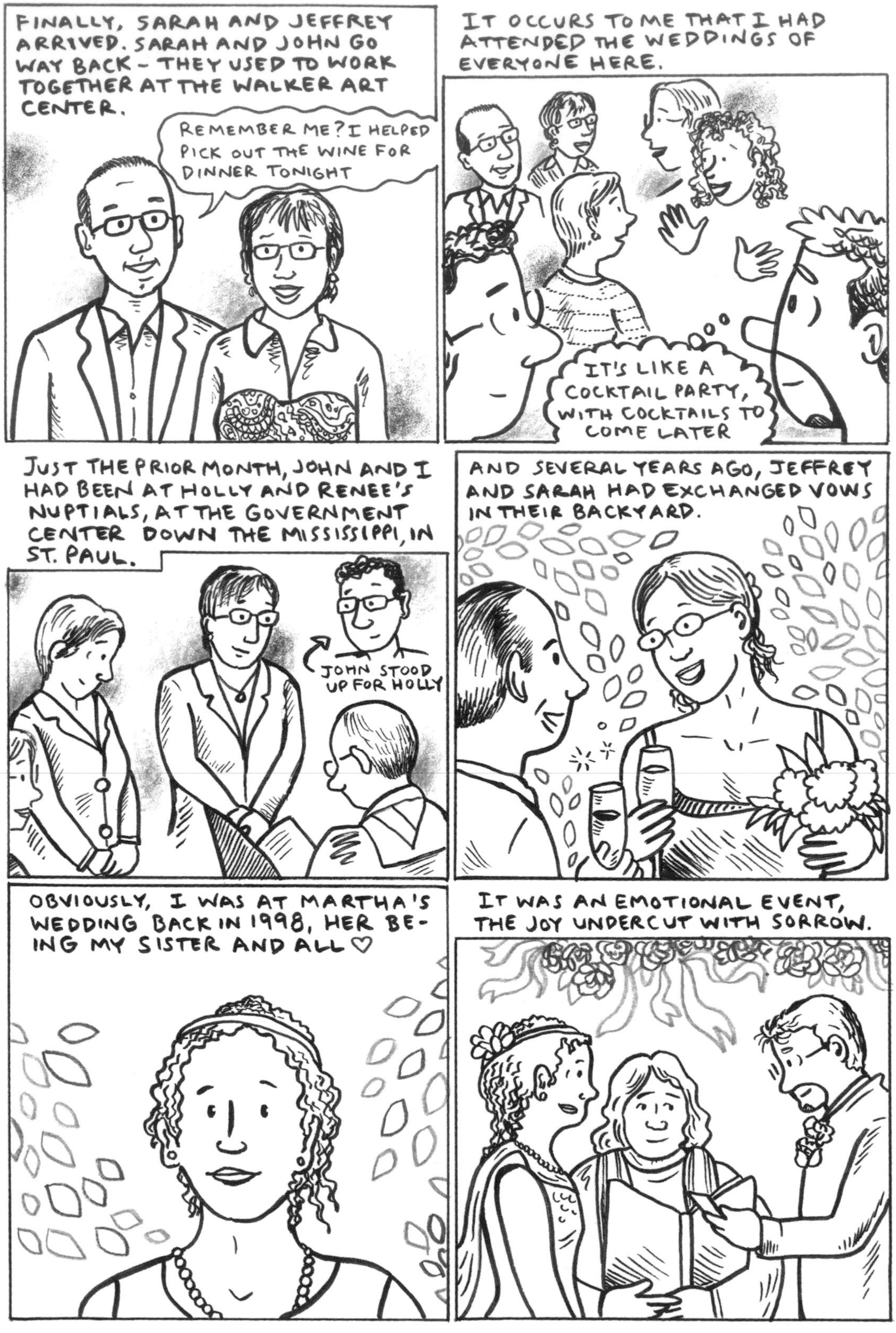
FINALLY, SARAH AND JEFFREY ARRIVED. SARAH AND JOHN GO WAY BACK – THEY USED TO WORK TOGETHER AT THE WALKER ART CENTER.
REMEMBER ME? I HELPED PICK OUT THE WINE FOR DINNER TONIGHT
IT OCCURS TO ME THAT I HAD ATTENDED THE WEDDINGS OF EVERYONE HERE.
IT'S LIKE A COCKTAIL PARTY, WITH COCKTAILS TO COME LATER
JUST THE PRIOR MONTH, JOHN AND I HAD BEEN AT HOLLY AND RENEE'S NUPTIALS, AT THE GOVERNMENT CENTER DOWN THE MISSISSIPPI, IN ST. PAUL.
JOHN STOOD UP FOR HOLLY
AND SEVERAL YEARS AGO, JEFFREY AND SARAH HAD EXCHANGED VOWS IN THEIR BACKYARD.
OBVIOUSLY, I WAS AT MARTHA'S WEDDING BACK IN 1998, HER BEING MY SISTER AND ALL ♡
IT WAS AN EMOTIONAL EVENT, THE JOY UNDERCUT WITH SORROW.

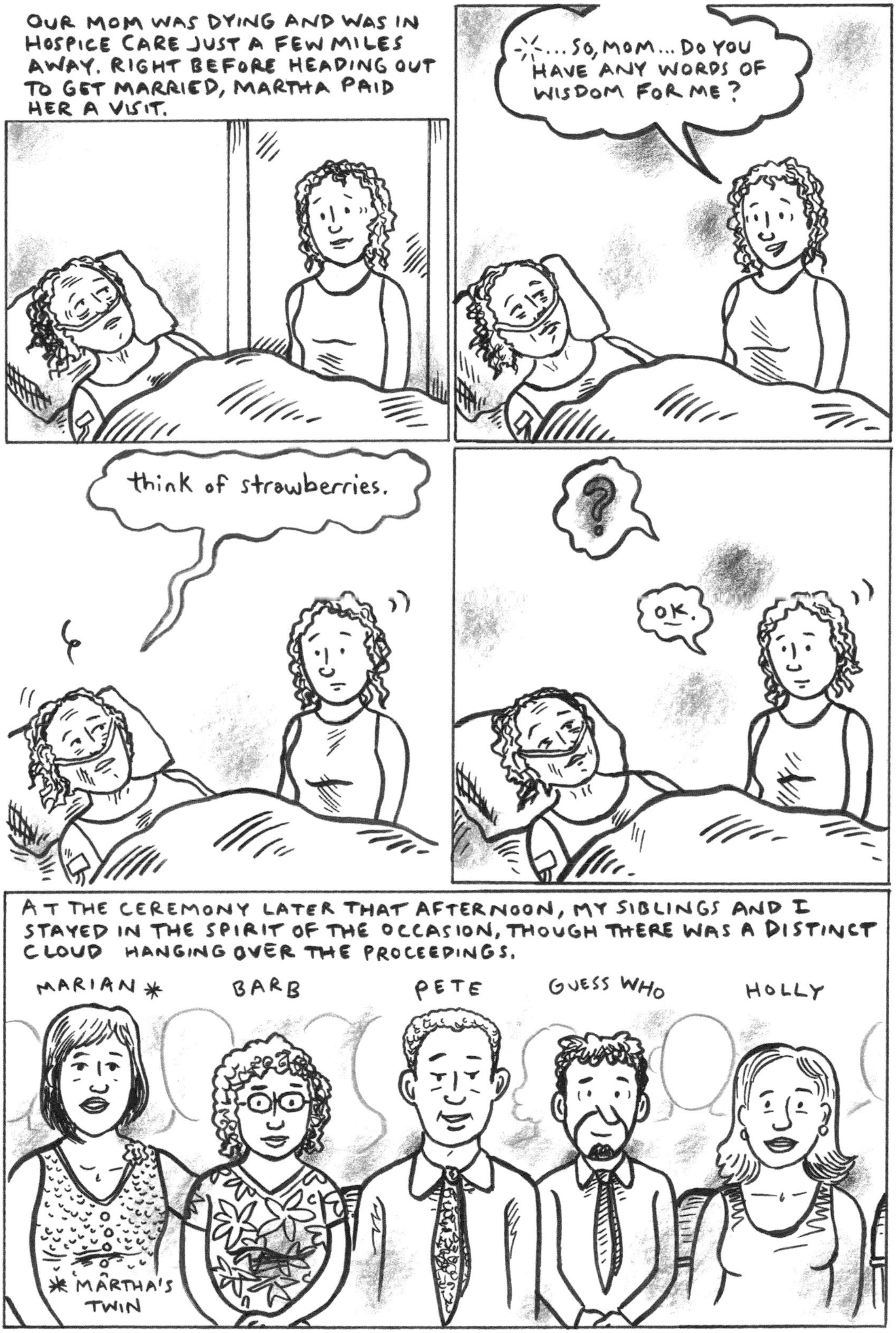
OUR MOM WAS DYING AND WAS IN HOSPICE CARE JUST A FEW MILES AWAY. RIGHT BEFORE HEADING OUT TO GET MARRIED, MARTHA PAID HER A VISIT.
...SO, MOM... DO YOU HAVE ANY WORDS OF WISDOM FOR ME?
think of strawberries.
?
OK.
AT THE CEREMONY LATER THAT AFTERNOON, MY SIBLINGS AND I STAYED IN THE SPIRIT OF THE OCCASION, THOUGH THERE WAS A DISTINCT CLOUD HANGING OVER THE PROCEEDINGS.
MARIAN *
BARB
PETE
GUESS WHO
HOLLY
* MARTHA'S TWIN

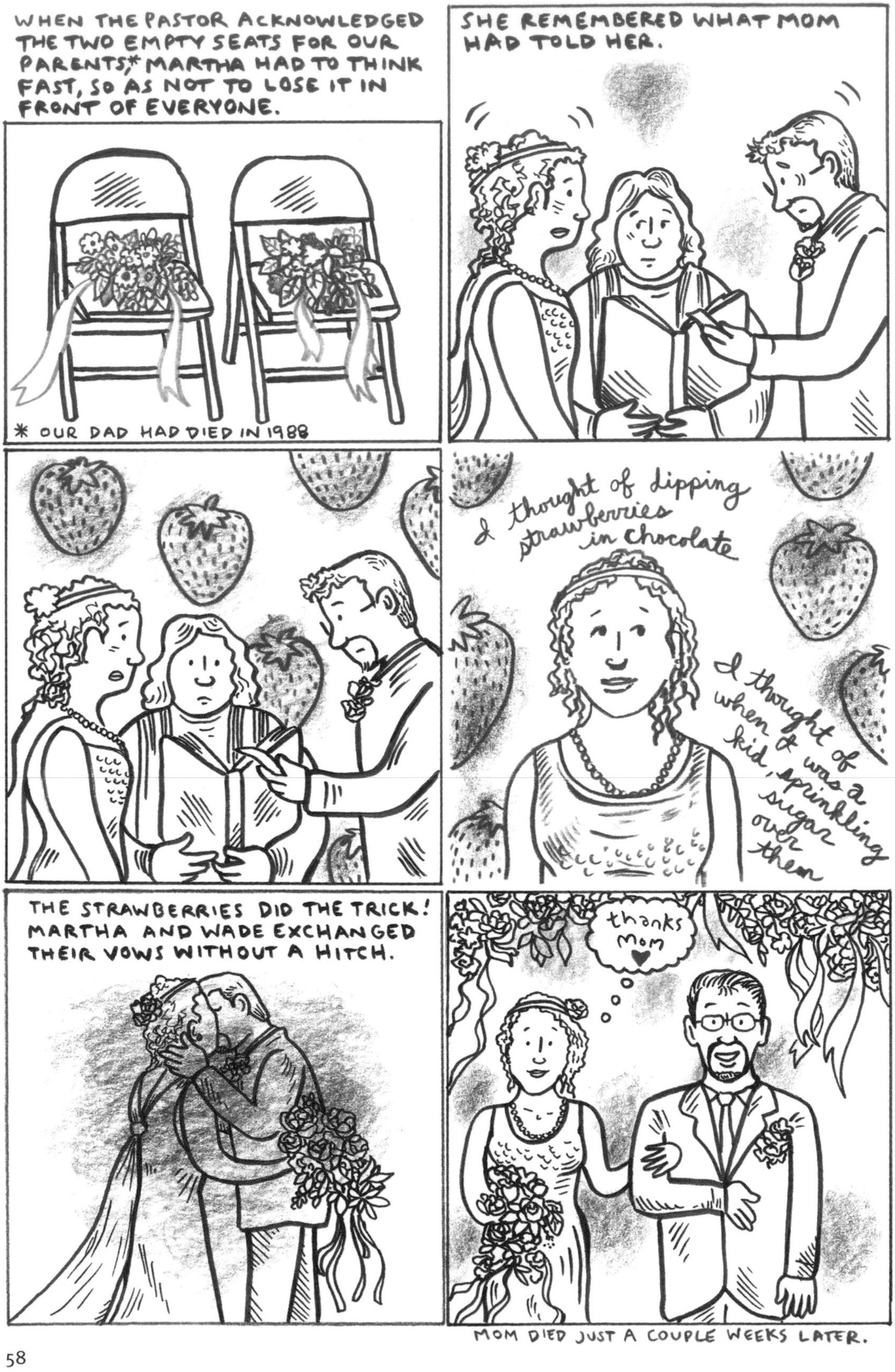
WHEN THE PASTOR ACKNOWLEDGED THE TWO EMPTY SEATS FOR OUR PARENTS,* MARTHA HAD TO THINK FAST, SO AS NOT TO LOSE IT IN FRONT OF EVERYONE.
* OUR DAD HAD DIED IN 1988
SHE REMEMBERED WHAT MOM HAD TOLD HER.
I thought of dipping strawberries in chocolate
I thought of when I was a kid, sprinkling sugar over them
THE STRAWBERRIES DID THE TRICK! MARTHA AND WADE EXCHANGED THEIR VOWS WITHOUT A HITCH.
thanks Mom
MOM DIED JUST A COUPLE WEEKS LATER.

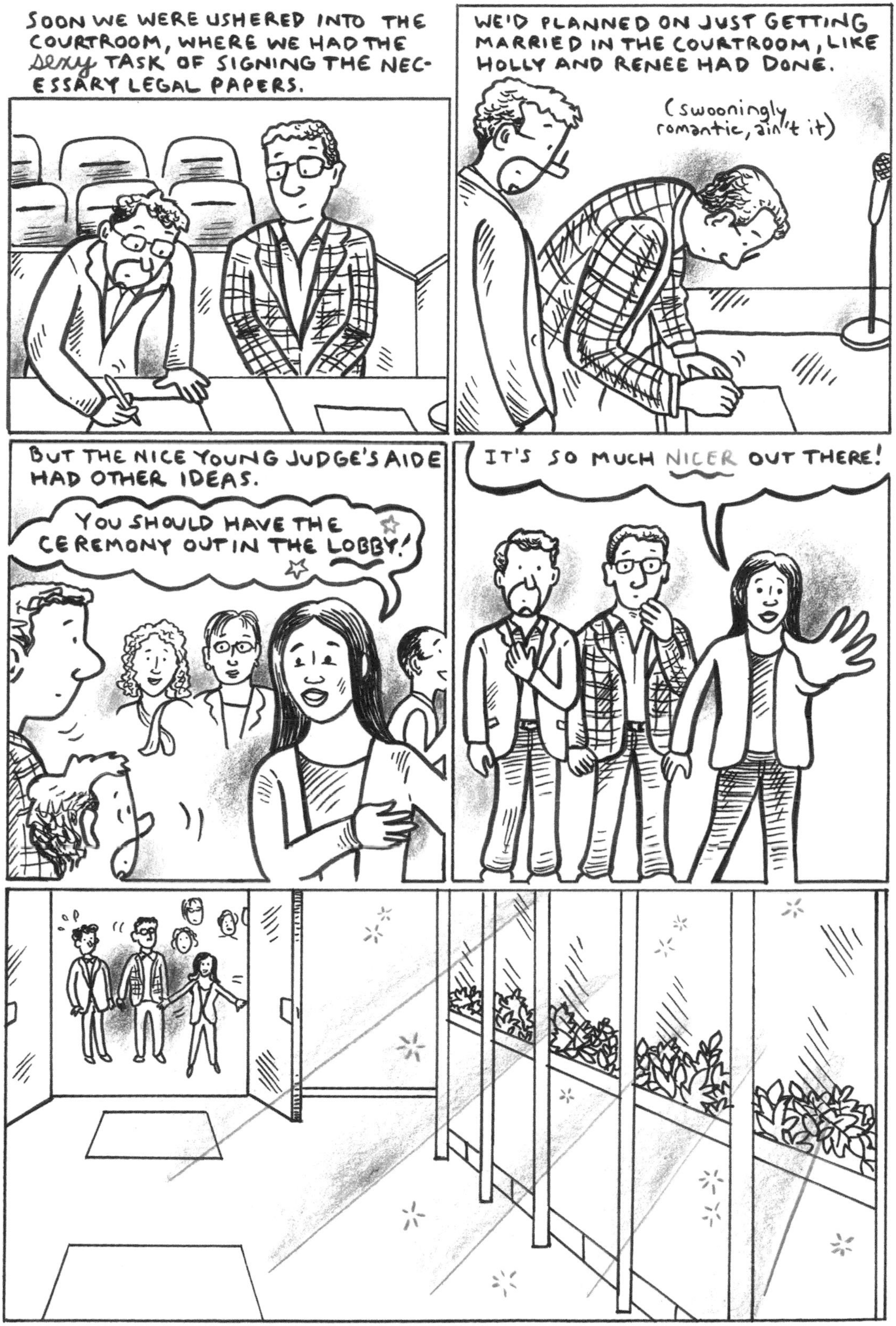
SOON WE WERE USHERED INTO THE COURTROOM, WHERE WE HAD THE *sexy* TASK OF SIGNING THE NEC-ESSARY LEGAL PAPERS.
WE'D PLANNED ON JUST GETTING MARRIED IN THE COURTROOM, LIKE HOLLY AND RENEE HAD DONE.
(swooningly romantic, ain't it)
BUT THE NICE YOUNG JUDGE'S AIDE HAD OTHER IDEAS.
YOU SHOULD HAVE THE CEREMONY OUT IN THE LOBBY!
IT'S SO MUCH NICER OUT THERE!

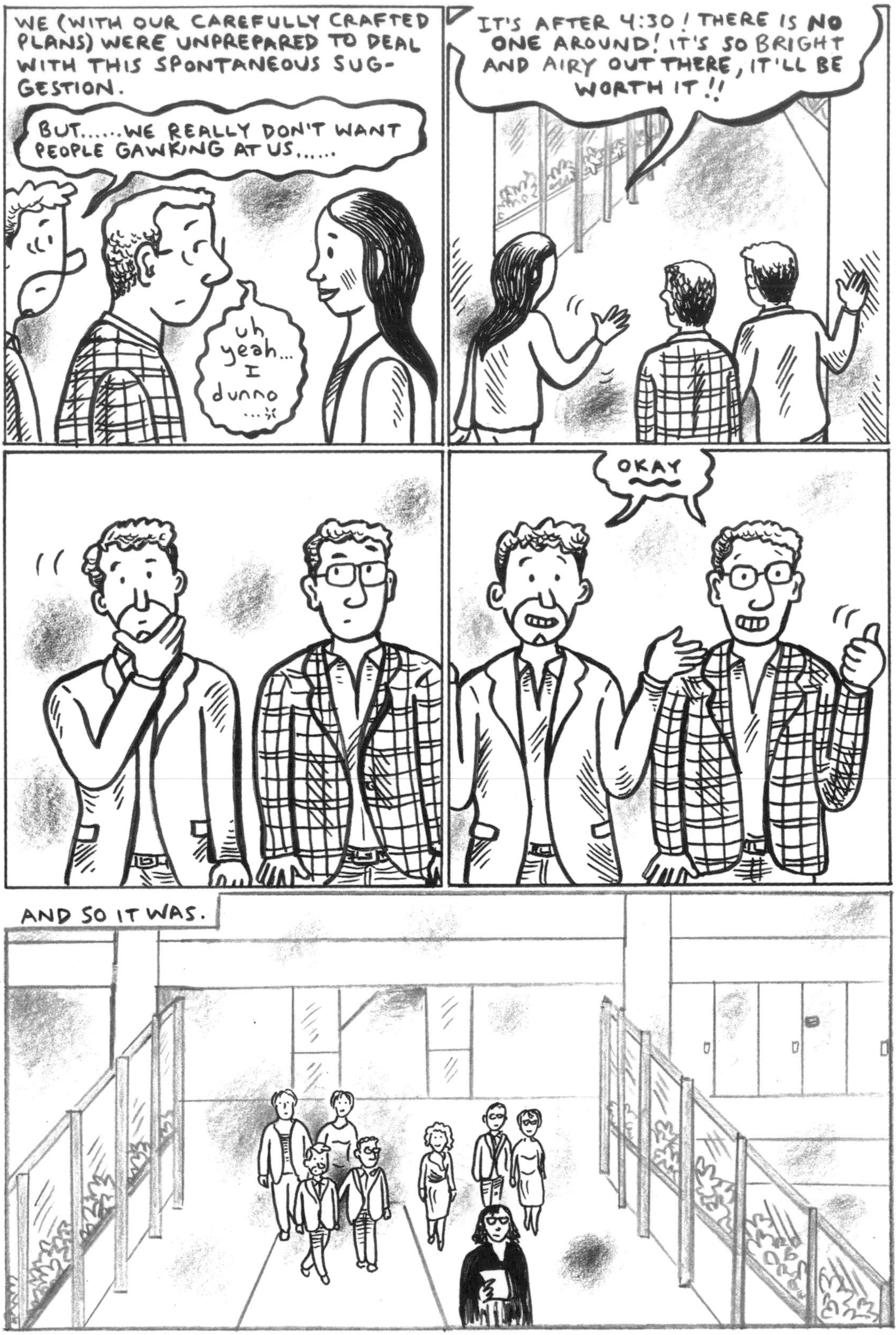

WE (WITH OUR CAREFULLY CRAFTED PLANS) WERE UNPREPARED TO DEAL WITH THIS SPONTANEOUS SUGGESTION.
BUT......WE REALLY DON'T WANT PEOPLE GAWKING AT US......
uh yeah... I dunno ...
IT'S AFTER 4:30! THERE IS NO ONE AROUND! IT'S SO BRIGHT AND AIRY OUT THERE, IT'LL BE WORTH IT!!
OKAY
AND SO IT WAS.

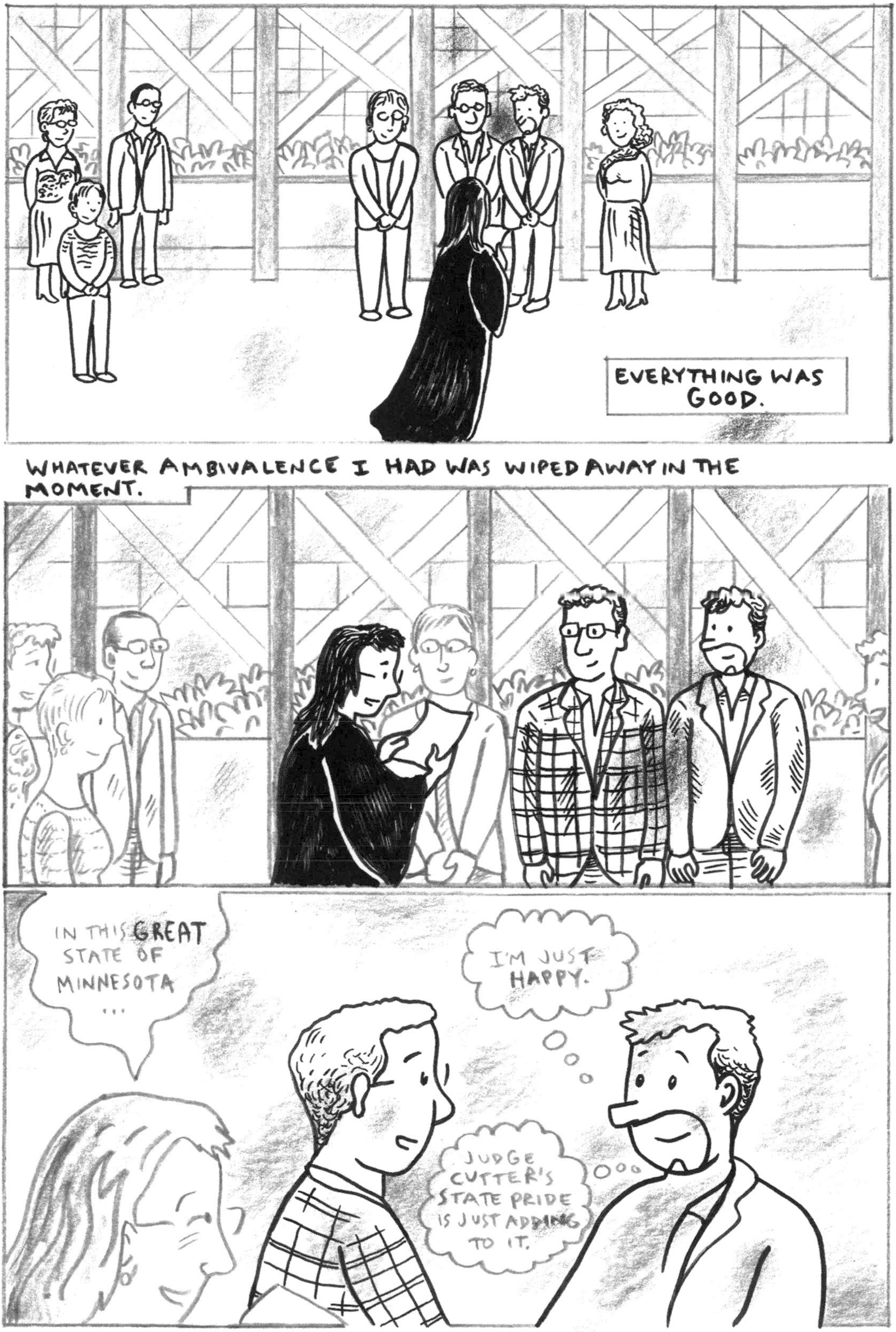
EVERYTHING WAS GOOD.
WHATEVER AMBIVALENCE I HAD WAS WIPED AWAY IN THE MOMENT.
IN THIS GREAT STATE OF MINNESOTA ...
I'M JUST HAPPY.
JUDGE CUTTER'S STATE PRIDE IS JUST ADDING TO IT.

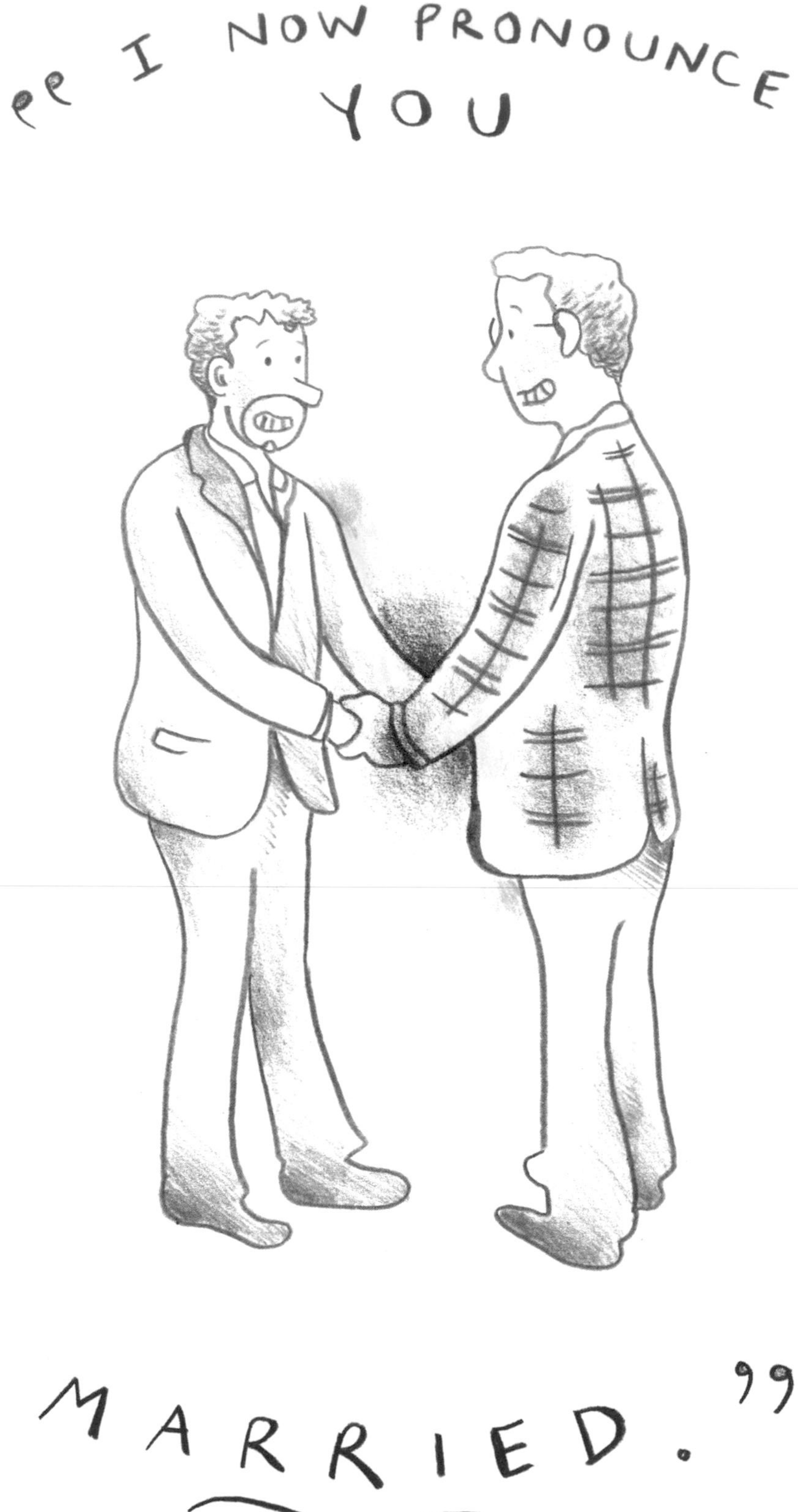
"I NOW PRONOUNCE YOU
MARRIED."

Sealed with a kiss

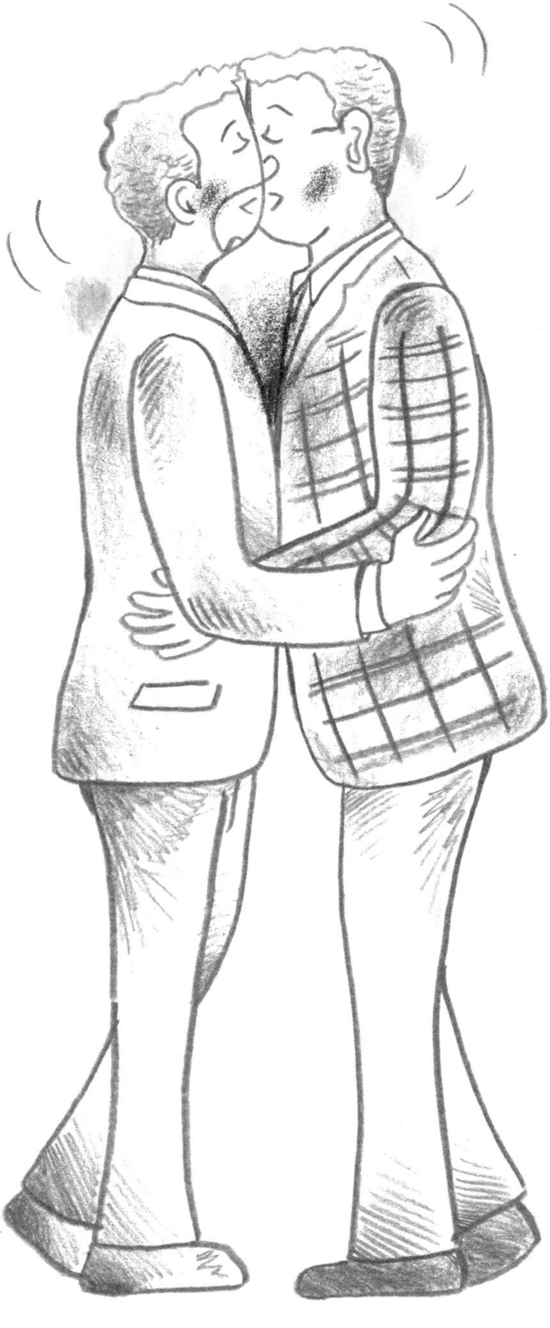

AFTERWARDS, THERE WERE PICTURES TO BE TAKEN, OF COURSE.

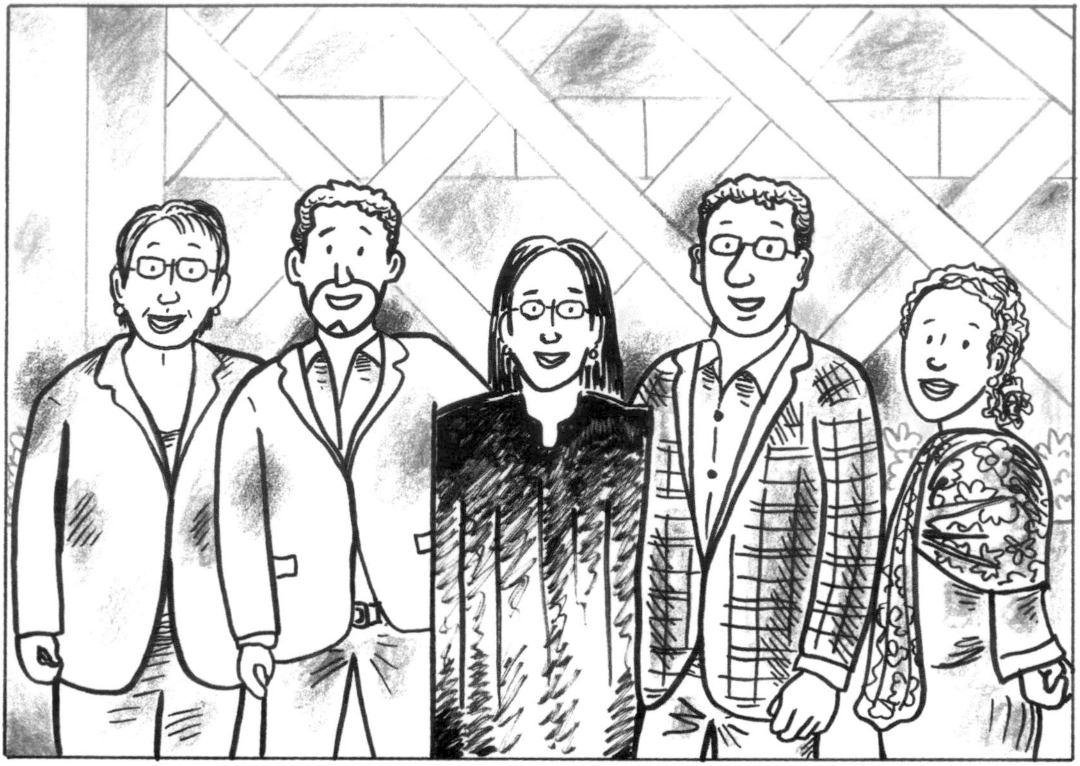

THROUGH IT ALL I CONTINUED TO HAVE THIS SORT OF FLOATY FEELING

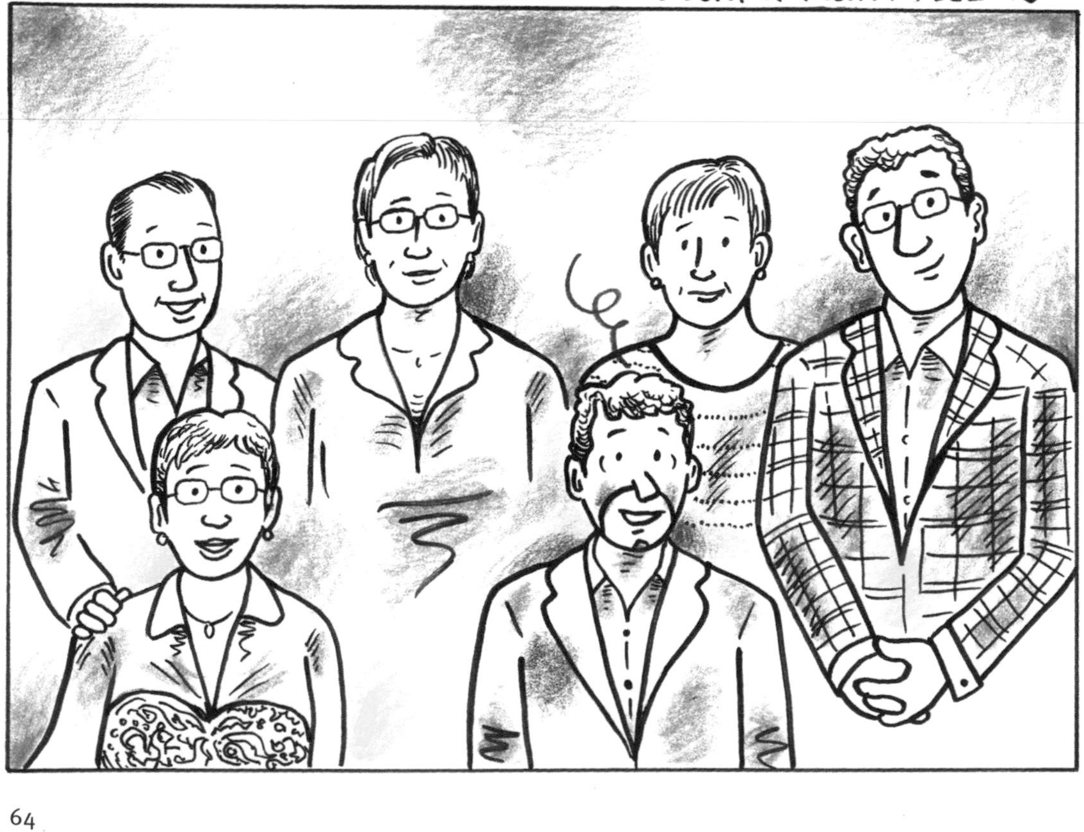

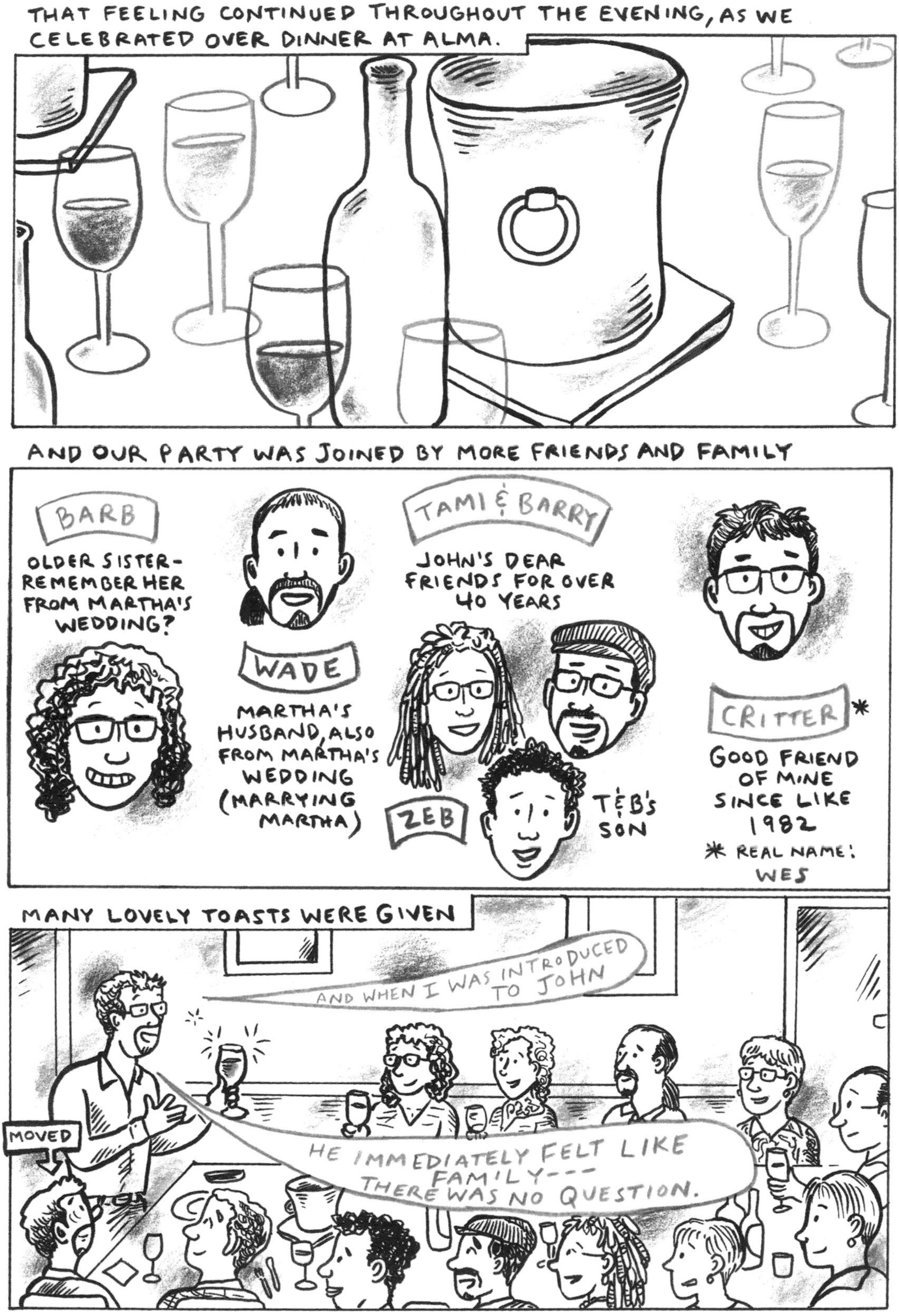
THAT FEELING CONTINUED THROUGHOUT THE EVENING, AS WE CELEBRATED OVER DINNER AT ALMA.
AND OUR PARTY WAS JOINED BY MORE FRIENDS AND FAMILY
BARB
OLDER SISTER- REMEMBER HER FROM MARTHA'S WEDDING?
WADE
MARTHA'S HUSBAND, ALSO FROM MARTHA'S WEDDING (MARRYING MARTHA)
TAMI & BARRY
JOHN'S DEAR FRIENDS FOR OVER 40 YEARS
ZEB
T&B'S SON
CRITTER*
GOOD FRIEND OF MINE SINCE LIKE 1982
* REAL NAME: WES
MANY LOVELY TOASTS WERE GIVEN
AND WHEN I WAS INTRODUCED TO JOHN
HE IMMEDIATELY FELT LIKE FAMILY--- THERE WAS NO QUESTION.
MOVED

(I THINK THE MAJOR REASON THAT CRITTER'S TOAST MADE ME TEAR UP A LITTLE IS THAT FROM THE MOMENT I MET JOHN I'VE ALWAYS HAD THE FEELING THAT I'VE KNOWN HIM ALL ALONG. IT'S NOT EXACTLY DÉJÀ VU.... CAN NEVER PUT MY FINGER ON JUST WHAT IT IS...)

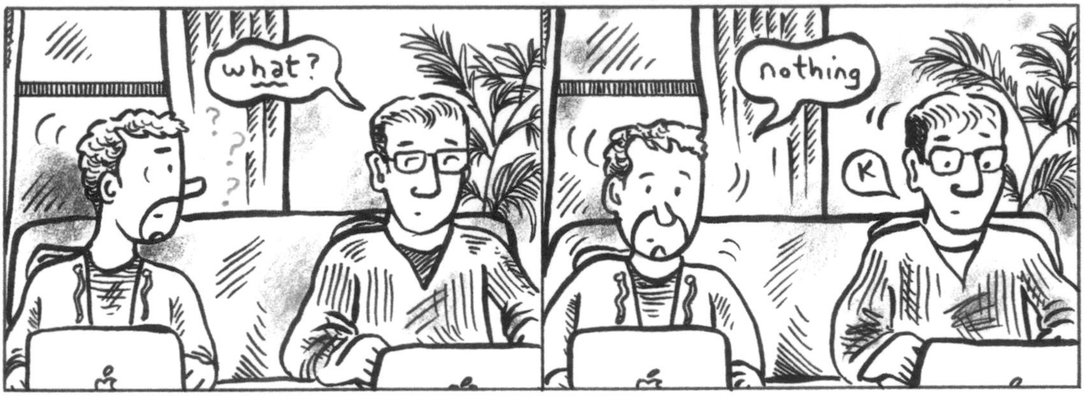
what?
nothing
K

ANYWAY, ANOTHER BIG HIGHLIGHT OF THE EVENING WAS THE AMAZING DINNER. EVERYONE WHO ATTENDED IS PRETTY MUCH A "FOODIE,"* SO WE WERE ALL LIKE YAY

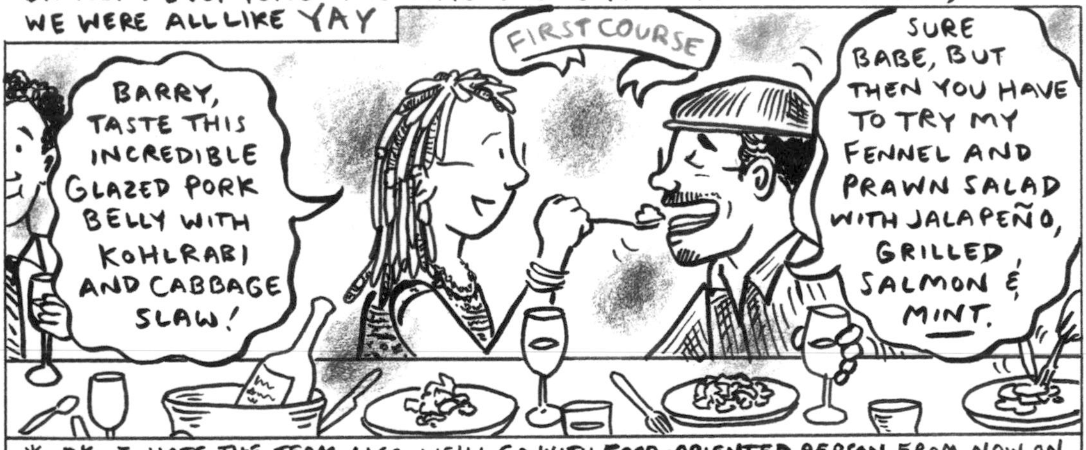
FIRST COURSE
BARRY, TASTE THIS INCREDIBLE GLAZED PORK BELLY WITH KOHLRABI AND CABBAGE SLAW!
SURE BABE, BUT THEN YOU HAVE TO TRY MY FENNEL AND PRAWN SALAD WITH JALAPEÑO, GRILLED SALMON & MINT.

* OK, I HATE THE TERM ALSO, WE'LL GO WITH **FOOD-ORIENTED PERSON** FROM NOW ON

IT WAS ALL JUST A LOT OF FUN.

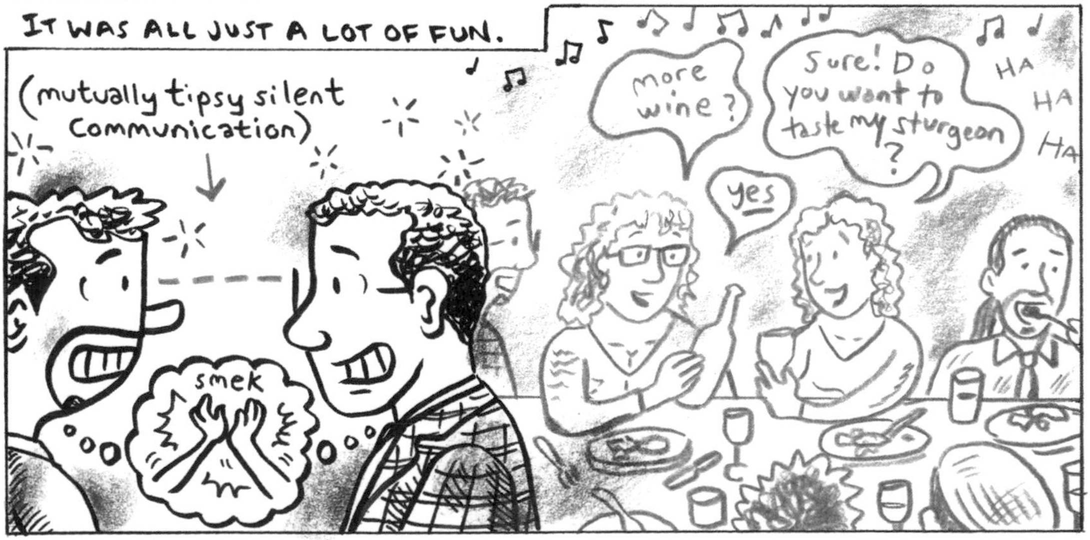
(mutually tipsy silent communication)
smek
more wine?
yes
Sure! Do you want to taste my sturgeon?
HA HA HA

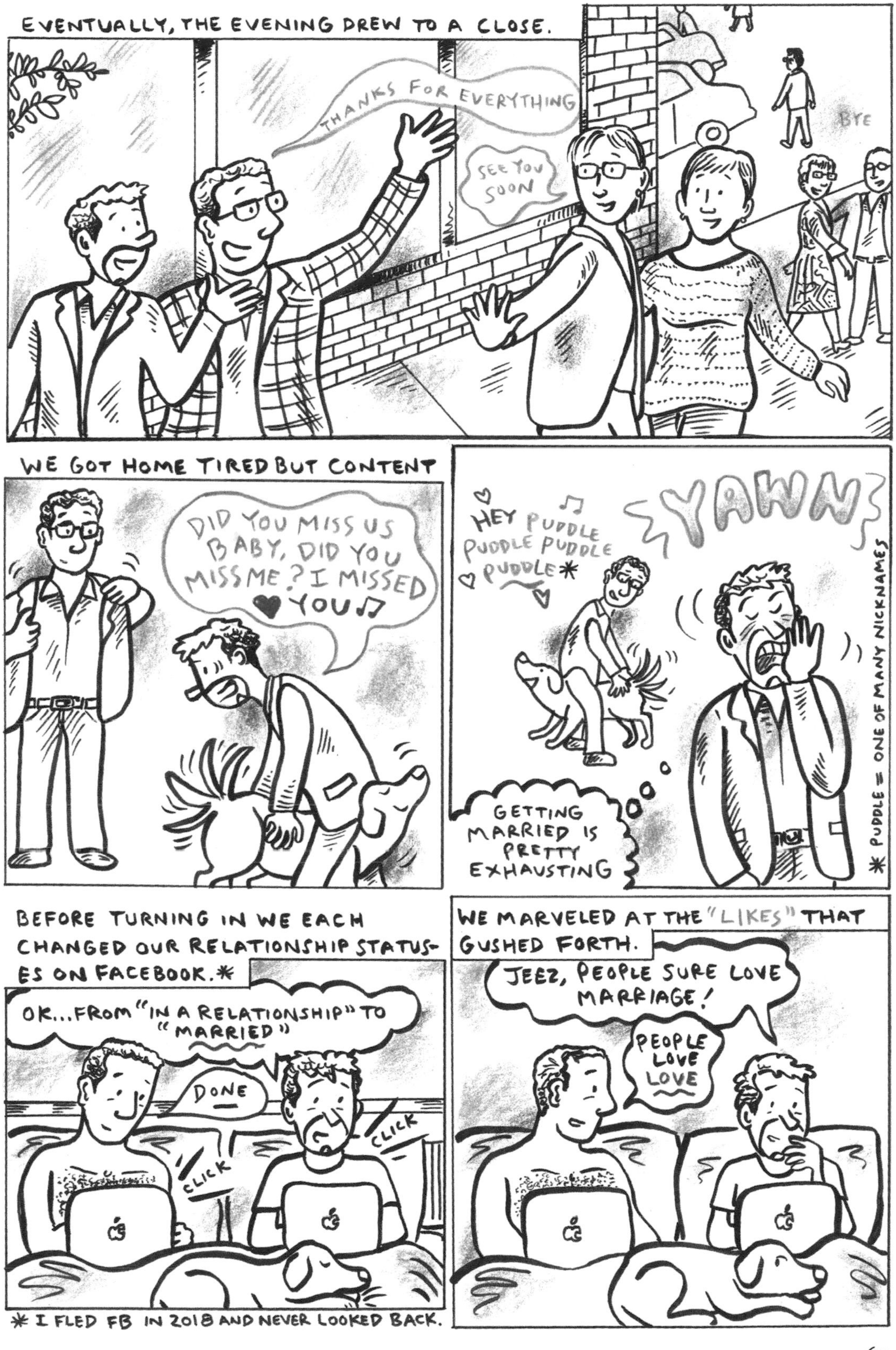
EVENTUALLY, THE EVENING DREW TO A CLOSE.
THANKS FOR EVERYTHING
SEE YOU SOON
BYE
WE GOT HOME TIRED BUT CONTENT
DID YOU MISS US BABY, DID YOU MISS ME? I MISSED ♥ YOU ♫
♡ ♫ HEY PUDDLE PUDDLE PUDDLE PUDDLE* ♡
YAWN
GETTING MARRIED IS PRETTY EXHAUSTING
* PUDDLE = ONE OF MANY NICKNAMES
BEFORE TURNING IN WE EACH CHANGED OUR RELATIONSHIP STATUSES ON FACEBOOK.*
OK...FROM "IN A RELATIONSHIP" TO "MARRIED"
DONE
CLICK
CLICK
* I FLED FB IN 2018 AND NEVER LOOKED BACK.
WE MARVELED AT THE "LIKES" THAT GUSHED FORTH.
JEEZ, PEOPLE SURE LOVE MARRIAGE!
PEOPLE LOVE LOVE

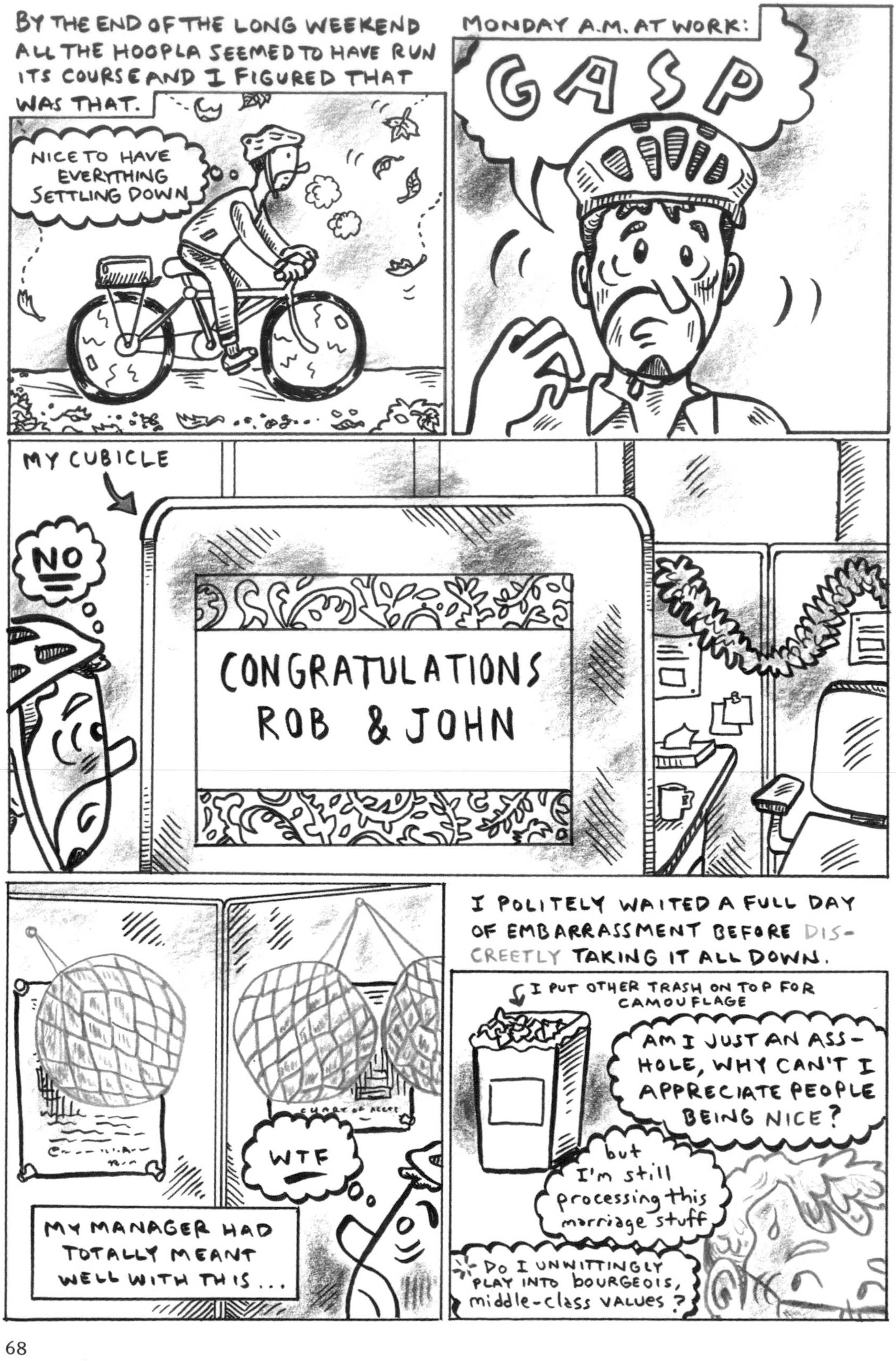
BY THE END OF THE LONG WEEKEND ALL THE HOOPLA SEEMED TO HAVE RUN ITS COURSE AND I FIGURED THAT WAS THAT.
NICE TO HAVE EVERYTHING SETTLING DOWN
MONDAY A.M. AT WORK:
GASP
MY CUBICLE
NO
CONGRATULATIONS ROB & JOHN
MY MANAGER HAD TOTALLY MEANT WELL WITH THIS...
WTF
I POLITELY WAITED A FULL DAY OF EMBARRASSMENT BEFORE DISCREETLY TAKING IT ALL DOWN.
I PUT OTHER TRASH ON TOP FOR CAMOUFLAGE
AM I JUST AN ASSHOLE, WHY CAN'T I APPRECIATE PEOPLE BEING NICE?
but I'm still processing this marriage stuff
DO I UNWITTINGLY PLAY INTO bourgeois, middle-class VALUES?

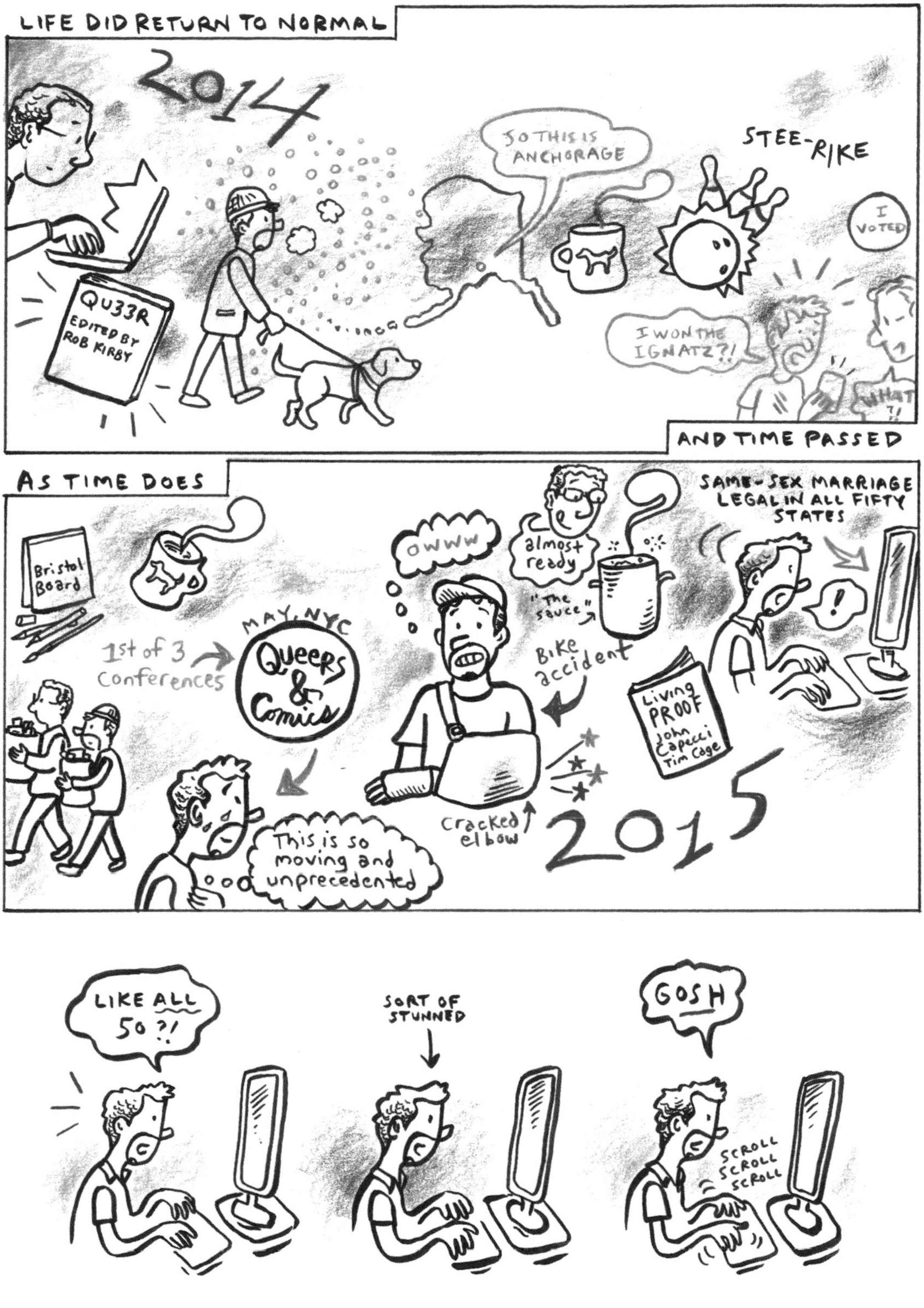
LIFE DID RETURN TO NORMAL
2014
QU33R
EDITED BY ROB KIRBY
SO THIS IS ANCHORAGE
STEE-RIKE
I VOTED
I WON THE IGNATZ?!
WHAT?!
AND TIME PASSED
AS TIME DOES
Bristol Board
1st of 3 conferences
MAY, NYC
Queers & Comics
This is so moving and unprecedented
OWWW
almost ready
"The sauce"
Bike accident
cracked elbow
Living PROOF John Capecci Tim Cage
2015
SAME-SEX MARRIAGE LEGAL IN ALL FIFTY STATES
!
LIKE ALL 50?!
SORT OF STUNNED
GOSH
SCROLL SCROLL SCROLL

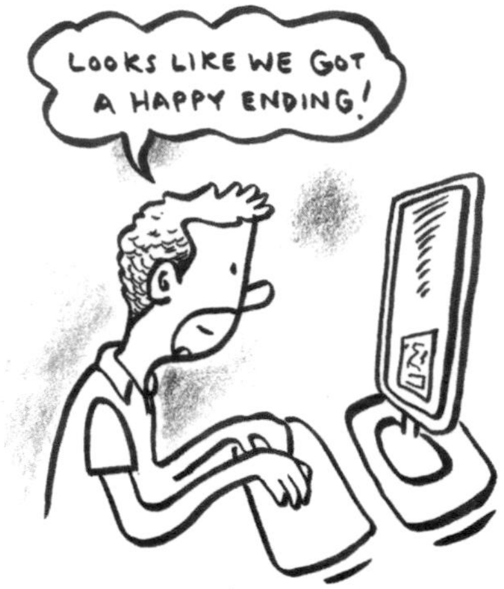
LOOKS LIKE WE GOT A HAPPY ENDING!

#SNOWFLAKE

I REMEMBER
THAT
HORRIBLE FEELING
ON ELECTION NIGHT,
WHEN IT
BECAME CLEAR
THINGS WERE RAPIDLY
GOING
SOUTH

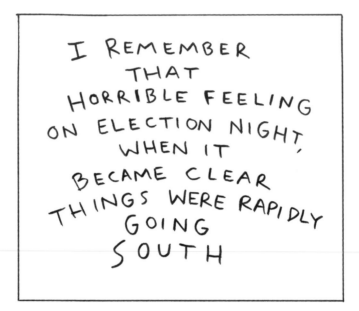

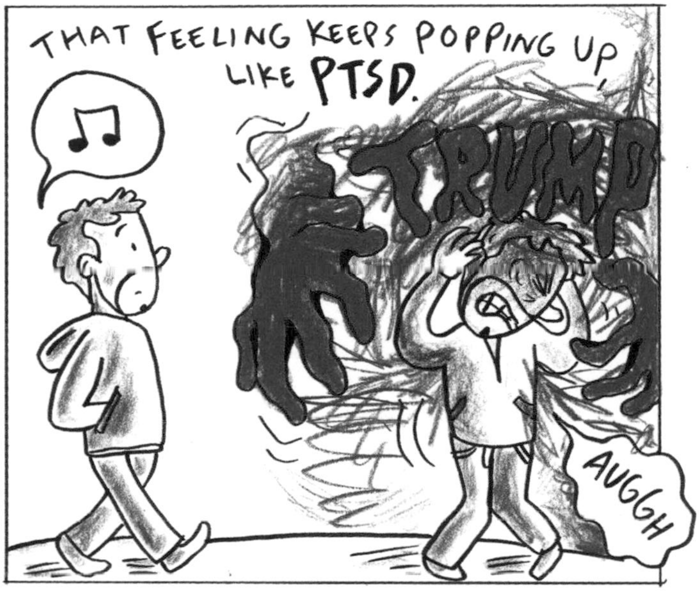
THAT FEELING KEEPS POPPING UP LIKE PTSD.
♫
TRUMP
AUGGH

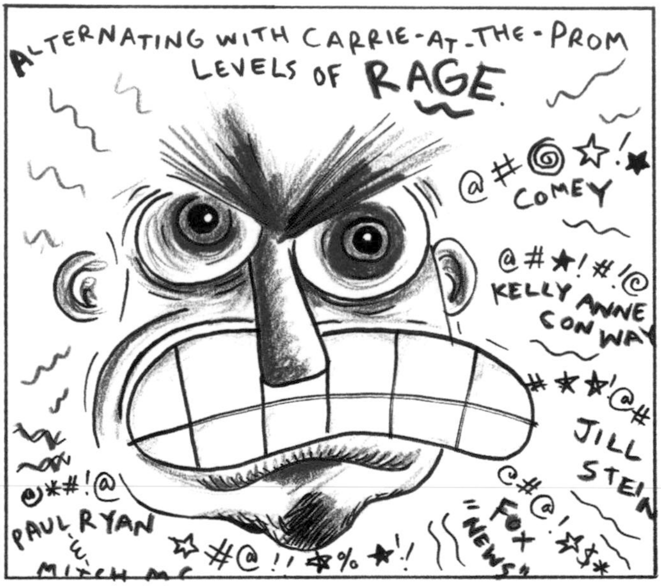
ALTERNATING WITH CARRIE-AT-THE-PROM LEVELS OF RAGE.
@#@☆!★ COMEY
@#★!#!@ KELLY ANNE CONWAY
#★★!@# JILL STEIN
@#@!☆$* "FOX NEWS"
@*#!@ PAUL RYAN
☆#@!!★%★!!

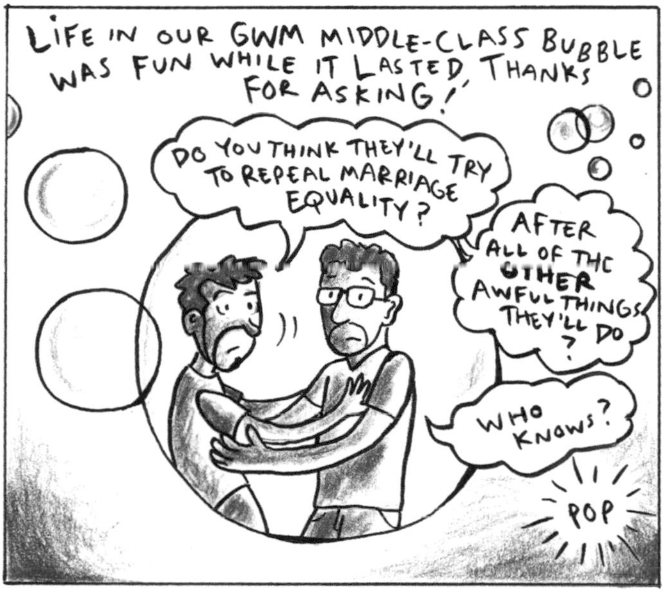
LIFE IN OUR GWM MIDDLE-CLASS BUBBLE WAS FUN WHILE IT LASTED, THANKS FOR ASKING!
DO YOU THINK THEY'LL TRY TO REPEAL MARRIAGE EQUALITY?
AFTER ALL OF THE OTHER AWFUL THINGS THEY'LL DO?
WHO KNOWS?
POP

IT'S
IMPORTANT
TO
COPE
IN A
POSITIVE
FASHION.

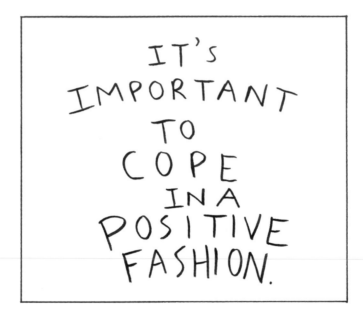

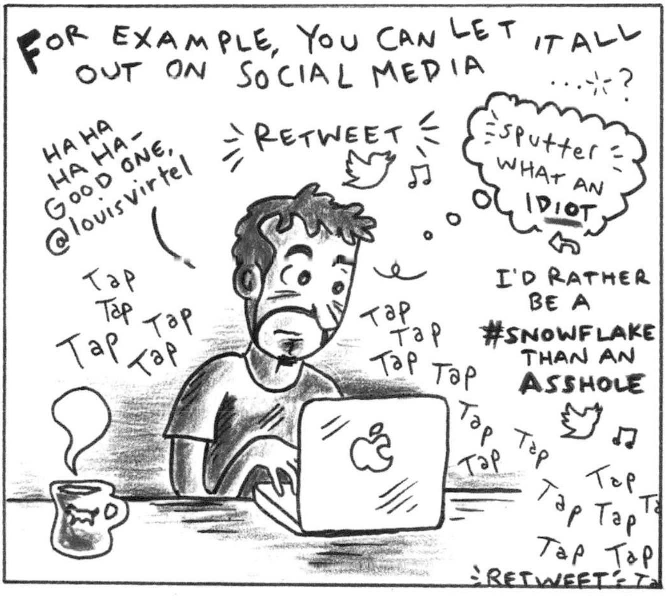
FOR EXAMPLE, YOU CAN LET IT ALL OUT ON SOCIAL MEDIA
...?
HA HA HA HA- GOOD ONE, @louisvirtel
RETWEET
sputter WHAT AN IDIOT
I'D RATHER BE A #SNOWFLAKE THAN AN ASSHOLE
Tap Tap Tap Tap Tap
Tap Tap Tap Tap
Tap Tap Tap Tap Tap Tap Tap Tap
RETWEET

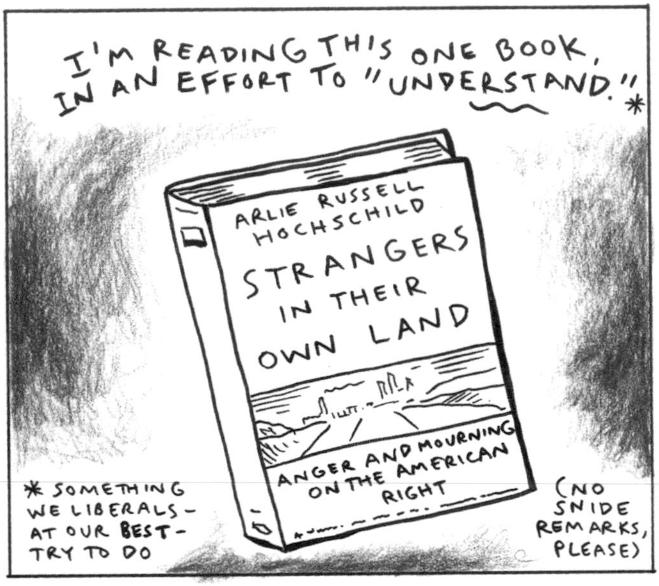
I'M READING THIS ONE BOOK, IN AN EFFORT TO "UNDERSTAND."*
ARLIE RUSSELL HOCHSCHILD
STRANGERS IN THEIR OWN LAND
ANGER AND MOURNING ON THE AMERICAN RIGHT
* SOMETHING WE LIBERALS - AT OUR BEST - TRY TO DO
(NO SNIDE REMARKS, PLEASE)

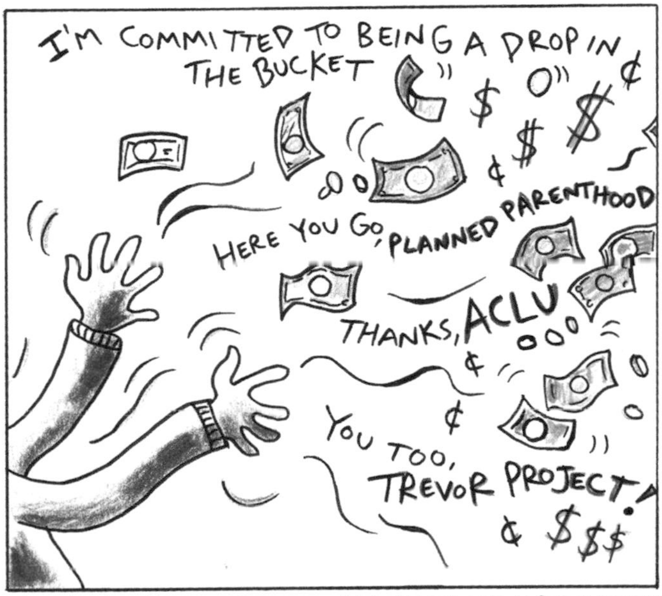
I'M COMMITTED TO BEING A DROP IN THE BUCKET
HERE YOU GO, PLANNED PARENTHOOD
THANKS, ACLU
YOU TOO, TREVOR PROJECT!
¢ $$$

NOTE: THIS PRESENTS ME AS FAR MORE UPWARDLY MOBILE THAN IN ACTUAL REALITY.

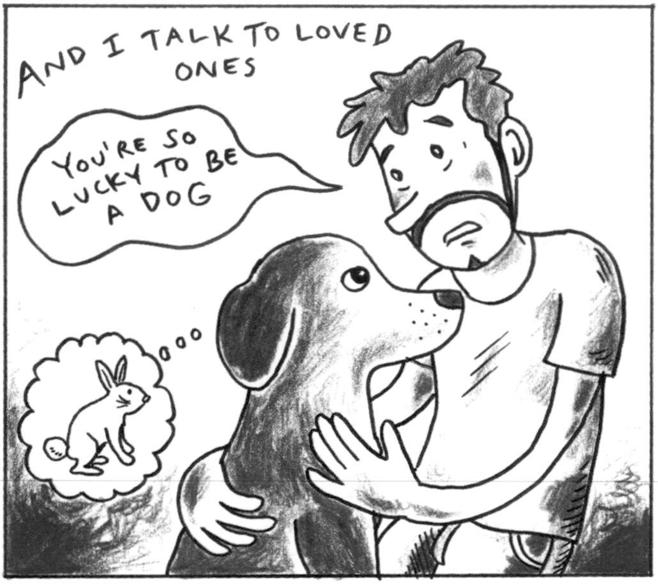
AND I TALK TO LOVED ONES
YOU'RE SO LUCKY TO BE A DOG

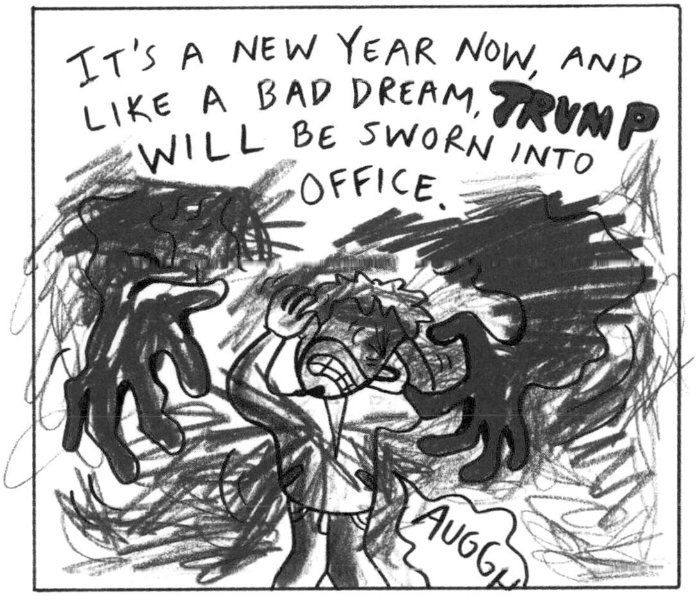
IT'S A NEW YEAR NOW, AND LIKE A BAD DREAM, TRUMP WILL BE SWORN INTO OFFICE.
AUGGH

BUT...

OPPOSITION TO THE **TRUMP** ADMINISTRATION — FROM PROGRESSIVES OF ALL STRIPES* — WILL BE FIERCE AND UNRELENTING.

IT MAKES ME FEEL A LITTLE BETTER JUST TO SAY THAT

* MAYBE EVEN THE DEMOCRATIC PARTY, THOUGH THAT MAY BE TOO MUCH TO WISH FOR.

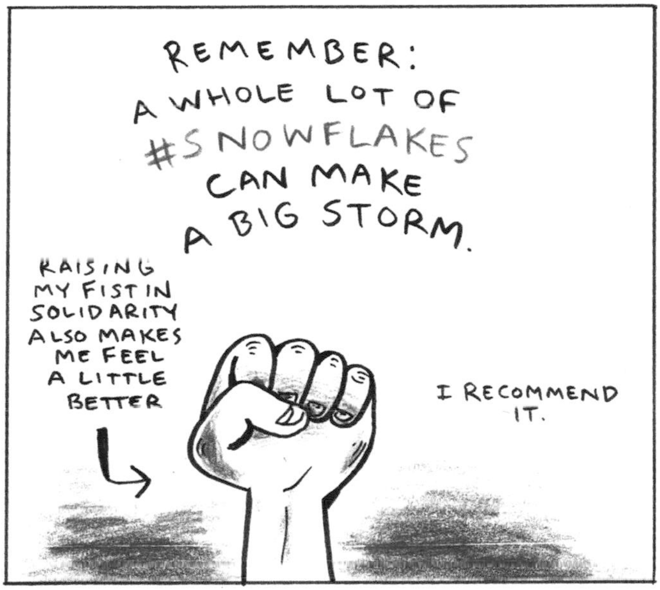
REMEMBER: A WHOLE LOT OF #SNOWFLAKES CAN MAKE A BIG STORM.
RAISING MY FIST IN SOLIDARITY ALSO MAKES ME FEEL A LITTLE BETTER
I RECOMMEND IT.

AMIDST ALL THE FEAR AND UNCERTAINTY SURROUNDING A NEW, FAR RIGHT POLITICAL REGIME IN THE WHITE HOUSE, THERE WAS AT LEAST ONE BRIGHT SPOT ILLUMINATING EARLY 2017.

THE WOMEN'S MARCH JANUARY 21ST

WHY ARE YOU SO OBSESSED WITH MY UTERUS

KEEP YOUR LITTLE HANDS OFF MY RIGHTS

MEN OF QUALITY RESPECT

THIS IS AMAZING

AMAZING

IT'S SO WORTH FREEZING OUR ASSES OFF FOR

MY BODY IS MY OWN

NOT USUALLY A SIGN GUY BUT GEEZ

Non-Consensual PRESIDENCY

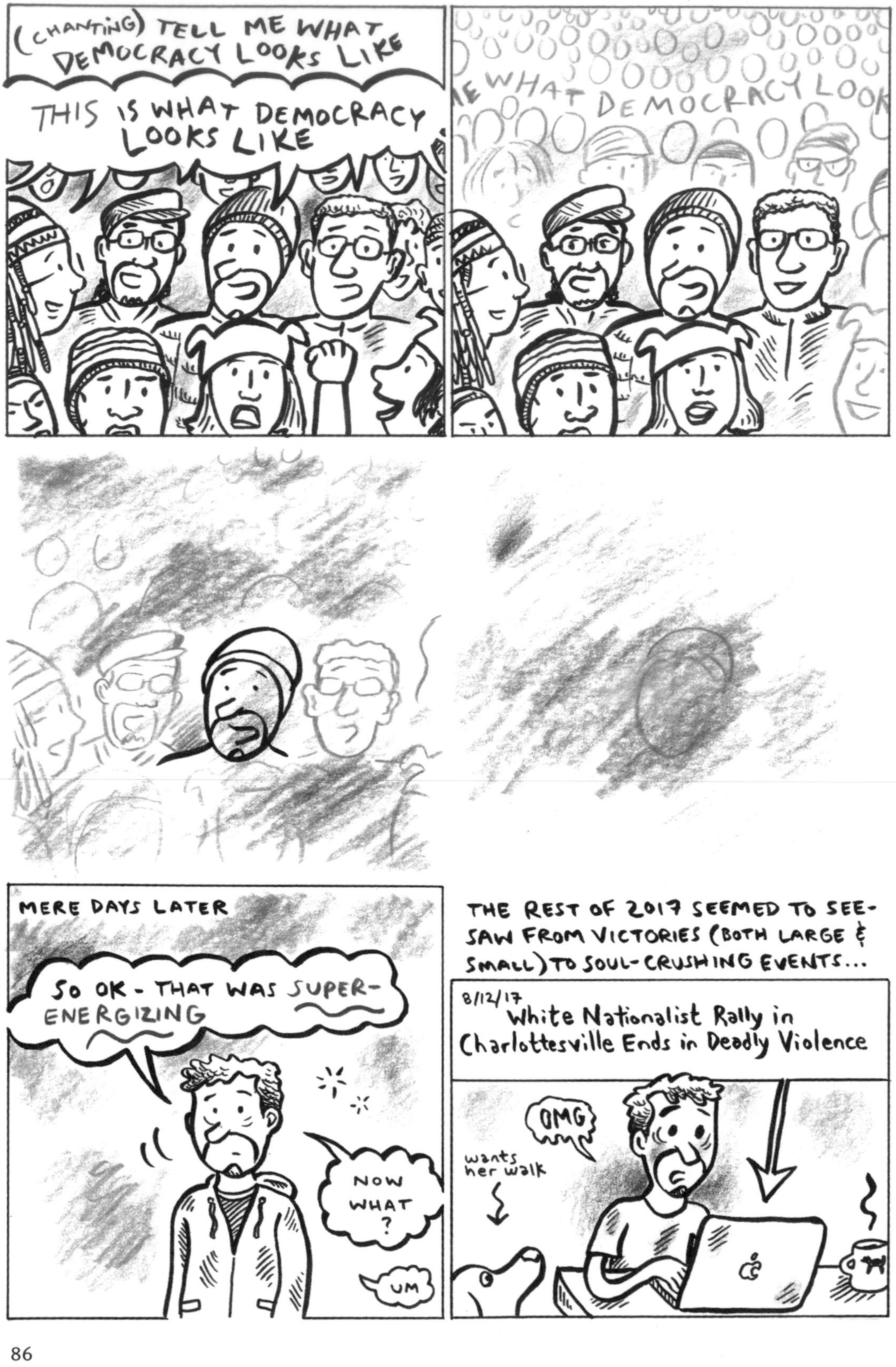
(CHANTING) TELL ME WHAT DEMOCRACY LOOKS LIKE
THIS IS WHAT DEMOCRACY LOOKS LIKE
ME WHAT DEMOCRACY LOOK
MERE DAYS LATER
SO OK - THAT WAS SUPER-ENERGIZING
NOW WHAT ?
UM
THE REST OF 2017 SEEMED TO SEE-SAW FROM VICTORIES (BOTH LARGE & SMALL) TO SOUL-CRUSHING EVENTS...
8/12/17
White Nationalist Rally in Charlottesville Ends in Deadly Violence
OMG
wants her walk

IT WAS NOT A GOOD YEAR FOR SLEEPING, OVERALL

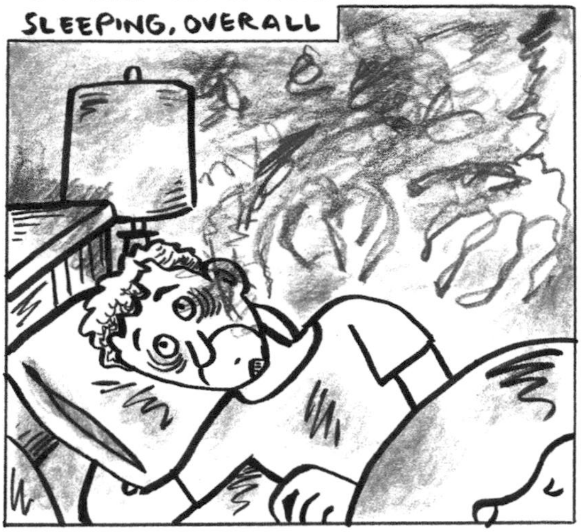

EVENTUALLY, I LEARNED NOT TO LISTEN TO THE NEWS AFTER 5PM IF I COULD HELP IT.

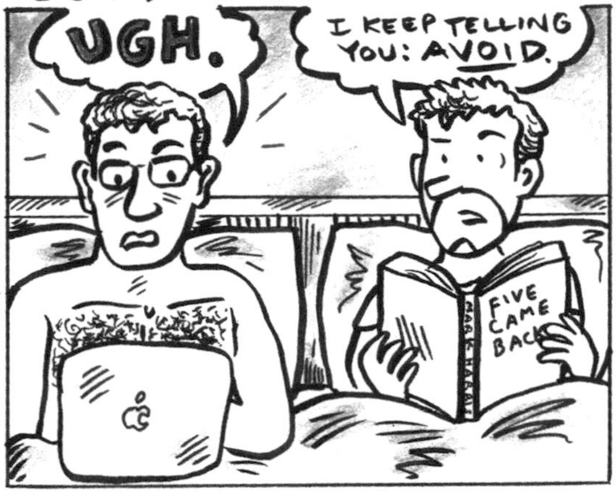
UGH.
I KEEP TELLING YOU: AVOID.
FIVE CAME BACK

AND I FINALLY REALIZED THE FUTILITY OF FIGHTING WITH STRANGERS ON THE INTERNET.

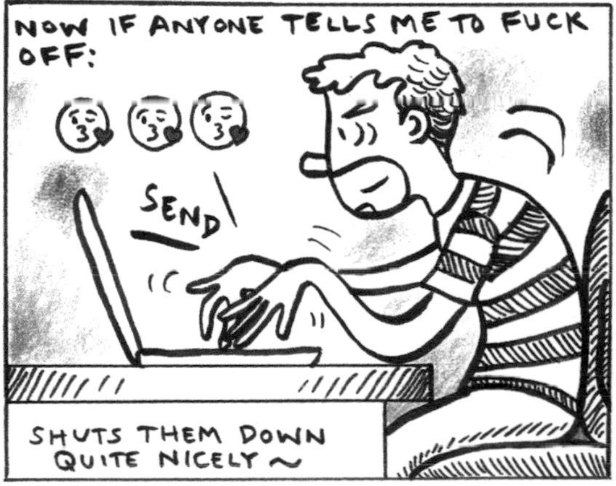
NOW IF ANYONE TELLS ME TO FUCK OFF:
SEND
SHUTS THEM DOWN QUITE NICELY ~

I BECAME NOSTALGIC FOR THE MORE INNOCENT TIME OF LIKE, EVEN JUST EIGHT MONTHS EARLIER.

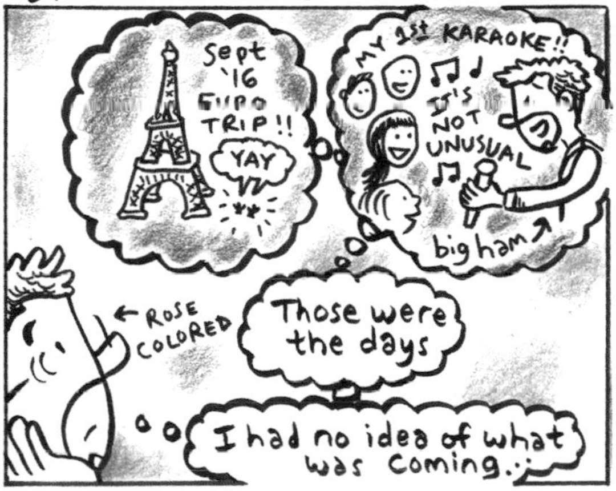
Sept '16 EURO TRIP!!
YAY
MY 1st KARAOKE!!
IT'S NOT UNUSUAL
big ham
← ROSE COLORED
Those were the days
I had no idea of what was coming...

THE TRUMP ADMINISTRATION DIDN'T SEEM TO HAVE ANY REAL INTEREST IN GOING AFTER MARRIAGE RIGHTS - DESPITE THE FACT THAT THE VICE PRESIDENT WAS A NOTORIOUS HOMOPHOBE. NOPE, THEY FOCUSED MAINLY ON TERRORIZING IMMIGRANTS, PERSECUTING TRANS PEOPLE, TRAMPLING ON THE RIGHTS OF PEOPLE OF COLOR & WOMEN, ETC.

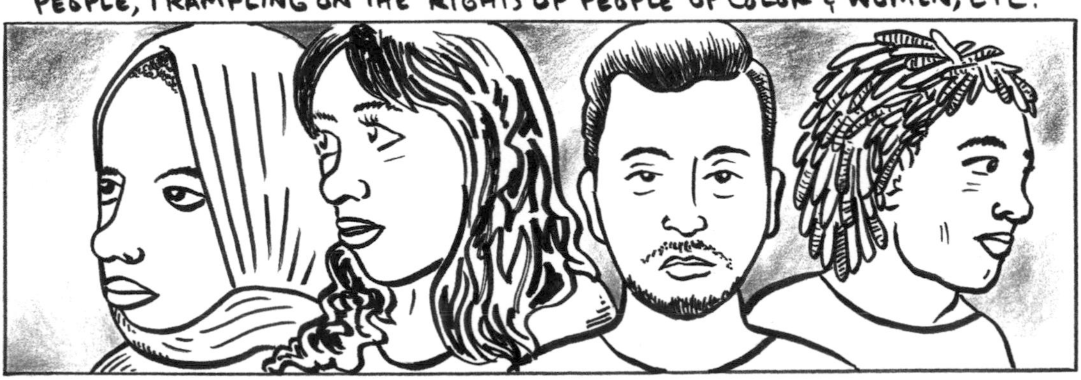

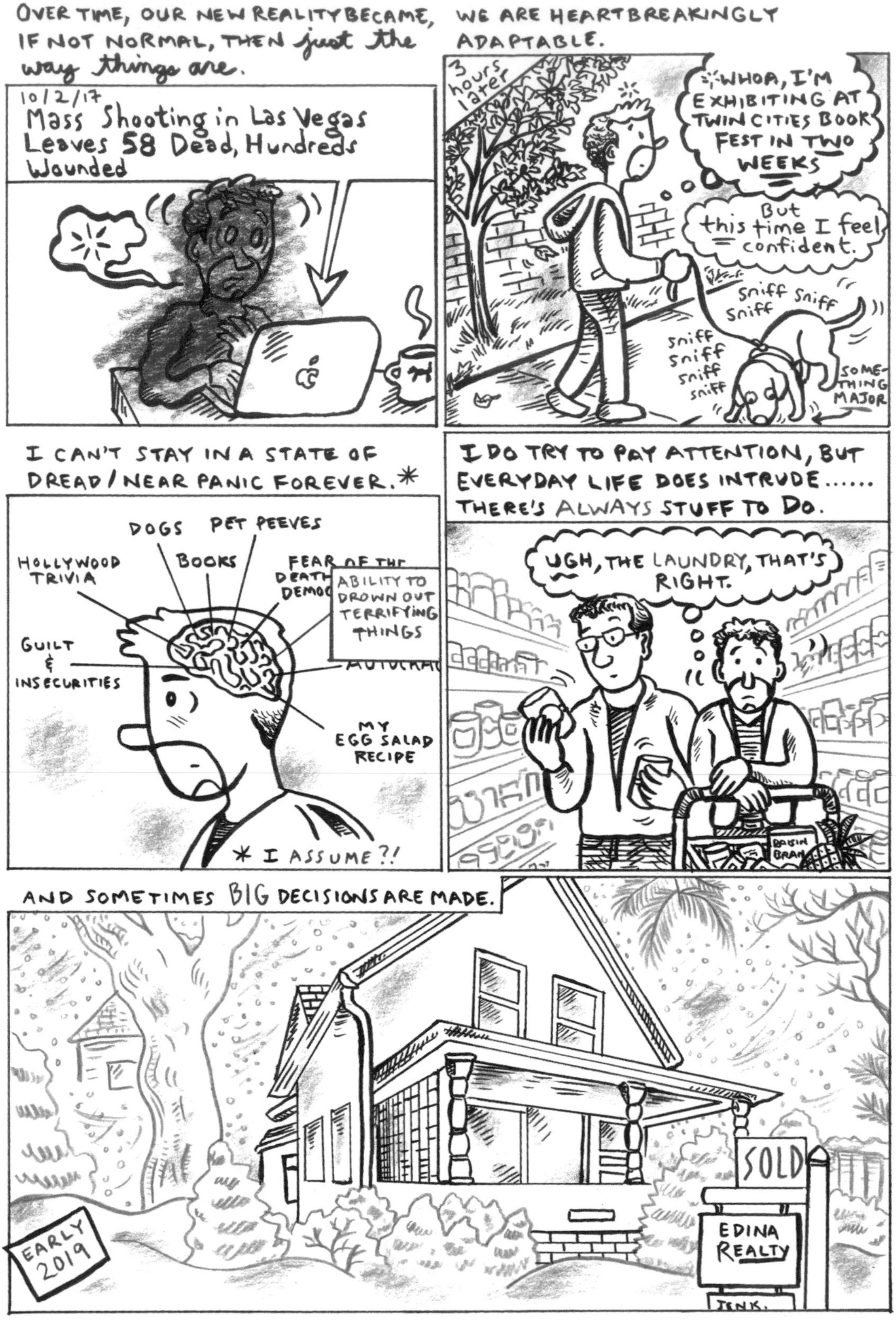
OVER TIME, OUR NEW REALITY BECAME, IF NOT NORMAL, THEN just the way things are.
10/2/17
Mass Shooting in Las Vegas Leaves 58 Dead, Hundreds Wounded
WE ARE HEARTBREAKINGLY ADAPTABLE.
3 hours later
WHOA, I'M EXHIBITING AT TWIN CITIES BOOK FEST IN TWO WEEKS
But this time I feel confident.
sniff sniff sniff
sniff sniff sniff sniff
SOMETHING MAJOR
I CAN'T STAY IN A STATE OF DREAD / NEAR PANIC FOREVER.*
DOGS
PET PEEVES
HOLLYWOOD TRIVIA
BOOKS
ABILITY TO DROWN OUT TERRIFYING THINGS
GUILT & INSECURITIES
MY EGG SALAD RECIPE
* I ASSUME?!
I DO TRY TO PAY ATTENTION, BUT EVERYDAY LIFE DOES INTRUDE...... THERE'S ALWAYS STUFF TO DO.
UGH, THE LAUNDRY, THAT'S RIGHT.
RAISIN BRAN
AND SOMETIMES BIG DECISIONS ARE MADE.
EARLY 2019
SOLD
EDINA REALTY

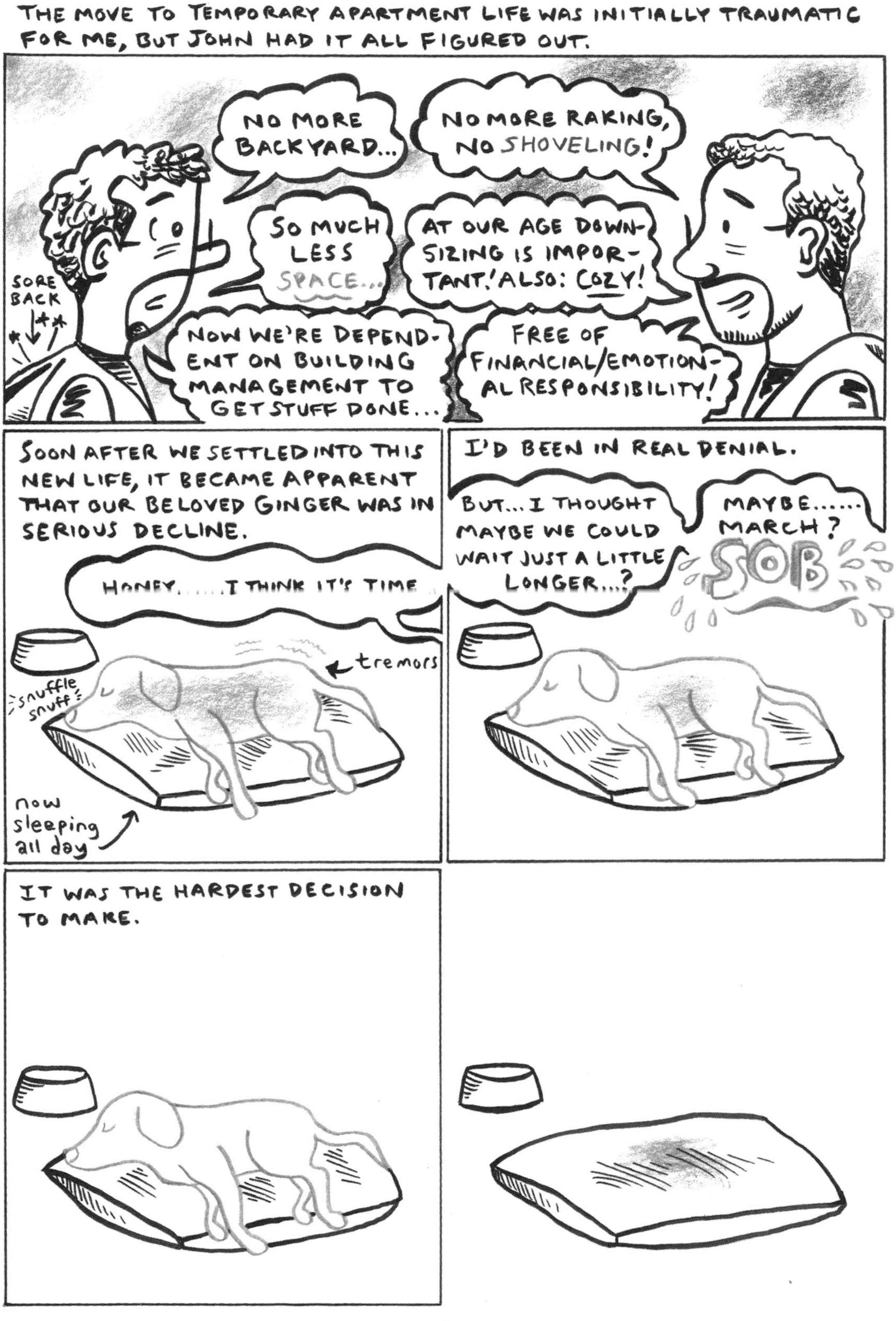
THE MOVE TO TEMPORARY APARTMENT LIFE WAS INITIALLY TRAUMATIC FOR ME, BUT JOHN HAD IT ALL FIGURED OUT.
NO MORE BACKYARD...
NO MORE RAKING, NO SHOVELING!
SO MUCH LESS SPACE...
AT OUR AGE DOWN-SIZING IS IMPOR-TANT! ALSO: COZY!
SORE BACK
NOW WE'RE DEPEND-ENT ON BUILDING MANAGEMENT TO GET STUFF DONE...
FREE OF FINANCIAL/EMOTION-AL RESPONSIBILITY!
SOON AFTER WE SETTLED INTO THIS NEW LIFE, IT BECAME APPARENT THAT OUR BELOVED GINGER WAS IN SERIOUS DECLINE.
HONEY......I THINK IT'S TIME
tremors
snuffle snuff
now sleeping all day
I'D BEEN IN REAL DENIAL.
BUT... I THOUGHT MAYBE WE COULD WAIT JUST A LITTLE LONGER...?
MAYBE...... MARCH?
SOB
IT WAS THE HARDEST DECISION TO MAKE.

WHILE I'M ADEPT AT PUTTING OFF/AVOIDING SCARY STUFF, I FIND THAT FOR ME GRIEF HAS A WILL-NOT-BE-DENIED STAYING POWER.

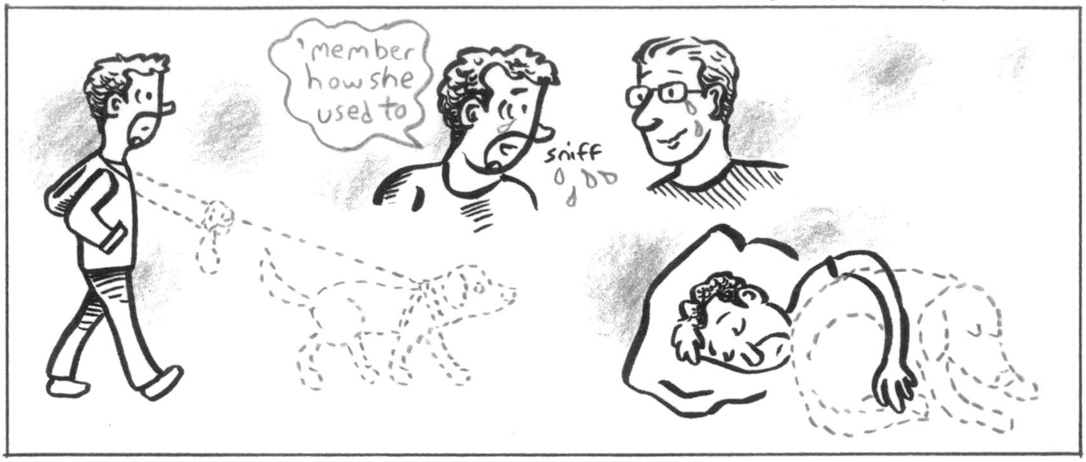
'member how she used to
sniff

JOHN IS FOND OF REPEATING SOMETHING HIS OLD THERAPIST TOLD HIM ONCE.

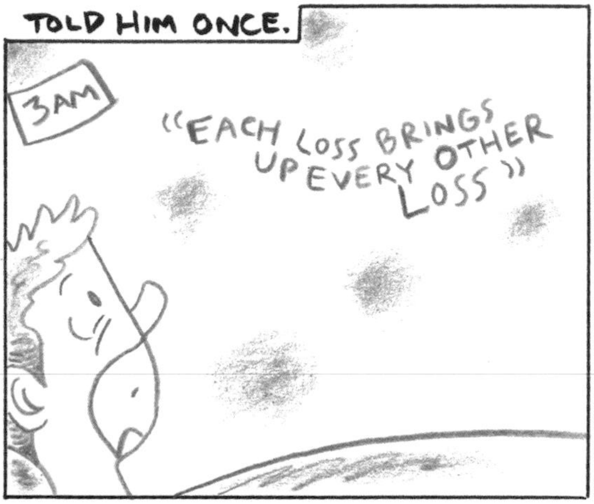
3AM
"EACH LOSS BRINGS UP EVERY OTHER LOSS"

EVENTUALLY GRIEF BECOMES A SORT OF FRIEND. IT KNOWS ALL YOUR STUFF, YOUR BAGGAGE, YOUR REGRETS.

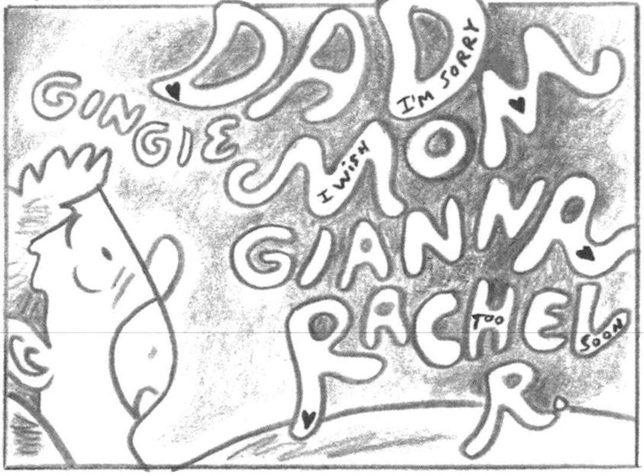
DAD
I'M SORRY
GONGIE
MOM
I WISH
GIANNA
RACHEL
TOO SOON
R.

YET ANOTHER REMINDER THAT WE'RE ALL PART OF SOMETHING BIGGER.

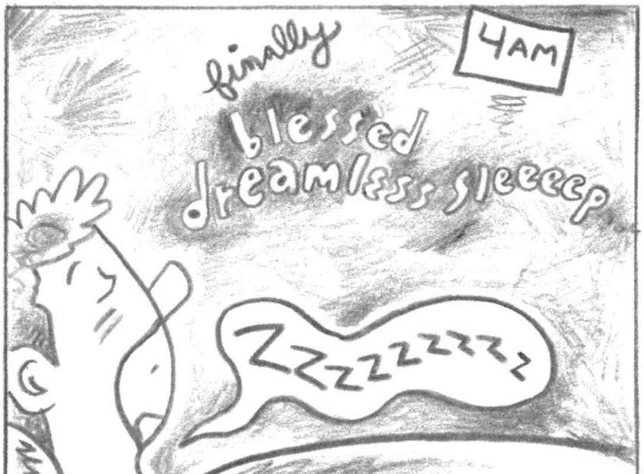
4AM
finally
blessed dreamlesss sleeeep
Zzzzzzzzz

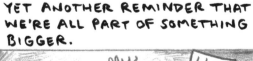

AND MORE TIME GOES BY...

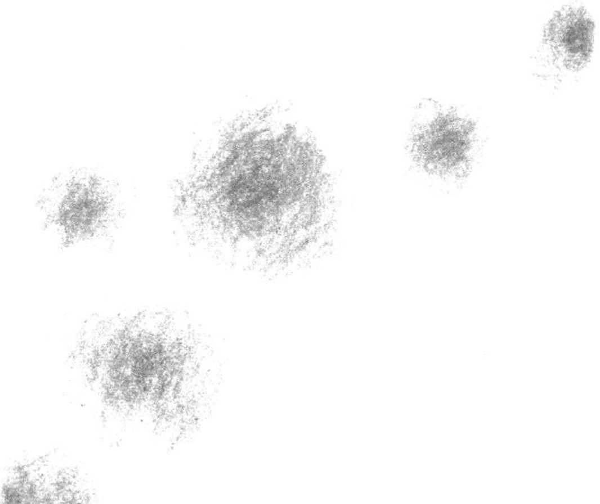

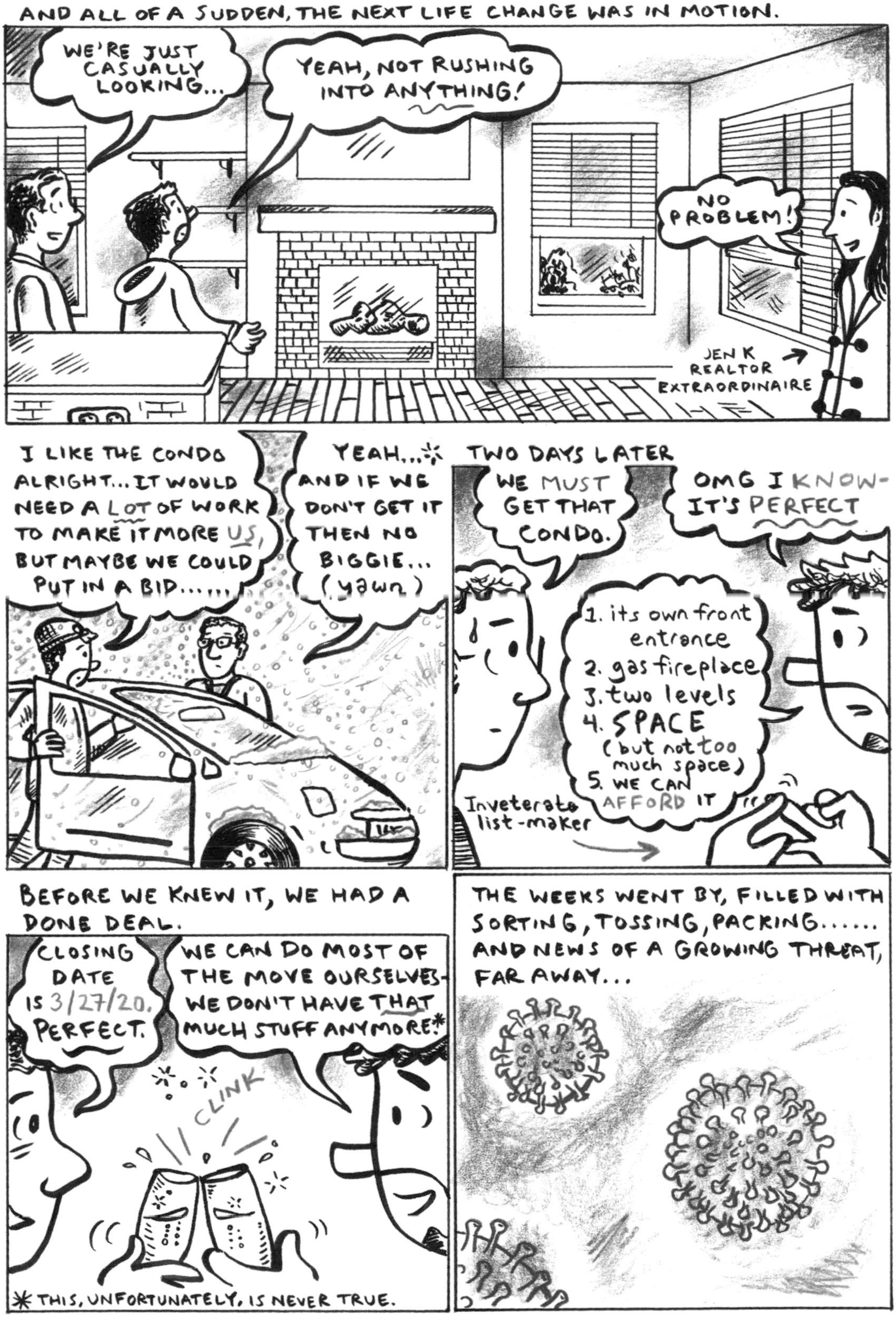
AND ALL OF A SUDDEN, THE NEXT LIFE CHANGE WAS IN MOTION.
WE'RE JUST CASUALLY LOOKING...
YEAH, NOT RUSHING INTO ANYTHING!
NO PROBLEM!
JEN K REALTOR EXTRAORDINAIRE
I LIKE THE CONDO ALRIGHT... IT WOULD NEED A LOT OF WORK TO MAKE IT MORE US, BUT MAYBE WE COULD PUT IN A BID.......
YEAH... AND IF WE DON'T GET IT THEN NO BIGGIE... (yawn)
TWO DAYS LATER
WE MUST GET THAT CONDO.
OMG I KNOW- IT'S PERFECT
1. its own front entrance
2. gas fireplace
3. two levels
4. SPACE (but not too much space)
5. WE CAN AFFORD IT
Inveterate list-maker
BEFORE WE KNEW IT, WE HAD A DONE DEAL.
CLOSING DATE IS 3/27/20. PERFECT.
WE CAN DO MOST OF THE MOVE OURSELVES- WE DON'T HAVE THAT MUCH STUFF ANYMORE!*
CLINK
* THIS, UNFORTUNATELY, IS NEVER TRUE.
THE WEEKS WENT BY, FILLED WITH SORTING, TOSSING, PACKING...... AND NEWS OF A GROWING THREAT, FAR AWAY...

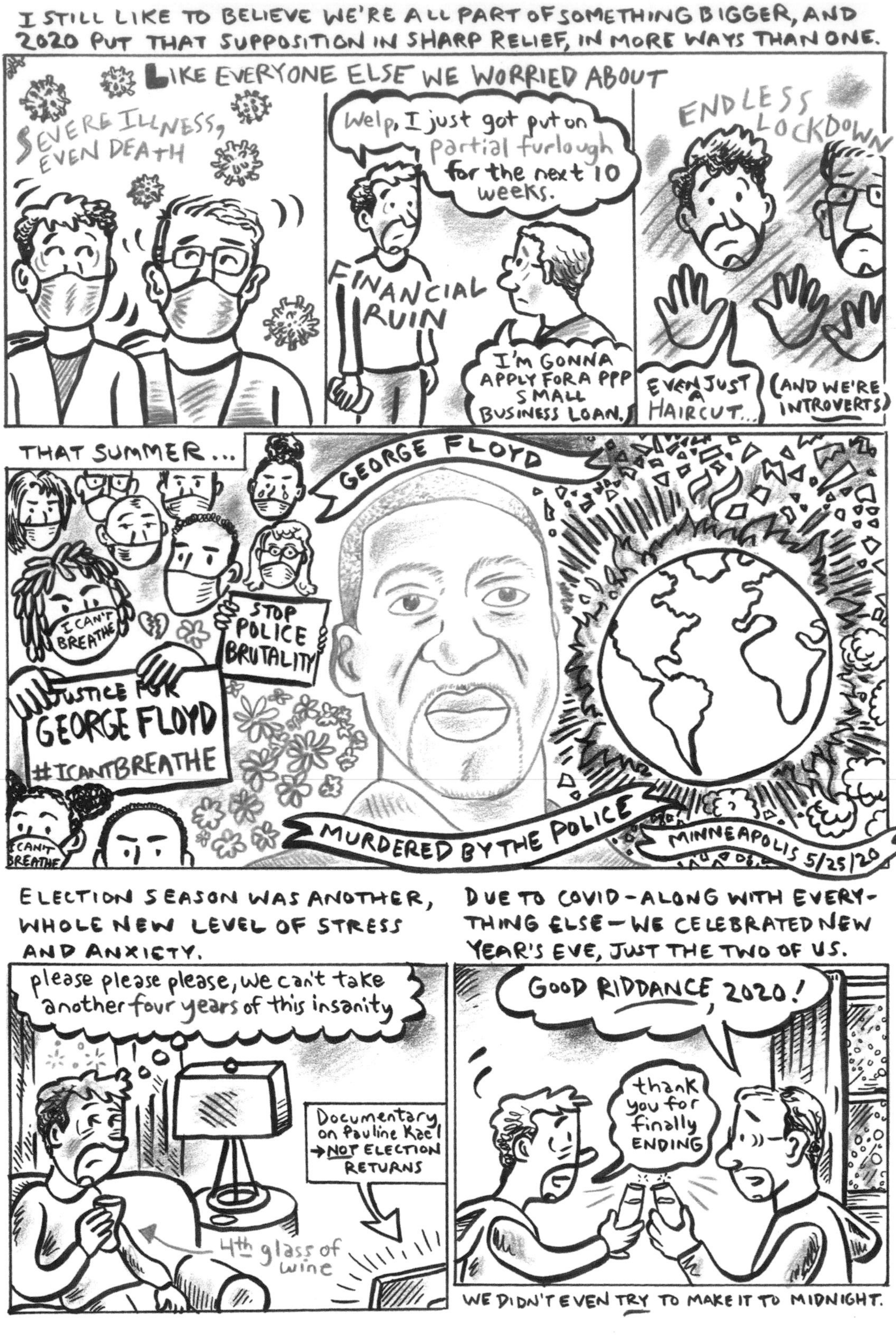
I STILL LIKE TO BELIEVE WE'RE ALL PART OF SOMETHING BIGGER, AND 2020 PUT THAT SUPPOSITION IN SHARP RELIEF, IN MORE WAYS THAN ONE.
LIKE EVERYONE ELSE WE WORRIED ABOUT
SEVERE ILLNESS, EVEN DEATH
Welp, I just got put on partial furlough for the next 10 weeks.
FINANCIAL RUIN
I'M GONNA APPLY FOR A PPP SMALL BUSINESS LOAN.
ENDLESS LOCKDOWN
EVEN JUST A HAIRCUT...
(AND WE'RE INTROVERTS)
THAT SUMMER...
GEORGE FLOYD
I CAN'T BREATHE
STOP POLICE BRUTALITY
JUSTICE FOR GEORGE FLOYD #ICANTBREATHE
I CAN'T BREATHE
MURDERED BY THE POLICE
MINNEAPOLIS 5/25/20
ELECTION SEASON WAS ANOTHER, WHOLE NEW LEVEL OF STRESS AND ANXIETY.
please please please, we can't take another four years of this insanity
Documentary on Pauline Kael → NOT ELECTION RETURNS
4th glass of wine
DUE TO COVID—ALONG WITH EVERYTHING ELSE—WE CELEBRATED NEW YEAR'S EVE, JUST THE TWO OF US.
GOOD RIDDANCE, 2020!
thank you for finally ENDING
WE DIDN'T EVEN TRY TO MAKE IT TO MIDNIGHT.

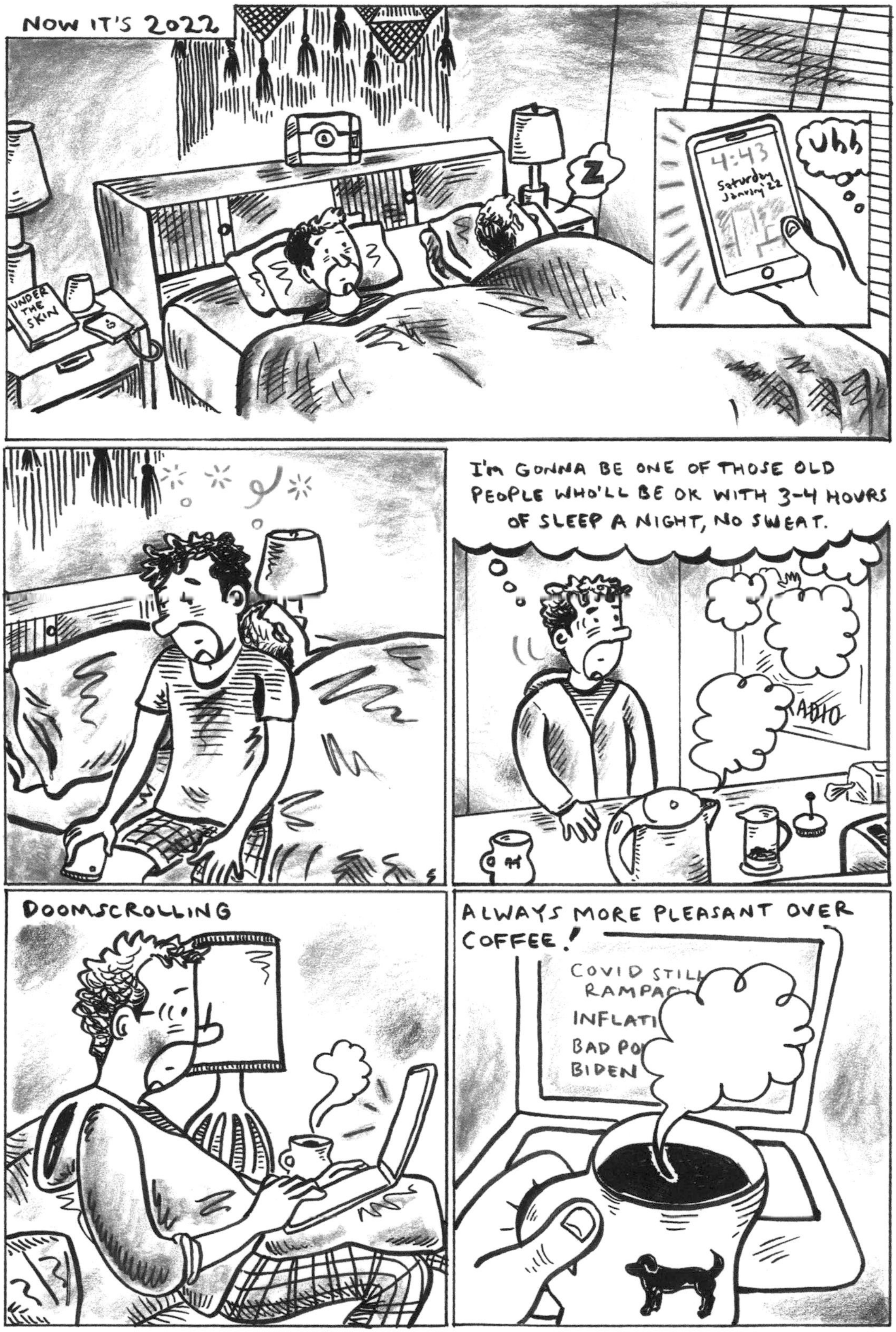

NOW IT'S 2022
UNDER THE SKIN
Z
4:43
Saturday January 22
Uhh
I'M GONNA BE ONE OF THOSE OLD PEOPLE WHO'LL BE OK WITH 3-4 HOURS OF SLEEP A NIGHT, NO SWEAT.
RADIO
DOOMSCROLLING
ALWAYS MORE PLEASANT OVER COFFEE!
COVID STILL RAMPA
INFLATI
BAD PO
BIDEN

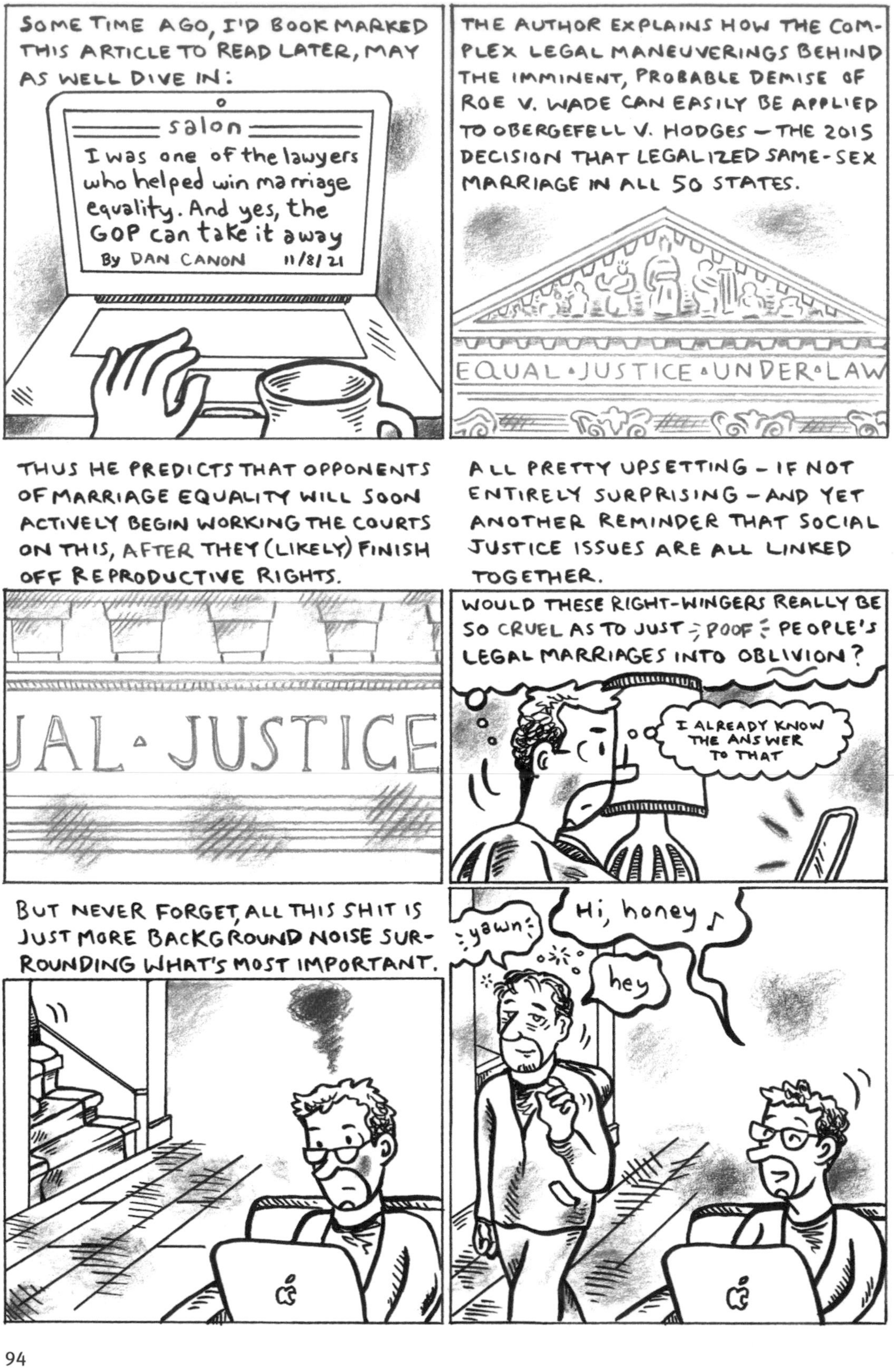
SOME TIME AGO, I'D BOOKMARKED THIS ARTICLE TO READ LATER, MAY AS WELL DIVE IN:
salon
I was one of the lawyers who helped win marriage equality. And yes, the GOP can take it away
By DAN CANON 11/8/21
THE AUTHOR EXPLAINS HOW THE COMPLEX LEGAL MANEUVERINGS BEHIND THE IMMINENT, PROBABLE DEMISE OF ROE V. WADE CAN EASILY BE APPLIED TO OBERGEFELL V. HODGES — THE 2015 DECISION THAT LEGALIZED SAME-SEX MARRIAGE IN ALL 50 STATES.
EQUAL • JUSTICE • UNDER • LAW
THUS HE PREDICTS THAT OPPONENTS OF MARRIAGE EQUALITY WILL SOON ACTIVELY BEGIN WORKING THE COURTS ON THIS, AFTER THEY (LIKELY) FINISH OFF REPRODUCTIVE RIGHTS.
ALL PRETTY UPSETTING — IF NOT ENTIRELY SURPRISING — AND YET ANOTHER REMINDER THAT SOCIAL JUSTICE ISSUES ARE ALL LINKED TOGETHER.
JAL • JUSTICE
WOULD THESE RIGHT-WINGERS REALLY BE SO CRUEL AS TO JUST POOF PEOPLE'S LEGAL MARRIAGES INTO OBLIVION?
I ALREADY KNOW THE ANSWER TO THAT
BUT NEVER FORGET, ALL THIS SHIT IS JUST MORE BACKGROUND NOISE SURROUNDING WHAT'S MOST IMPORTANT.
yawn
Hi, honey ♪
hey

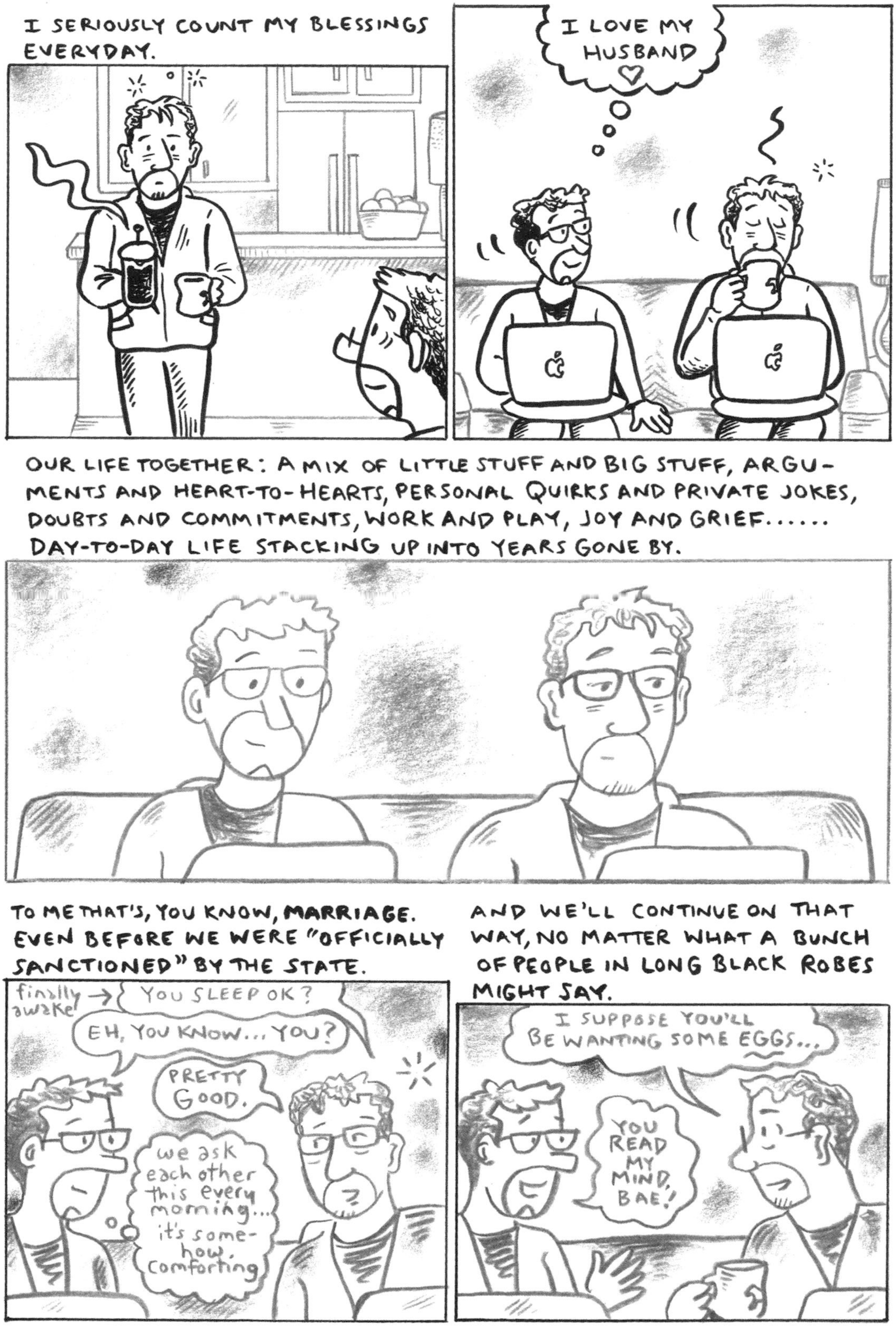
I SERIOUSLY COUNT MY BLESSINGS EVERYDAY.
I LOVE MY HUSBAND
OUR LIFE TOGETHER: A MIX OF LITTLE STUFF AND BIG STUFF, ARGUMENTS AND HEART-TO-HEARTS, PERSONAL QUIRKS AND PRIVATE JOKES, DOUBTS AND COMMITMENTS, WORK AND PLAY, JOY AND GRIEF...... DAY-TO-DAY LIFE STACKING UP INTO YEARS GONE BY.
TO ME THAT'S, YOU KNOW, MARRIAGE. EVEN BEFORE WE WERE "OFFICIALLY SANCTIONED" BY THE STATE.
finally awake →
YOU SLEEP OK?
EH, YOU KNOW... YOU?
PRETTY GOOD.
we ask each other this every morning... it's somehow comforting
AND WE'LL CONTINUE ON THAT WAY, NO MATTER WHAT A BUNCH OF PEOPLE IN LONG BLACK ROBES MIGHT SAY.
I SUPPOSE YOU'LL BE WANTING SOME EGGS...
YOU READ MY MIND, BAE!

MARRIAGE
DOESN'T DEFINE A RELATIONSHIP

UNLESS YOU WANT IT TO.

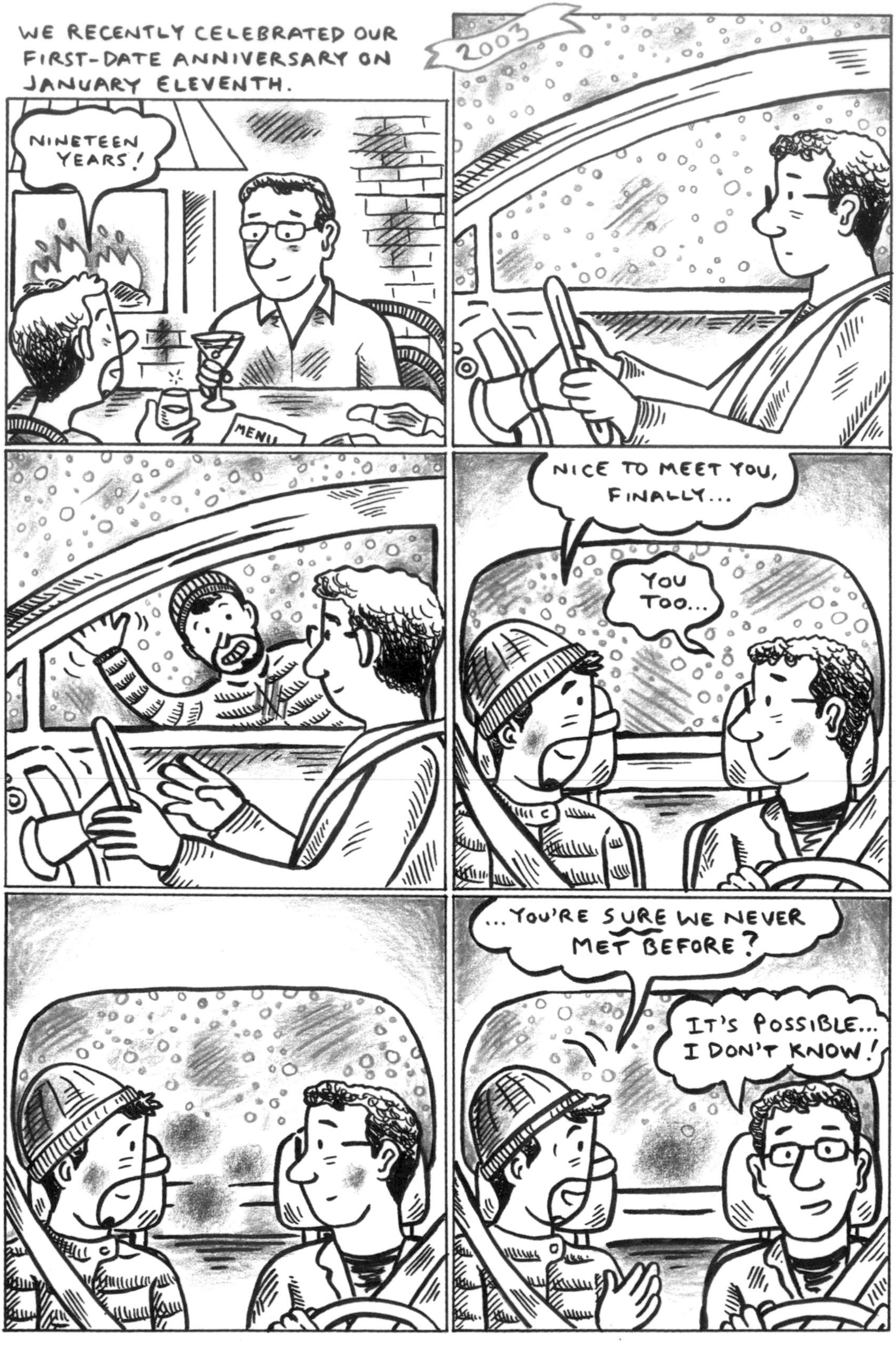
WE RECENTLY CELEBRATED OUR FIRST-DATE ANNIVERSARY ON JANUARY ELEVENTH.
NINETEEN YEARS!
MENU
2003
NICE TO MEET YOU, FINALLY...
YOU TOO...
...YOU'RE SURE WE NEVER MET BEFORE?
IT'S POSSIBLE... I DON'T KNOW!

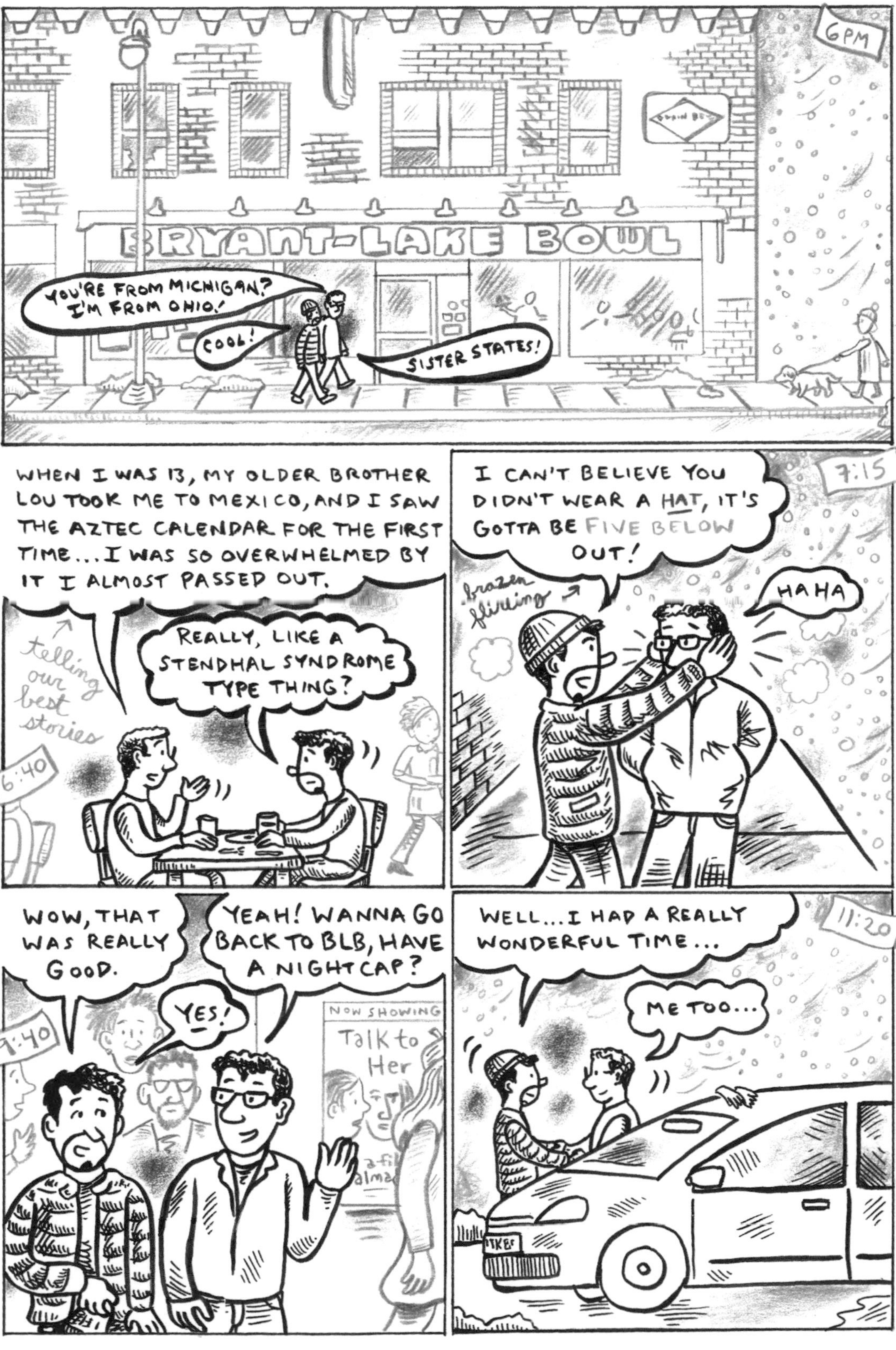
6PM
BRYANT-LAKE BOWL
YOU'RE FROM MICHIGAN? I'M FROM OHIO!
COOL!
SISTER STATES!
WHEN I WAS 13, MY OLDER BROTHER LOU TOOK ME TO MEXICO, AND I SAW THE AZTEC CALENDAR FOR THE FIRST TIME... I WAS SO OVERWHELMED BY IT I ALMOST PASSED OUT.
telling our best stories
REALLY, LIKE A STENDHAL SYNDROME TYPE THING?
6:40
I CAN'T BELIEVE YOU DIDN'T WEAR A HAT, IT'S GOTTA BE FIVE BELOW OUT!
7:15
brazen flirting
HAHA
WOW, THAT WAS REALLY GOOD.
YEAH! WANNA GO BACK TO BLB, HAVE A NIGHTCAP?
9:40
YES!
NOW SHOWING
Talk to Her
WELL... I HAD A REALLY WONDERFUL TIME...
11:20
ME TOO...

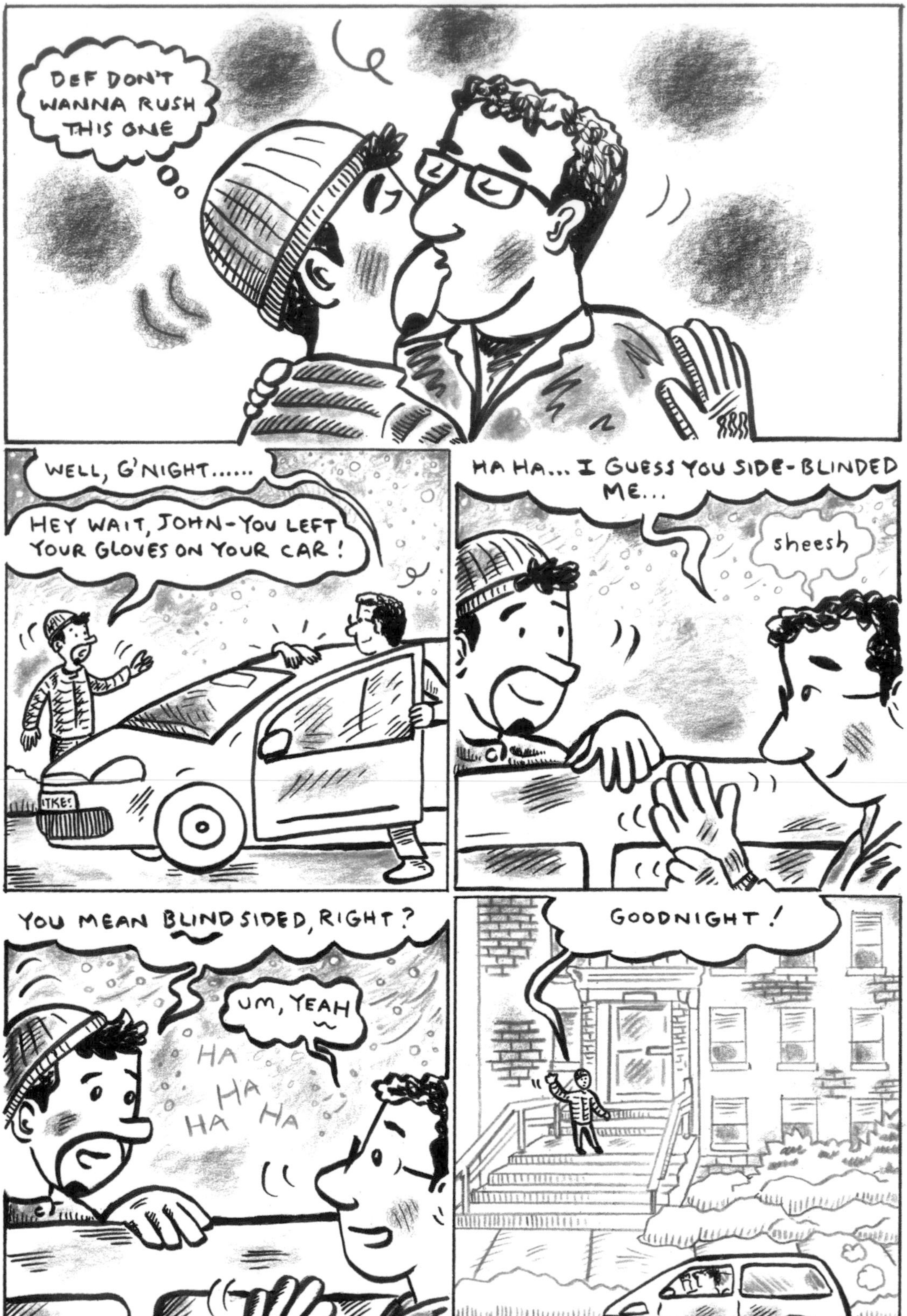
DEF DON'T WANNA RUSH THIS ONE
WELL, G'NIGHT......
HEY WAIT, JOHN - YOU LEFT YOUR GLOVES ON YOUR CAR!
HA HA... I GUESS YOU SIDE-BLINDED ME...
sheesh
YOU MEAN BLIND SIDED, RIGHT?
UM, YEAH
HA HA HA HA
GOODNIGHT!

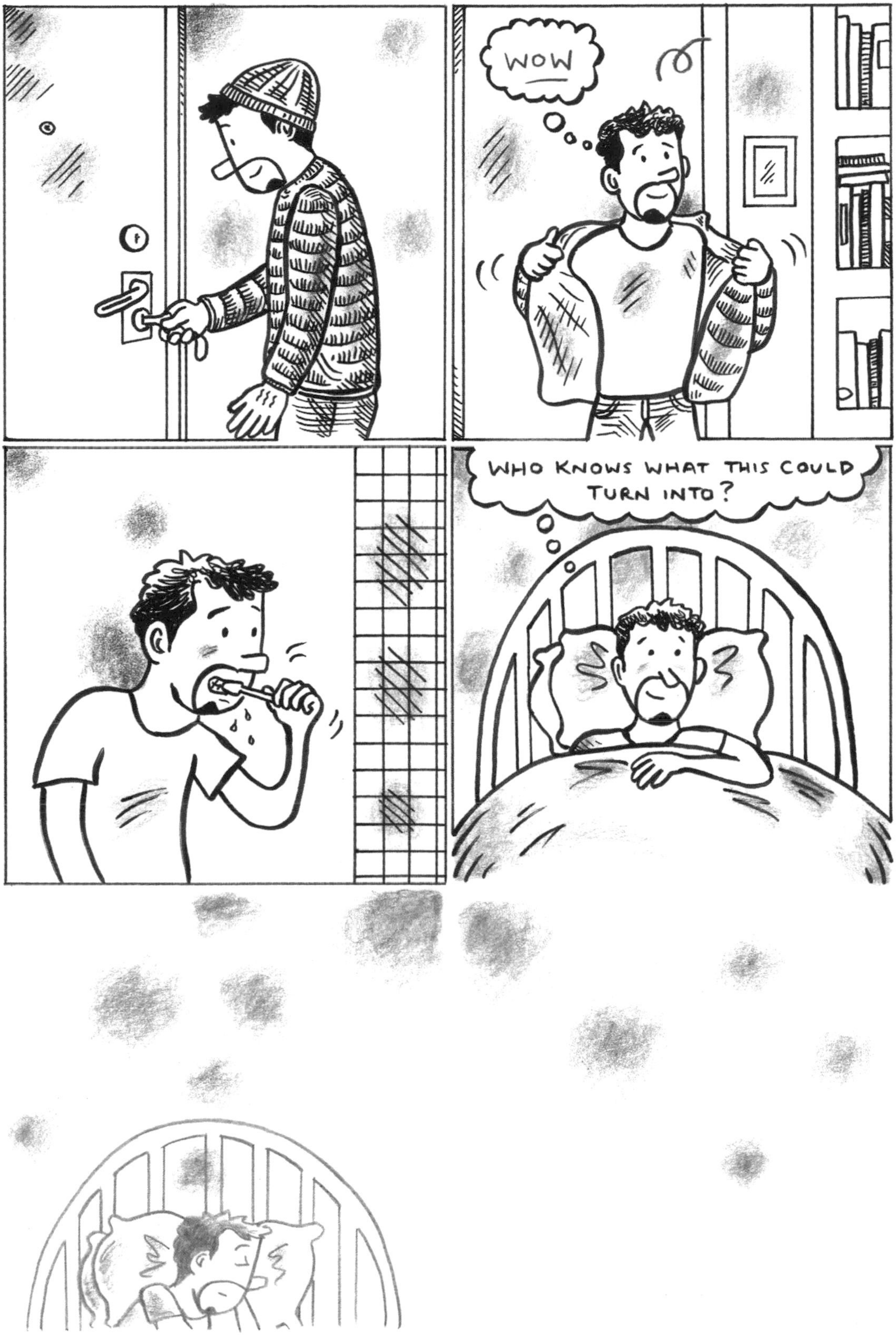
WOW
WHO KNOWS WHAT THIS COULD TURN INTO?

acknowledgments

I'm very grateful to all the folks who were present on 10/3/13. You made the whole thing a lot of fun! And a shout out to all our friends and family who were with us there in spirit, obviously.

Special thanks to Cathy Camper, Justin Hall, and Eric Orner for their camaraderie and support. I'm always very grateful to MariNaomi for her friendship, unflagging enthusiasm, and advocacy for my work. Thanks also to Rob Clough, Senator Scott Dibble, Meg Lemke, and a big shout out to everyone who supports my Patreon. Finally, many thanks to Kendra Boileau, Cate Fricke, and everyone else at Graphic Mundi.